Short Loan

T   er
If yr wish to
_____

Focal Guide to Safety in Live Performance

This is the first book in the Live Performance Technology Series

Series Editor: John Offord,
        Editor of Lighting & Sound International and
        Chief Executive of the Professional Lighting and Sound Association

PROFESSIONAL LIGHTING
AND SOUND ASSOCIATION

Future titles in the series will cover all areas of entertainment and presentation technology, including:
    lighting design, control and effects
    performance sound
    projection
    rigging and trussing

Focal Guide to Safety in Live Performance

Edited by
George Thompson, CEng, MIEE
Standards Officer,
Professional Lighting and Sound Association

Focal Press
An imprint of Butterworth-Heinemann Ltd
Linacre House, Jordan Hill, Oxford OX2 8DP

℞ A member of the Reed Elsevier plc group

OXFORD   LONDON   BOSTON
MUNICH   NEW DELHI   SINGAPORE   SYDNEY
TOKYO   TORONTO   WELLINGTON

First published 1993
Reprinted 1995

British Library Cataloguing in Publication Data
Focal Guide to Safety in Live Performance
  I. Thompson, George
  363.14

ISBN 0 240 51319 3

Library of Congress Cataloguing in Publication Data
Focal guide to safety in live performance/edited by George Thompson.
  p.   cm.
  Includes bibliographical references and index.
  ISBN 0 240 51319 3
  1. Theaters – Fires and fire prevention.   2. Theaters – Safety measures.
  I. Thompson, George.
  TH9445.T3F63   1993
  628.9'22 – dc20   93–18063   CIP

Typeset by Vision Typesetting, Manchester
Printed and bound in Great Britain by
Redwood Books, Trowbridge, Wiltshire

Contents

Contributors

Bob Anderson, BEng, CEng, MIEE, MCIBSE
Consultant

Terry Ashton, PEng, MSFE
Warrington Fire Research Consultants Ltd

David Bertenshaw, EurIng, BSc(Eng), ACGI, CEng, MIEE, MCIBSE
Strand Lighting Ltd

Richard Brett, BSc, CEng, FIEE
Technical Planning International

Tony Brown, BEng
Strand Lighting Ltd

Rodney Clark
Indoor Shows and Touring Productions Manager, Le Maitre Fireworks Ltd

Stephen Day, BSc, MIOSH
Senior Consultant, Rendel Science & Environment Ltd

Ken Dibble, MIoA, MASA, MAES, FInstSCE
Consultant, Ken Dibble Acoustics

Graeme Hansell, BSc, CEng, MCIBSE, AIFireE
Fire Research Consultant, Colt International Ltd

John Landamore
Ark Light

John Shaughnessy, MInstSPP(Dip), MRIPHH
Principal Inspector, Health, Safety & Licensing Division, Brent Council

Kevin Sivyer, MIOSH
Safety Manager, Royal Shakespeare Company

George Thompson, CEng, MIEE
Standards Officer, Professional Lighting and Sound Association

Graham Walne
Chairman, Arts & Entertainment Technical Training Initiative (AETTI)

1

Safety, risk and hazard

George Thompson

There is no such thing as an accident! If we look at the causes of what are called accidents, in almost every case there is a reason which could have been foreseen or avoided if someone had taken sufficient care or had been in possession of the necessary knowledge. It is the purpose of this book to provide that knowledge across the field of live entertainment, both indoors and out, either directly by providing detailed techniques which are complete in themselves, or indirectly by pointing the reader in the direction of authoritative sources. It is not of course possible for a book to cover every eventuality, but it is hoped that study of the material gathered here will alert workers in the industry to the dangers involved in almost all operations and will induce in them a feeling for safety – first, last, and all the time.

Workers in the entertainments industry have a reputation for a 'macho' attitude, encouraged by the old cliché 'the show must go on.' There is no doubt that if an essential feature happens to malfunction half-an-hour before hundreds or even thousands of people are due to be spectacularly entertained, there is considerable pressure from all sides to get something done, with the consequence that desperate – and therefore dangerous – measures can ensue. However, with the amount of new and complex equipment around nowadays, this attitude must be tempered with a suitable degree of caution and thought for the safety of oneself and others. Attention paid to the safety and maintenance procedures in the rest of this book could prevent an unexpected malfunction in the first place.

The theme of the safety of oneself and especially others for whom one may be responsible is being taken up more and more in modern legislation, which will be considered again and again throughout the book. Under much current and almost certainly all future law, people are being held responsible for their actions (or lack of them) and in many cases a liability under criminal law may exist. In this connection there is a worrying tendency in European Community law that proof of innocence lies with the defendant, and not with the accuser. This change is shown by the relatively new Electricity at Work Regulations 1989, in which the defendant in any Court action will have to prove that 'all reasonable steps were taken and all due diligence exercised' to avoid committing the offence. If an accident occurs, the employer is therefore automatically guilty of an offence unless he can prove that reasonable methods and procedures were in place to prevent it. This is a reversal of English law as it is commonly understood, where the prosecution would normally have had to prove negligence, and this shift of the burden of proof will have far-reaching implications for the maintenance of equipment.

Safety is a difficult word to define, although everybody knows what it means. All of life is a risk, of course, but this risk is often considerably increased at work, a fact which is generally recognized throughout industry. Even the august British Standards Institution, dedicated to providing authoritative guidance on how to make industrial and commercial products safe to use and handle, has to admit that there is a certain degree of 'unsafety' in life. This is shown in the British Standard which governs all other Standards, BS 0 'A standard for standards', which states quite bluntly that 'It is impossible to make any product or process absolutely safe.' Whilst true, this does not give anyone an excuse for sloppy thinking and haphazard methods of working.

BS 4778 'Quality vocabulary' extends our conception of safety by stating that 'Safety is the freedom from unacceptable risks of personal harm'. In this definition everything turns on what is meant by 'unacceptable', a word which obviously implies that some risks are acceptable. The question of who decides whether a risk is acceptable, and to whom, needs careful consideration in any particular work situation. In the final analysis, only an individual can decide which risks he will accept and which he will not. Of course, it is not quite so easy as that, as he may not be able to perceive the risk, either because the hazard is hidden from him, or because he does not have sufficient knowledge to judge if it presents an acceptable risk or not. It is precisely in this area that this book hopes to give some guidance to the hazards abounding in any kind of live entertainment and provide the knowledge on which the judgement of an acceptable risk can be made.

Under current legislation, not only is an employer responsible for the safety of his workers, but the workers themselves have a duty to see that others are not put in danger by their own actions. 'Safety from personal harm' therefore means not just one's own safety, but the safety of all persons, however remote, who may be affected by an action.

Economics is a factor in safety: whilst it would be possible to make almost any operation safe if enough money were spent on it, there comes a point beyond which the project just does not make economic sense. Unfortunately this is particularly so in entertainment, where after most of the production budget has been spent on spectacular effects, not much is left over to ensure the absolute safety of people working 'at the coal-face'. It should be borne in mind by such people that most safety legislation, as mentioned above, only asks an employer to take reasonable and practicable precautions, and leaves it to the Courts to decide what is reasonable or practicable in a specific case. This is all the more reason for an individual to take such precautions as are available, many of which are indicated in the following chapters.

Having mentioned legislation, at this point it is necessary to consider in more detail the terms 'hazard' and 'risk', which are widely used in the various laws on safety. Most people use these words more or less indiscriminately, but a hazard is some object, substance or circumstance which has the *potential* to cause harm, whereas risk is the *probability* that the hazard will cause actual harm. For example, travelling through the air in an aluminium tube at over 1000 mph and 30,000 ft above the ground is obviously hazardous, but statistics of the Concorde flights to date show the risk to be negligible.

To ensure safety, everyone must therefore look at the hazards around them and use their best endeavours to reduce the risk to vanishing point. This means thinking about the possible dangers before embarking on any undertaking, and a safety assessment should be a routine preliminary to all work. It is surprising how many common objects and systems are so obviously hazardous when serious consideration is given to the potential they have for causing damage. This is especially so in the theatre, where heavy objects are constantly being moved by powerful machinery, but here it is often the case that familiarity breeds contempt.

Finally, paraphrasing the well-known saying of John Philpot Curran, the price of safety is eternal vigilance.

(References to British Standards by kind permission of the British Standards Institute.)

2
Audience and crowd control

John Shaughnessy

Introduction

Indoor venues have been regulated by public authorities since the last century, and many model codes have developed to ensure safety standards in buildings. Large outdoor events, however, are relatively recent developments which began in the 1960s. When in 1971 a young girl died in dense crowd conditions on a front-of-stage barrier at a David Cassidy concert, crowd management became a feature of all subsequent events of this type.

Capacities over the years have increased from 10,000 seated in arenas to standing audiences of 120,000. The entertainments industry moved from buildings where physical conditions could be easily controlled, into open field sites where it was much more difficult.

By comparison with football matches, large outdoor pop concerts and similar events take place infrequently, and this undoubtedly contributes to keeping fatalities low. This does not mean, however, that the risk factors are low. It is necessary to use knowledge to minimize the risk through the introduction of practical safety measures.

Public safety at major events is a tightrope for the safety officer. Some events sail too close to the wind, relying heavily on crowd control measures rather than crowd management. These events are potentially damaging to the whole industry, and it is hoped that the guidance given in this chapter will help both producers and promoters avoid such dangerous entertainments.

Outdoor events can attract large audiences, in some cases in excess of 100,000, and are held at locations which vary from open fields to national stadiums (Figure 2.1). The former require a complex engineering infrastructure to be imported to the site, whereas the latter will have much of the necessary provision already there. By contrast, sports stadiums may require significant temporary alterations to be made to their structure in order to guarantee public and occupational safety, in cases where they are not used for their original purpose.

In the wake of the Bradford, King's Cross and Hillsborough disasters, both

Figure 2.1   *Live Aid Concert, Wembley, 1985 (photo courtesy Wembley Stadium Ltd)*

public authorities and central government departments have become more active in establishing safety criteria for all places of public assembly. There is a tendency to link sporting events with pop concerts simply on the basis of similar holding capacities. There are, however, fundamental differences in crowd behaviour, structural provision and the general management of sport and entertainment. By comparison with football, public order disturbances at pop concerts are rare and organized crowd violence is virtually unknown. An assessment of the reasonable practicability of safety provisions should take this into account. The direct linking of sport and entertainment in this way should be discouraged, since the lack of an accurate perception of the event can lead to expensive and inappropriate provision.

In applying safety criteria we should be wary of allowing myth to obscure fact. Environmental psychologists have in recent years caused safety professionals to question deeply their response to the potential of disaster. Many assumptions about how people behave in emergencies have been shown to be fundamentally flawed. The work of the psychologists has focused attention on information and management systems rather than a purely engineering response. For instance, the proposal that even in the late stages of an emergency people behave in a normative fashion and do not panic,[1] provided adequate verbal information and intrusive signage are available, may affect a whole range of decisions made by safety professionals who have responsibility for controlling the movements of large numbers of people at public events.

Crowd *control* implies that crowds are intrinsically dangerous. They are not: they are simply made dangerous by insufficient or inappropriate provision for their demands. Crowd *management* is the business of ensuring that the demands of a large body of people in one place are analysed and met by a combination of forward planning, engineering response, adequate information systems and alert general management. Some leading entertainment security companies use tabards emblazoned with the words 'crowd control'. Unfortunately 'crowd control' is their function: they are the first and last hope for people in difficulty. Because of poor planning, management has failed to assess the risk and provide effective safety measures. The aim should be to make crowd control a redundant activity by the implementation of crowd management. This is not simply a matter of semantics but a fundamental principle which all those involved in public safety should understand.

The intention of this chapter is to draw attention to the characteristics of crowd movement within a venue used for pop concerts and other events where large numbers are gathered together. It suggests procedures and gives practical advice for those new to the business. The remainder of the chapter is divided into sections as follows:

Risk evaluation   Making an early risk evaluation of a performance.
Licensing and inspection   Procedures for local authorities, and strategies for inspection.
Event analysis   Analysis of an event in detail to produce effective crowd management measures from the time the spectators arrive to the time they leave.
Stage front   Making safe provision for front-of-stage crowd management.
Indoor events   A safe approach to crowd management at indoor venues.
Outdoor events   A safe approach to crowd management at seated outdoor venues.

Particular attention should be paid to the stage front section: this can be an area of considerable risk if safe structural and management provisions are not in place.

Risk evaluation

At an early stage in the planning of an event, a basic risk evaluation needs to be made of the nature of the performance. Promoters, licensees and other public authorities may be very helpful in providing information. By considering the points below, an early assessment can be made of the atmosphere likely to prevail at the site on the day of the event. This will give management a valuable aid to determining reasonable practicable provisions at the site.

The nature of performers

Some performers may throw items into the audience; some may wish to throw themselves into the audience; and others may wish to perform in the audience! Some acts may encourage audiences to move towards the stage. These are exceptions rather than the rule. Management should ask how security will deal with such occasions if they arise. Behaviour as described could lead to sudden crowd movement involving large numbers of people surging and subsequently crushing others. Such performances therefore need prevention or control.

Audience behaviour

The behaviour of people who follow particular performers is often well documented and therefore predictable. Sometimes fans consume large quantities of alcohol, whilst at other times they dance aggressively. In both cases public order problems may arise, especially if a young and hysterical following attaches itself to the act. Management should be aware that this type of following exists and ensure that measures are in place to deal with it.

Many performers attract a mature audience and many acts pride themselves on the behaviour of their followers. Where audiences are known to be calm, certain requirements may be relaxed, but management should be clear as to why this has been permitted. Examples of this might be the provision of a rope barrier rather than a crowd-loaded barrier where the audience is seated. Stage thrusts can be constructed in the audience area when performers and their fans are known to have a responsible attitude.

Support acts

It is important not just to assess the main act in terms of the previous paragraphs but also to apply the same criteria to performers of lesser status lower down the bill. They may attract a small following, but their partisanship can occasionally cause friction between themselves and other groups.

Multi-act performances

Similarly, where several major acts appear on the same bill, each attracting a different following, considerable crowd movement may be observed between the acts. This movement may be perfectly orderly and present no risk, but consideration should be given to the case where one particular performer has a large or enthusiastic following, as an apparently relaxed crowd may suddenly surge and dynamic load crushing may result.

Under 16s audiences

Popular performers may attract audiences of children as young as 5 years of age. Local authorities will not usually issue licences for standing shows where performers attract a mainly under 16s audience. For a seated under 16s audience, special conditions will probably be attached to Entertainments Licences or consents. Structural and management provisions must be made to ensure the safety of children. A minimum supervision guideline used in London that seems to work well is 1 steward to every 30 children (former GLC adopted rules).

Alcohol sales

As described earlier, some gatherings may be associated with heavy drinking over a short period. Even when this is not the case, on warm summer days the spectators may drink steadily throughout the day. Although this situation may cause public order problems rather than those associated with crowd management, one may impact upon the other. Police officers have responsibility for control of alcohol sales, and good liaison and exchange of information may prevent problems before they arise.[2]

Length of performance

At large outdoor events some people may arrive at the venue the night before. Hot summer days and a long show can result in some of them being exhausted by the time of the main evening performance, which can lead to a high incidence of fainting and falling in dense crowds. Provision of effective rescue and first-aid arrangements must be made.

Experience of the promoter/licensee

On some occasions the promoter may both organize the event and be licensed by the local authority. In the case of most major events, however, the promoter will not be the licensee and the two may have different vested interests. This is not an obstacle to running a safe event, but the legal implications of this situation must be considered in terms of how to secure appropriate crowd management measures. Ultimately the licensee is responsible for meeting the terms and conditions of the Entertainments Licence, but certain critical responsibilities may be subcontracted quite properly to the promoter, e.g. control of the pit area in the front of the stage.

The organizers should assure themselves that any delegation of responsibility for matters of crowd management is appropriate. Furthermore, they must ensure that licensees or promoters are qualified by experience to cope with whatever may arise. Written records should be kept of agreements made in this respect. Where there is no track record and the competency of a promoter or licensee is unknown, references can be taken from trade associations, local authorities or police regarding a particular company or individual's ability to provide proper controls.

Police intelligence and emergency services

An important question to be answered here is: do the police have sufficient resources to commit to the event for both their public order and their traffic management responsibilities? Where police intelligence indicates that an act may have a political following or high-profile political allegiances, consultation should take place with senior police officers regarding the possibility of bomb threats. There should be a search procedure and evacuation contingency plan. Although evacuation in these circumstances is primarily a police responsibility, the means-of-escape provision is usually set as a condition of an Entertainments Licence. Clear evacuation procedures should therefore be understood by all.

Fire and ambulance services should be satisfied with access routes for emergency vehicles, and these should be remote from pedestrian areas.

Condition of venue (suitability survey)

A suitability survey will generally be carried out by the licensing authority at a venue which is not annually licensed for public entertainment. Where a venue is unsafe but can be made good, the licence applicant will be told how to remedy the situation as soon as possible. Where a venue is thoroughly unsuitable, the entertainments licence application will be refused by the local authority, which will give clear reasons in writing. Reasons for refusal could be: inadequate means of escape, unsafe structures or dangerous slopes on the site.

The organizer must be sure that whatever remedial work is promised can realistically be carried out within the time available, obviously well before the event takes place.

Other major events

Other major events may occur in the vicinity on the same day. Whilst facilities may be adequate for the planned concert, the unforeseen additional crowd loading on existing public facilities may create unpleasant or even dangerous conditions. Where temporary arrangements cannot be made to secure public safety in these circumstances, alternative times, dates or even venues should be considered.

Infrastructure

Questions to be answered about the local infrastructure are as follows. Can the public authorities guarantee sufficient rail and bus links to the site? Are access roads sufficient for the expected traffic load, and is street lighting adequate? Can water supplies, drainage and sewage facilities be connected? Any unsatisfactory answers should be addressed well in advance of the performance.

General

By applying risk evaluation criteria at an early stage, it is possible to reasonably foresee what structural and management measures are necessary to achieve safe crowd management. Wherever practicable, risk should be removed; where it cannot be removed, it should be managed. Where risk management fails, control measures should be in place to safeguard spectators.

Local authority procedures and safety inspection strategy

Licensing of places of public entertainment and other legislation

Public entertainments are licensed both in and outside London.[3, 4] There is a presumption in law that licences should be granted subject to such conditions as may be necessary. They may be issued either annually or occasionally for one or more occasions.

Local authorities are empowered to attach technical conditions to licences which must be met by the licensee. Failure to meet these conditions is a criminal offence. The authorities may refuse to issue licences, but in doing so they must be seen to be acting reasonably. Also, in setting conditions for the licence they must only require that which is reasonable and practicable. Applicants who have been refused a licence, or who feel that the conditions are either unreasonable or impractical, may appeal firstly to a Magistrates' Court and subsequently to a Crown Court against the local authority's decision.

Employers (and the self-employed) have a duty to protect the health, safety and welfare of *persons other than their employees*,[5] and it is a criminal offence to fail in that duty. Recent advice from the Health and Safety Executive suggests that greater emphasis will be placed on this legislation, not only in relation to this specific duty to audiences under Section 3 of the Health and Safety at Work Act 1974, but also in respect of the occupational safety of workers in the entertainments industry.

Local authority inspectors hold statutory warrants and are empowered to enter licensed entertainments premises at reasonable times to ensure that all is well. It is a criminal offence to obstruct them.

Premises such as football grounds are subject to additional special legal requirements,[6] and Safety Certificates are issued under the Safety at Sports Grounds Act 1975. Usually these do not cover pop concerts, and the local authority will issue a Special Safety Certificate for such events.

Having looked at our legal responsibilities, we now need to establish management protocols in the form of meetings and inspections to ensure that we meet those responsibilities.

Pre-production meeting

Large outdoor or major indoor concerts require a pre-production meeting to evaluate risk factors and to determine what is necessary in terms of crowd management measures. It is sometimes a matter of legal consent under an Entertainments Licence condition for any pop concert to take place at all. Before issuing such a consent, local authority inspectors may decide a pre-production meeting is necessary. Each proposal will be evaluated on its own merits. For events in occasionally licensed premises there should always be a pre-production meeting, because the venue is not in regular use for entertainments.

The pre-production meeting should consider crowd management measures. Subcontractors to the promoter or licensee should be present to answer questions regarding provisions necessary to comply with the conditions of the Entertainments Licence. Plans, drawings, calculations and material samples should be submitted for approval or testing at this stage.

Matters of particular concern for crowd management (Figure 2.2) might be:

- barriers and fencing
- means of access and escape
- public address installation
- staging arrangements
- mixers, delay towers and temporary structures
- emergency and management lighting
- sightlines
- production detail
- policing, security, stewarding, first-aid and emergency services provision
- evacuation plan.

All of these elements impact upon crowd management measures, and the local authority inspectors will assess what is reasonable to set as the conditions of licence in the light of the proposals.

Programme of event inspections

In order to ensure that events proceed in line with agreements at the pre-production meeting and the conditions set down, a series of inspections should be carried out as follows.

Suitability survey

A site inspection should be carried out to determine possible capacities, means of escape and the practicality of compliance with any entertainments technical regulations. Reference has already been made to this inspection under 'Risk evaluation'. This inspection should be carried out as early as possible, when the location of the event is announced.

Figure 2.2   *Curved barrier, Monsters of Rock, Castle Donington. Note the raised decking and disciplined stewards standing well back to avoid interfering with fan sightlines (photo courtesy Midland Concert Promotions Ltd)*

Pre-event inspections
For a large outdoor event, it is necessary to hold a series of programmed safety inspections during the days leading up to the event. With temporary installations and structures, the finished article is not always as shown on the plan. Indeed, it may not even be in the presumed location. Checks should be made to assess whether such changes will affect crowd movements or create dangerous situations, for example reduction of exit widths, reduction of available viewing area, and places narrowing into funnels which might cause crushing in dense crowds. It is important that safety professionals are present at the setting out of major structures, such as the perimeter fence, the stage, the stage barrier, and the mixer and delay towers to ensure compliance with any licence conditions. Because of time restrictions, these structures are often difficult or impossible to move and it is therefore imperative to get it right first time.

During-performance inspection
In order for those responsible for large-scale entertainments to understand the results of their work and gain skills in crowd management measures, it is necessary for them to attend performances and to observe how structural control measures affect crowd movement. In doing so, they may also gain skill in assessing how different types of performers or audiences require different responses.

Ideally crowd movements should be watched from a vantage point and particular observation made of the following:

- access control, and whether the arrangements lead to crushing due to poor directional feeding or poor sightlines
- exit arrangements, and whether in practice they meet the theoretical escape times
- the area immediately in front of the stage and the operation of the pit.

The front-of-stage and pit area is critical to crowd safety. Barrier design at this location is very important as the highest crowd densities are found there. It is also where there is most crowd movement, and sudden unexpected surges may occur. Close observation should be made of faces in the crowd for signs of distress or panic. Rescue tactics for distressed spectators should be evaluated and the complementary first-aid operation should also be observed. The structural provisions in these areas must assist security and first-aid personnel to do their job properly. Production detail, filming or staging arrangements must not be allowed to interfere with this priority. Safety inspectors should check these areas personally to ensure that provisions are in place and management is working efficiently.

Event analysis

Having established a broad view of the event by risk evaluation, examined the legal responsibilities and set out an inspection strategy, we now need to look specifically at locations where crowding may occur and decide to manage those situations (Figures 2.3, 2.4). Safety officers should evaluate all places where there may be a potential for high crowd density and subsequent crushing. This analysis of crowd movement should begin when spectators arrive and end when they leave the area. Those responsible should not restrict their assessment to the performance arena alone.

Public transport arrival

Liaison should be established with public transport authorities and an assessment made by them of the handling potential of stations, bus depots, drop-off points etc. These facilities must be suitable for the expected crowd loads. Suitability should be judged by density and flow rate against a time scale.

Particular attention should be paid to narrowing passageways where funnelling may occur and cause crushing. Any tunnel should be inspected in detail, always looking for dead ends or trapping points, as often such structures were not built with high crowd loading in mind.

Where station platforms are used, assurances should be obtained from the transport authorities either that they are adequate in themselves or that crowd

Figure 2.3   *'We will, we will, rock you': Freddie Mercury and Queen rock the Wembley Stadium. Note the wide fan sightlines which thin the crowd density stage centre (photo courtesy Wembley Stadium Ltd)*

management measures can be put in place to prevent overcrowding, particularly on exit from the event. In the case of major events, extra trains may be necessary to prevent a backlog of pedestrians. Contingency plans should exist to deal with this, in the form of pedestrian holding areas, usually managed by police officers.

Car parking and approach roads

It goes without saying that sufficient parking facilities should be available. Approach roads must be suitable for pedestrians to walk safely to and from the venue, and the general principle should be to separate pedestrians from vehicles. It should be remembered that at major events many thousands of people leave the site within a very short time. In many instances the only safe procedure is to close certain roads to vehicular traffic, and the police traffic division and local authority traffic engineers can usually provide traffic schemes for such occasions.

Safe queuing areas, gates and turnstiles

It is difficult to give specific advice regarding provision in these areas. However, the following points should be considered when setting technical standards.

The turnstiles in sports stadiums will already be subject to detailed inspection.[6] The maximum notional rate through any turnstile in one hour should be 660 persons (i.e. 5.45 seconds for each person), as recommended in the final report into

Figure 2.4   *Nelson Mandela Birthday Concert, Wembley Stadium. Note how the delay tower in the foreground is raised to allow a sightline through the structure. Large vision screens stage right and left also help (photo courtesy Wembley Stadium Ltd)*

the Hillsborough disaster.[7] This standard was recommended to take account of the way football supporters arrive within one hour of the start of the match. At other events the audience may generally be better behaved and arrive over a much longer period of time. Where management can guarantee a slow arrival it may be appropriate to reduce the turnstile flow rate.

Ticket sale points should be remote from the turnstiles, as should pick-up points for credit card sales. Essential security and camera checks usually cause enough delay.

Serious crowd conditions can occur, particularly at evening concerts in situations where the access system cannot process people into the venue quickly enough. This can be compounded if those outside can hear their favourite performer already on stage. Management must be sure that there are areas sufficient to hold those awaiting access and that barriers, fences, gates and turnstiles are suitable and sufficient for foreseeable crowd loads.

There must also be some method of counting individuals as they enter the site or building, so that an assessment can be quickly made of capacity remaining.

Site layout

To prevent overcrowding at an outdoor site a substantial perimeter fence should be built, 3–3.5 m in height and able to withstand crowd loading where it is predictable that this may occur. Metal track is often used for this purpose. Within the site any structure which may suffer crowd loading should either be designed to withstand right angle and parallel loads or be protected by a fence or barrier which can withstand such loads. Examples could be the mixer platform, delay speaker towers, catering points and fences in certain private areas. In designing fences or barriers one should be aware that they may create excellent viewing positions. In instances where security staff do not protect these structures by standing within the barriers, they should be close boarded to a height of 2.4 m, thus making them difficult to climb.[8]

Barriers should be designed to the following standards. Right angle loads should be taken as 3.4 kN per metre run (kN/m) and parallel loads as 2.2 kN/m (design force) at a height of 1.1 m. These are the standards for handrails and walls and have been found to be useful where crowd conditions are not excessively dense, i.e. 0.5 m² per person or looser.[8]

For a 2.4 m fence the horizontal load at 1.1 m should be 3.4 kN/m (right angle) or 2.2 kN/m (parallel) design force, and the horizontal load at 2.4 m should be 0.73 kN/m. The vertical load at 2.4 m should be 1.46 kN/m. This is a standard that was used by the former GLC for pitch perimeter fences at football grounds, and it proved effective in deterring occasional revellers safely whilst protecting loose crowds.[9] Again, these standards are not appropriate to higher-density crowds and would need to be increased for such situations.

Arena area viewing slopes

Without further structural safety provisions, viewing slopes with a gradient of in excess of 1 in 6 (9.5 degrees) are unacceptable.[10] Areas immediately in front of the stage should not slope at all and should be a flat even surface. Slopes in sports stadiums will already be subject to these technical standards.[9]

Management of access

Spectators should not be fed directly into the front-of-stage area from stage right or left. This can lead to serious overcrowding and subsequent crushing, especially when areas are simultaneously filled from the rear. Stewarding, barriers and manipulation of side-stage sightlines can help to ensure that this does not happen. Care should be taken with stage sightlines not to compress the crowd shape into a wedge as this will create discomfort. The golden rule is to always feed from the opposite end of the venue to the stage, closing off stage right and left access temporarily if necessary. Once the crowd is in, it will self-regulate. Lines of stewards may be employed across the area on entry to prevent people running down the site towards the stage, and their actions can be reinforced by complementary public address announcements.

Once people arrive at the front of the stage area, they should be allowed to stand or preferably encouraged to sit as close as possible to the stage security barrier. If security staff hold a gap and then later move back behind the barrier, the audience will immediately assume that the concert is about to start and crush towards the barrier. This phenomenon can often be observed hours before the first performer is due to arrive on stage, and leaves fans standing uncomfortably for a long period in dense crowd conditions. There may of course be major crowd movements during intervals. Also, at the programmed end of the concert the artiste(s) may begin an encore, thus causing the departing audience to re-enter the venue. Structural and stewarding preparations should take this into account.

Disabled persons access and egress

Every opportunity should be taken to make provision for disabled persons to attend major events. Provision of level access for wheelchair users, avoiding densely crowded areas, should be arranged. One way to achieve this would be to offer wheelchair users the option of entering the site prior to the normal gate time, thus avoiding congestion.

Wheelchair users will require elevated sightlines in standing audiences. Platforms built for this purpose should not be remote from the stage or crowd but should blend into the event naturally, e.g. they could be built into the terraces of seated bays at football grounds. Toilets for the disabled should be close at hand. On open field sites, tracking may need to be laid, particularly in poor weather conditions. Note that there are specific technical standards for means of escape from buildings for the disabled.[11, 12]

Dense, volatile crowd conditions are dangerous even for the able-bodied, but the disabled and wheelchair users are at an additional disadvantage in these situations. If it is possible to provide a dedicated access and egress system at the event, this can be a great help. Where it is not possible, this should not be used as an excuse to prevent wheelchair users attending major events, and other alternative methods to achieve safe access and egress should be sought.

Organizers should remember that not all disabled people are in wheelchairs or mobility impaired! Some may be vision or hearing impaired, and provision should be made for them to enjoy the show as safely and comfortably as the able-bodied.

Holding capacity

Standards have in the past been considered appropriate to assess safe overall capacity for an event. The holding capacity of any space occupied by the audience should be based on the following:[10]

1 The number of seats where seating accommodation is provided.
2 One person for each 450 mm (1 ft 6 in) length of seating where bench seating is provided.
3 One person per 0.5 m² (5 ft²) on stepped terraces. This standard is reasonable for one-day events or evening performances.

4 One person per 0.75 m² (8 ft²) on sloping terraces and arenas, whether indoor or outdoor. This is more of a comfort standard, and is probably excessive for the average short event: it may be more appropriate to two-day festivals.

These standards are in line with current Home Office guidelines.[13] However, it is felt that safe events can be held based on a 0.5 m²/person density standard, which is also the accepted norm for standing audiences at indoor premises.

It should be remembered that for short-duration events or for areas immediately in front of the stage, crowd densities may be well in excess of these figures. For practical purposes this is the approximate density of a crowded bar area. The notional mathematical calculation is all very well, but it should be remembered that 0.3 m²/person will be the real density close to the stage even if only 50 tickets are sold.

In some circumstances other legislation and technical standards may be applicable, e.g. at a certificated sports ground.[7] Where there is a conflict of standards, it is reasonable to interpolate the figures by taking into account the different activities and lengths of time around which the codes are intended to apply.

Deduction should be made of areas taken up by mixer, delay towers, merchandising and catering units etc. Sightline-obscured areas must also be deducted. There should be sound reasons for whatever final holding capacity is decided, and the decision and the reasons should be given in writing. The calculated area and crowd density are not, however, the only factors in assessing capacity. The density and capacity should never exceed the available overall calculated means of escape.

Means of escape

It is essential for effective crowd management during emergencies and evacuations that a first-class means of escape exists at the venue.

Outdoor sites and sports grounds

A 15 minute evacuation time is recommended for outdoor sites.[10] Where concerts are held at sports grounds or certificated stadiums the exit times should be between 2 minutes 30 seconds and 8 minutes, with a travel distance of 30 m to a place of safety.[9] These standards represent good general guidelines and should be thought of as maximum escape times dependent upon otherwise safe conditions at the venue.

Escape times may be calculated through exits at outdoor events using the standard flow rates of 40 persons/minute. Flow rates of 60 persons/minute may be used from wide gangways or open areas. Unit widths (person widths) should be taken as 0.55 m/person.

Example
To calculate the holding capacity based on the exit potential of a venue, the width
of an individual exit should be divided by the number of unit (person) widths and
multiplied by the flow rate. That result should again be multiplied by the required
exit time and then by the number of exits; this gives the exit capacity. For example:

2.2 m exit divided by 0.55 m = 4 unit widths (or persons)
   (where 0.55 m is the notional width of a person)
4 unit widths × 40 persons/minute = 160 persons/minute/exit
   (where 40 persons/minute is the flow rate)
160 persons/minute × 8 minutes = 1280 persons/exit in 8 minutes
   (where 8 minutes is the exit time appropriate to that venue)

Assuming the site has 10 evenly distributed 2.2 m exits, the notional capacity
would be 12,800 persons (based on exit only). This capacity figure should then be
compared with the area and density calculation which, if it is greater, should be
reduced accordingly.

Canter *et al.*[14] have suggested that the flow rates used extensively in the UK
understate the real speed but experience at Wembley Stadium is that the 40
persons/minute standard delivers people through exits slightly quicker than the
mathematical notional time. This should not be a surprise, since real flow rate is
dependent upon the particular structural arrangements present and not a
mathematical formula. Exit flow time should never be viewed in isolation, and flow
rates can often be adjusted between 20 and 60 persons/minute dependent upon
external factors. Again, whatever is decided should be based on sound reasoning
and written down.

Indoor premises
A variable evacuation time between 2 and 3 minutes is acceptable dependent upon
conditions.[13] Travel distances may vary between 12 m and 30 m depending upon
the arrangements at the venue.[15] Matters which should be considered include such
issues as exit widths, structural provisions (particularly fire separation) and fire
warning and detection systems.[16] For the purposes of this chapter, 'means of
escape' is only discussed as an element of crowd management.

Public address systems and signage
Studies have shown that where persons are subjected to overcrowded conditions
and excess stimulation they subsequently suffer problems of orientation.[17] This
American research has demonstrated that after exposure to high-density crowds,
people are unable to draw an accurate map of the area and even find a map of the
area to be unhelpful. In conditions of excess stimulation, as found in pop concert
audiences, signage and public address announcements should be intrusive, to be
sure that the message is clearly understood. Signage may be subject to specific
rules of management.[16, 18-20]

Emergency plans

There should always be an emergency evacuation plan, agreed between the management, the emergency services and the local authority. The details of this plan should be attached to either the occasional music licence, the annual music licence, or the special safety certificate in the case of a certificated sports ground.

The plan should provide arrangements for the following:

- identification of key decision-taking personnel
- location of a central control point equipped with a communications network
- arrangements for stopping the concert in an emergency
- identification of sterile emergency routes
- rendezvous points for emergency vehicles
- identification of road closures and holding areas for members of the public
- detail of the script of coded messages to management and stewards, for example to open gates
- detail of the script of coded 'stand down' messages
- detail of the script of public address announcements
- detail of first-aid casualty arrangements together with lists of hospitals in the area prepared for major catastrophes.

In an emergency, on no account should music suddenly be turned off. This can cause major public disorder and crowd disturbance, exacerbating the work of the police, security and first-aid staff. Volume should be reduced gradually, or if possible authorities should wait until the end of that part of the performance.

Emergency announcements should not be left to performers – but their assistance may be enlisted in calming the crowd. Persons making emergency announcements should work from a prepared script and should be experienced in doing so.

Stage and front barrier area

Introduction

The area directly in front of the stage barrier is perhaps the most critical to consider (Figure 2.5). Crowd densities here may be very high. Crowd surges may be experienced, and subsequent dynamic loads on those at the front of the stage may be considerable. Such surges and loads however are generally instantaneous, and experience at sports stadiums together with research suggests that the greatest danger is not dynamic load crushing but crowd collapse and subsequent traumatic asphyxiation.[21, 22] Most sites are wide open areas and therefore not subject to the overcrowding and static load crushing potential of an enclosed bay at a football ground. Static loads do not appear to play a significant part in causing injury at major events such as pop concerts: the vast majority of first-aid cases reported are fainting and exhaustion. These conditions may also be due in part to other factors

Figure 2.5 *Curved scaffold barrier. Note A-brace construction and tubes to the stage to prevent lateral movement (photo courtesy Wembley Stadium Ltd)*

(heat, alcohol, hysteria etc.). People may however fall into the crowd as a result of the surge and heave motion and be trampled, possibly resulting in serious injury or even death. Fortunately, experience shows that this is rare. Injury may also occur on occasion due to public order disturbance, and good security provision in this area is vital.

Although to some people the thought of such crowd conditions may be an anathema, to others it is part of their enjoyment. Provided that adequate provisions are made, a great deal can be achieved not only to make the area safe, but also to introduce comfort.

There are four major potential hazards for concert-goers at standing shows:

1 crowd surges (causing injuries to legs, feet etc.)
2 dynamic load crushing on the front barrier (as a result of crowd surges)

3 potential trampling (again as a result of falling in a crowd surge)
4 injury due to public order disturbance.

The following section seeks to provide a strategy to apply in order to deal with these hazards. Those regularly involved in events will develop skills in applying the safety criteria since there is an interrelationship between all the provisions which ultimately creates a safe event.

Stages

Stages should be positioned so that the area immediately in front is level and even. Surfaces should not be slippery. The heights of the stage and the screamers (platforms extending out stage right and left to the extremities of the PA wings and used by performers) should be set to afford good sightlines, particularly from the front of the stage barrier. The performers' stage position should be downstage where side stages or drapes do not obscure side views; where performers must be located upstage for production reasons, consideration should be given to setting back side stages. Promoters should be encouraged to provide video or projection screens. Good sightlines are critical in reducing front-of-stage crowd density and avoiding surges and subsequent crushing.

Sightlines

The general principle should be to achieve the widest possible sightline in an arc from stage right to stage left. If this is ensured then a comfortable and safe crowd shape is created, and fans do not need to crush to the front or stage centre to obtain a satisfactory view.

Front-of-stage barriers

Various types of barrier are currently in use in the entertainments industry:

- An A-frame scaffold barrier. This normally has a 1 m tread at the front. In some cases it is tied to the stage to prevent lateral movement.
- A demountable barrier system. This is custom built and easily transported. It is also A-framed and relies upon a tread plate at the front to maintain stability. It is free standing.
- A barrier constructed from staging sections with additional bracing to meet loading requirements. These may be box-section steel structures.

For many years a loading standard of 3 kN per metre run at a height of 1.2 m was required.[10] Current standards are more of the order of 5 kN/m in line with sports ground codes.[8] In addition, 1.02–1.12 m has been shown to be the height at which most people can withstand the greatest pressure.[21, 22] The loading factors on the barrier are set at a standard to avoid structural collapse, and not at a pressure limit which can be endured by human beings.

Where it is foreseeable that standing audiences are expected to produce crowd loading, a barrier should always be required as a condition of the local authority licence. Where a seated audience at an indoor concert is not expected to migrate into the gangways, it may be acceptable not to use a barrier, but this will depend upon the performer and his/her following. Barriers should be set at a minimum distance of 3.05 m from the downstage edge.[10] It is reasonable to reduce this to 2.44 m for closely seated audiences. These distances may appear to be onerous for the performer who wishes to be close to the audience, but the intention is to prevent enthusiastic members of that audience from jumping on to the stage. Once space is deducted for bass bins in the pit and braces from the barrier, the pit security and first aid have as little as a 1 m gangway in which to work.

The downstage edge should be taken as the last edge of the stage structure and not the edge of the performance area: camera platforms may protrude a number of metres beyond the latter. This does not include thrusts.

Although in many cases straight barriers have been the norm, wide convex curved barriers (as recommended in the Health and Safety Commission guide[10]) have been shown to provide considerable safety benefits where standing audiences are concerned. *Concave stage barriers should never be permitted as they form dangerous trapping areas* (Figures 2.6, 2.7).

The curve of a convex barrier should be across the main performance area, terminating close to the ends of the side stages. Curved barriers have the following advantages over straight barriers:

1 They have the effect of dissipating crowds away from the centre of the stage and, when used in conjunction with escapes at stage right and left, form a valuable adjunct to means-of-escape provision.

Figure 2.6 *How not to do it! A concave barrier arrangement, Rolling Stones concert, East Berlin. The centre of this barrier forms a dangerous trapping area where crowd density and compression will be at its highest*

Figure 2.7   *Straight barriers made from staging sections, Rolling Stones concert, East Berlin. Note that the stewards' platform is too high and has a camera track obstructing their gangway, i.e. there is no pit*

2 Because they have a greater length, they provide a wider front row sightline.
3 They improve security by placing a greater distance between the downstage edge and the barrier, making it difficult for enthusiastic fans to jump the stage.
4 They provide a wider area for rescue and first aid to operate within the pit should it be necessary.

A production argument may be put forward that the performer wishes to be closer to the audience. However, this should never be a basis for accepting a straight barrier. As an alternative, stage thrusts may be acceptable to achieve this production requirement. It is a good general principle that straight barriers are only suitable for seated audiences. Density appears to be uniformly high along the length of a straight barrier, rather than concentrated in the centre and thinning towards the edges as with a curved (convex) barrier.

When evaluating a barrier, plans and calculations should show that not only the structure but also the individual elements are suitable for the purpose. Metal barriers should be smooth with no rough edges or trapping points. The top of the front plate or board should be padded to prevent injury. Scaffold barriers should have all exposed couplers padded as they may cause injury. Where ply is used as a front board it should be 18 mm. If a satisfactory curve cannot be obtained and the thickness is reduced to 12 mm, then the board should be treated to achieve a standard of BS 476 Class 1 surface spread of flame and should be no lower standard throughout its thickness.[16]

The design of stage barriers should include a raised deck between the barrier and the stage. The tread plate on some barriers is essential to the integrity and stability of the structure and ideally it should be low in profile. Some scaffolds may not allow this, in which case the tread should be gently feathered to ground level.

Where staging sections are used as a barrier, the elements and overall structure should meet the general design criteria and loading requirements of stage barriers. Such arrangements should be system designed and not *ad hoc* provisions based on spare staging.

Side-stage barrier or fences

On wide outdoor concert stages the 1.2 m stage barrier will need to rise to 2.4 m at some point towards the extremities. The design of this feature regulates the shape of the crowd to either a wide fan or a narrow wedge. Management may wish to have a narrow crowd wedge to make the pit manageable with limited numbers of stewards. However, a wide fan is likely to create a thinner crowd density, which is preferable.

The high fence at stage right and left provides an excellent sightline obstruction at the ends of the side stages. This is helpful where pressure relief or evacuation exits are provided in these locations. This high barrier ensures that these important exits are kept clear and ready for use in an emergency. Where the site or building is suitable, escapes at stage right and left should be provided for standing audiences.

Security or rescue personnel may need to go into the crowd to assist individuals or to deal with public disorder. Access gates should be provided at the far ends of the high side-stage barriers to facilitate this. The high side-stage barriers also provide ideal locations to place spotter platforms to allow security or rescue staff to watch the crowds without interfering with sightlines.

Rescue and security in the pit area

A specialist team of experienced and disciplined stewards should be available within the pit. They should work in conjunction with first-aid personnel and be under the direction of a senior steward. Stewards working in this area must be trained to recognize distressed individuals in the crowd. They must be physically capable of dealing with both disorder and rescue as necessary. To assist their work, first-aid points should be in close proximity to the stage.

Thrusts within the barrier

Should thrusts be used within the barrier, care should be taken not to allow interference with the rescue, security or first-aid operation. They should be a sufficient distance from the stage to prevent stage jumping.

Other obstacles within the barrier

Sub-bass bins, camera track and large numbers of press photographers may obstruct access in the pit area, prejudicing safety arrangements. Clear agreements should exist as to exactly what structural and management provisions are to be in place. Safety officers should ensure that all agreements are fully met in this critical area. Authorized senior rescue and first-aid staff should remove anything or anybody who interferes with the safe operation of the pit.

Pens on open air arenas or sites for standing audiences

Penning of audiences in these situations is not reasonably practicable and is generally an unsafe procedure. It is difficult to meet the necessary structural loading requirements without major works to achieve footings. Alternatively, penning requires a vast amount of suitable demountable barrier. Planning adequate means of escape is often impractical. Penning is not recommended as an appropriate crowd management measure, except as a result of a multiple barrier installation (see below).

Multiple barrier arrangements

It may be possible to introduce double or triple barrier arrangements radiating out from the front of the stage, thus forming pens. The barriers should be convex curves with escapes at both ends. Where such barriers are installed, arrangements must secure evacuation within a specified time. A calculation must be made of the overall impact upon means of escape from the arena or site when crowd loads are aggregated. Double or triple systems can reduce the incidence of crowd surges and subsequent crushing to zero, provided that a comfortable capacity calculation is made and the structure is managed properly. Each curved barrier can be provided with a sterile corridor behind it, to enable stewards and first-aid personnel to have access to the public. The barriers used to achieve this should meet the required loading of 5 kN per metre run.[8]

Sterile areas must be maintained at the ends of the barriers laterally up and down the site, to ensure an absence of congestion and guarantee a means of escape at stage right and left. Escape routes can be maintained as sterile areas by gates at the edges of the barrier furthest from the stage. Trapping points can easily be created at these access gates and these may be dealt with by sightline obscuration. Great care needs to be taken in applying principles of means of escape to these structures. All gates must open in the direction of the exit and no gate should impede the path of another exit route. Some sites will be wholly unsuitable for these arrangements.

With multiple barrier systems, strict control of capacity must be achieved. The capacity for the pens therefore will be set as a condition of the Entertainments Licence. One system that has proved effective in controlling access is the use of colour-coded wrist bands for fans (one colour for each pen). A fixed number is

Figure 2.8 *Curved demountable barrier used in a multiple system, Feyenoord Stadium, Rotterdam. Note the sterile gangway for rescue/first aid*

issued to security personnel, corresponding to the capacity of the pens. If a band is removed to pass to others, the fastening is destroyed and entry to the pen is refused.

Where enthusiastic audiences are concerned, it is likely that many of the problems normally encountered at the front-of-stage barrier will be experienced at the barrier furthest from the stage. First-aid and security management arrangements should therefore reflect this hazard. The indications are, however, that because of the wider sightline potential (75% in some cases) and the increased distance from the stage, the incidence of crowd surge and crushing is vastly reduced.

Multiple barrier systems may not be suitable for all sites or buildings. They are more suitable for pop concerts in sports stadiums because of the advantage of pitch perimeter fencing in controlling sterile side escapes. These crowd-loaded structures would be difficult and expensive to achieve on open sites and may not be reasonably practicable. If the means-of-escape requirements are not considered with great care, multiple barriers can become a system of dangerous pens, but if properly installed they can perform admirably in making the event much more comfortable and safe (Figure 2.8).

Crowd management at indoor concerts

Standing indoor concerts

These events will generally be permitted by local authorities for audiences largely under 16 years of age.

The holding capacity should be assessed using the criteria set out earlier under 'Holding capacity' and 'Means of escape', i.e. the calculation is based on area, but with priority given to available means of escape within a specified time. A suitable convex crowd-loaded curved barrier should be installed, to meet the criteria set out under 'Front-of-stage barriers'.

There should be careful control of floor capacity to prevent overcrowding. A suitable method would be utilizing the coloured wrist band method, as detailed under 'Multiple barrier arrangements'.

Mixed standing and seated indoor concerts

Where standing and seated areas are mixed at the same event, the standing area should be nearest to the stage. The seated area should be at the rear of the hall, and on raked tiers so that sightlines are not obscured. Where this situation is reversed, i.e. the seats are in front of a standing audience, crowd control problems can occur at the access points to the seating area as members of the audience try to get closer to the stage.

Seated indoor concerts

With closely seated audiences a straight barrier presents no problems (Figure 2.9). The front row of seats should be only one seatway distance from the front barrier (where sightlines permit). Escape gangways along the front row should not be permitted as they become gathering areas for members of the audience and, once full, can become unmanageable and dangerous.

House management should of course not permit standing on seats, but it is usually quite safe for the audience to stand in their seat place. After all, that is the position they would be in directly prior to evacuation. On the other hand it should be appreciated that standing audiences can cause irritation if those behind wish to remain seated.

Indoor concerts (general)

There should be sufficient safe holding areas for the public outside the building. Where temporary barriers are used for queues, they should not be of a design that will topple easily. Most police control barriers have extended feet that are a serious trip hazard. Queues should not force other pedestrians to walk in the road.

Rules of management or technical regulations adopted by the local authority

Figure 2.9   *Indoor seated concert at Wembley arena: Kenny Rogers. Note the absence of a stage barrier and wide gangways for this relaxed country and western singer (photo courtesy Wembley Stadium Ltd)*

may specify crowd management conditions for concerts at indoor venues. Detailed technical standards do exist on seating provision, means of escape, notification of concerts etc., and it is wise to check the legal requirements.

An evacuation procedure should exist for premises whether they are licensed annually or occasionally, and all stewards should be fully briefed in these procedures. Experience shows that closely seated audiences evacuate more slowly than standing audiences, but this is offset by the fact that evacuation is more orderly.

With occasionally licensed indoor premises, it is again critical that an early suitability survey is carried out, as detailed earlier under 'Programme of event inspections'.

Seated outdoor concerts

Seated outdoor concerts are popular in the US but are still the exception rather than the rule in Great Britain, no doubt due to climatic conditions (Figure 2.10). Control of audience migration is the most formidable problem, and adequate

Figure 2.10 *Seated outdoor concert: Amitabh Bachan. Note the use of perimeter fence controlling access to seat blocks on the pitch area (photo courtesy Wembley Stadium Ltd)*

structural and management methods must be employed to prevent it. If not controlled properly, such events can become volatile and consequently dangerous.

General technical guidance on seatways should be followed.[15, 16, 18] Particular care should be taken to ensure sound fixing of individual seats, seat rows and seat blocks, which can be difficult to achieve at open air venues. Floor bar systems may be permitted, provided they are not a trip hazard.

There should be adequate control between areas of differently priced seats. If barriers are used in gangways they must be instantly removable, or must be fixed securely and must open in the direction of escape. They must not topple easily.

Where seated concerts take place in sports grounds, pitch perimeter fences or moats may be utilized as a control feature between differently priced seats. Pass-out arrangements must be made to allow access to toilets and refreshment facilities in other parts of the site. Adequate means-of-escape provision must be maintained from the arena area directly to final exits. Alternatively, exits may be provided through the bays, as long as evacuation criteria are met. In all cases the evacuation times must comply with current legislation.

Gangways should be adequate for means of escape but not too wide. Wide escape gangways can become uncontrollable in situations of audience migration, and consideration should be given to providing a number of narrower gangways. As with indoor seated audiences, the front row should only be one seatway width from the barrier. Gangways should therefore not be provided between the front row and the pit barrier, as this creates an ideal location for migrating members of the audience to watch the show.

For a show which is half seated and half standing, it is not recommended that the seating is placed closest to the stage. This creates crowd migration problems at the barrier or gate where access is gained to the seating compound. Standing audiences should always be closest to the stage, and any seating behind them should be tiered to provide a good sightline.

Ticket sales should be known in advance. This is important, as if there are large areas of vacant seating near to the stage, impatient audiences will try to migrate closer. Subsequently, when the rightful holders of tickets for those seats arrive, the interlopers have to be moved on and may congregate in the fire lanes, at which point it is difficult to move them back to their proper seats. The coloured wrist band system would again prove useful for different price blocks to prevent overcrowding, as explained under 'Multiple barrier arrangements'.

Acknowledgement

I should like to thank my colleague Colin Wickes for his help in the preparation of this chapter.

References

1 Wardlaw, G. 'Human behaviour in emergencies', *Fire International*, no. 80, 1983.
2 Licensing Act 1964, Chapter 26, HMSO.
3 London Government Act 1963, Schedule 12, HMSO.
4 Local Government (Miscellaneous Provisions) Act 1982, Schedule 1, HMSO.
5 Health and Safety at Work (etc.) Act 1974, HMSO.
6 Safety of Sports Grounds Act 1975, Chapter 52, HMSO.
7 Rt Hon. Lord Justice Taylor. *The Hillsborough Stadium Disaster Final Report*, HMSO, 1990.
8 Home Office and Scottish Office. *Guide to Safety at Sports Grounds* (The Green Guide), HMSO, 1990.
9 Greater London Council. *Safety of Sports Grounds*, practice note 5, unpublished.
10 Health and Safety Commission. *Guide to Health Safety and Welfare at Pop Concerts and similar events*, in press, 1993.
11 BS 5588: Part 8: 1988. Code of Practice for Means of Escape for Disabled People.
12 Building Regulations 1985. *Approved Document M: Access for Disabled People*, HMSO.

13 Home Office and Scottish Home and Health Department. *Guide to Fire Precautions in Existing Places of Entertainment and Like Premises*, HMSO, 1990.

14 Canter, D., Comber, M. and Uzzell, D. *Football in its Place: An Environmental Psychology of Football*, Routledge, 1989.

15 Greater London Council. *Code of Practice: Means of Escape in Case of Fire* (The Orange Guide), 1983.

16 London District Surveyors Association. *Model Technical Regulations for Places of Public Entertainment*, 1991.

17 MacKintosh, E., Saggert, S. and West, S. 'Two studies of crowding in urban places', *Environment and Behaviour*, vol. 7, no. 2, 1975.

18 London District Surveyors Association. *Model Rules of Management for Places of Public Entertainment*, 1989.

19 Safety Signs Regulations 1980, HMSO.

20 BS 5378: Part 1: 1980.

21 Thompson, Janet. Home Office paper, March 1973 (unpublished).

22 Evans, E.J. and Hayden, F. *Tests on Live Subjects to Determine the Tolerable Forces that may be Exerted by Crowd Control Crush Barriers*, November 1971 (unpublished).

3
Fire safety precautions

Terry Ashton

Introduction

Much has been written about fire and its causes and it is therefore difficult to add anything original, but this chapter will review the precautions to be taken and give guidance to the sources of authoritative advice.

If one had to choose, death by fire would be one of the least popular, even if it occurred whilst doing something enjoyable. This is all the more reason why places of entertainment should have proper systems of fire safety management and why safety precautions should be strictly enforced. Most fires are preventable, and all staff should be vigilant about ensuring that they are not responsible for setting up circumstances in which a fire could begin. If a fire should break out, early and positive action will ensure there are no casualties.

Fire casualties

Fire is an ever-present threat to human life. It is an unfortunate fact that over 90% of the casualties occur in the home, where it is difficult to introduce much worthwhile legislation. However, we should not be complacent about this in considering precautions in places of entertainment. Deaths from fire in such places are both politically and socially unacceptable, as well as in many cases being entirely needless. There have been numerous fires in places of public entertainment resulting in large casualties, and each significant fire in the United Kingdom has resulted in extensive investigation, public enquiries or even legislation.

A few examples of fires in places of public entertainment worldwide are as follows:

- In 1970, 142 people lost their lives in the Cinq-Sept dance hall in Saint Laurent-du-Pont, France.
- In 1972, 172 people lost their lives in a night-club in Osaka, Japan.

- In the same year, 37 people died in the Wagon Wheel Lounge, a night-club in Montreal, Canada.
- In 1975, 15 people died in a fire in the Six Nine Discothèque, a dance hall in La Louvière, Belgium.
- In 1977, 164 people lost their lives in a fire in the Kentucky Supper Club, a restaurant and night-club in Southgate, Kentucky, USA.
- In 1981 a fire in the Stardust Disco in Dublin, Eire was responsible for 48 fatalities.
- In 1985 a fire in a football stand at Bradford City Football Club in Bradford, UK caused 56 people to lose their lives.

There is no common thread running through all these fires. Locked or blocked exists were one of the causes in some of the cases; highly flammable wall linings or decorations contributed to the severity of the fire in other cases; whilst in yet others the fatalities might have been reduced if the occupants had been given earlier warning (or any warning at all) of the outbreak of fire. It is undoubtedly true, however, that locked exits or overcrowding or the lack of warning given to the occupants of the building point to bad management. This illustrates that good management of places of public entertainment is a crucial element in the provision of public safety, if not the most important element.

The law governing public entertainment

Almost every conceivable type of public entertainment, from the public performance of plays to the showing of films and videos in hotel bedrooms, and from skating to music and dancing, is governed by statute and licensed, generally by local authorities. It would not be appropriate or possible to list all the various statutes applicable to entertainment here, but the principal ones are as follows:

- Theatres Act 1968
- Cinematograph (Safety) Regulations 1955
- Cinematograph (Children) Regulations 1955
- London Government Act 1963 (which applies to Greater London only)
- Local Government (Miscellaneous Provisions) Act 1981.

These are generally enforced by local or district authorities with a varying degree of input from the fire authorities (fire brigades).

One Act of Parliament which can impinge on the activities of entertainers, but which is not specifically related to entertainment as such, is the Fire Precautions Act 1971 (as amended by the Health and Safety at Work Act 1974 and the Fire Safety and Safety of Places of Sports Act 1987). This Act can be called upon by local authorities to secure closure or part closure of buildings used for entertainment where there is 'excessive risk to persons in case of fire'. It is, therefore, an important enactment and should be carefully studied.

We have already mentioned another statute which is not specifically related to places of public entertainment but which has far-reaching implications for those employed in such places: the Health and Safety at Work Act 1974. This Act is extremely important, and everyone in the entertainments industry should by now be aware of its general principles. In simple terms, the Act places a responsibility on management *and on individuals* to ensure the safety of their colleagues and others working around them.

Functions of the licensing authorities

As the name suggests, licensing authorities grant licences for public entertainment and so they are said to license premises. Initially they will have to be satisfied that a building or part of a building is suitable for the grant of the licence applied for, taking into account the views of their own technical staff and the fire brigade regarding suitability in fire safety terms but also the views of the police, local residents etc.

Licences are generally renewed annually on payment of the appropriate fee. This is not an automatic process, however, and if buildings have been allowed to deteriorate such that they have become unsafe or have not been managed properly the licensing authority will refuse to renew the licence.

Depending upon the staffing levels in authorities, premises will be visited periodically to see that their fire and public safety arrangements are being adequately maintained. Visits will also be made unannounced during performances to see that the premises are being properly run. In theatres, visits will be made when a change of production is to take place. Frequently, inspections will be made by the fire authority as well as the local authority.

Most, if not all, licences issued by the licensing authorities will contain special conditions under which the licence may operate. These conditions normally relate to the numbers of persons that may be admitted to the premises, or to how the premises and its infrastructure should be operated.

Licensing authorities frequently have their own rules of management which they issue to licensees and which relate, among other things, to the conduct of a licensed premises. A good example of these is the *Model Rules of Management for Places of Public Entertainment* issued by the London District Surveyors Association.[1]

Some authorities may grant occasional licences. These are generally granted to premises which are, as the name suggests, used only occasionally for public entertainment, but they may also be granted to premises which would not be regarded as suitable for the grant of licences which could be used at any time. They are generally for specific events in places such as church halls, tented structures or even open air venues. It might be thought that the safety standards which are provided in premises occasionally licensed are inferior to those provided in high street cinemas and theatres: this is not necessarily the case, as temporary arrangements could be made in a building to render it suitable for use for public entertainment.

Fire precautions

Fire precautions can be divided into passive and active measures to deal with fire safety. Passive measures generally describe structural fire precautions, for example measures to contain fire, to separate escape routes from fire sources, and to protect the structure of buildings against premature collapse in fire. Active measures include installations which react to fire such as sprinklers, smoke detection systems, and smoke control systems.

It will be obvious that active systems need to be adequately maintained in order to be effective, but it is not so obvious that the effectiveness of passive measures can also be seriously compromised by the lack of proper maintenance or unauthorized tampering.

Technical guidance

There is sufficient technical guidance available to satisfy the needs of everybody involved in the entertainments industry, from designers of new buildings through to their end users. It would not be appropriate to list every guide or code of practice that has ever been produced, but it is worth identifying the major guidance documents with which everyone connected with the entertainments industry should familiarize themselves.

There can be little doubt that the former Greater London Council was responsible for producing the most comprehensive and the most widely used guidance until recent years. The GLC's *Places of Public Entertainment: Technical Regulations,*[2] as with those produced by its predecessor the London County Council, have been widely used in the UK, together with its *Code of Practice: Means of Escape in Case of Fire.*[3] The *Technical Regulations* have been used not only for purpose-built or new places of public entertainment but also for the adaptation of existing buildings. The London District Surveyors Association has produced a replacement for the GLC *Technical Regulations*, the *Model Technical Regulations for Places of Public Entertainment.*[4] This publication brings the technical standards closer to those contained in guidance issued by the Department of the Environment in support of the Building Regulations 1991.[5]

The value of the GLC documents may well now be historical, as newer documents have arrived on the scene which have built on the work done by the GLC. Anybody who is connected with a place of public entertainment which was licensed by the GLC may wish to use the documents as workshop manuals, as they indicate how places of public entertainment should have been arranged, what areas were required to be fire separated from public areas, and so on. Sadly, neither of the two GLC documents is readily available, although some local authorities in London have technical regulations based on the GLC document.

Another GLC publication which is most useful but which is also not readily available is the *Code of Practice for Pop Concerts.*[6] No explanation is needed as to the subject matter of the 'Pop code', as it became known. There is, however, no comparable guidance available at present.

Another essential document is the Home Office *Guide to Fire Precautions in Existing Places of Entertainment and Like Premises.*[7] This must be regarded as the bible for people adapting existing buildings or parts of buildings into places of public entertainment. It was published in 1990 as a replacement for guidance issued by the Home Office in 1934![8] The *Guide* not only advises on how to adapt an existing building to render it suitable for public entertainment, but also gives information on the safe operation of electrical and gas equipment, the selection of appropriate fire extinguishing apparatus for the different parts of the building, how to use special effects, pyrotechnics and firearms safely, and what precautions need to be taken with entertainments provided in tents or with circuses. An interesting feature is that it identifies three separate classes of building according to their construction and recommends different evacuation times and other standards for the three classes.

A new British Standard has been published, BS 5588: Part 6: 1991,[9] dealing with fire precautions in the design, construction, and use of places of assembly. This is essentially a guide for the design of new buildings, although it is also intended to apply to alterations to existing buildings. It contains a sizeable section on the safe management of places of assembly. Unlike most other published guidance on places of entertainment, but in common with the Home Office *Guide* referred to earlier, it gives a rationale for its recommendations in the form of commentary. This commentary gives the reasoning behind each recommendation and helps considerably when it comes to applying the advice. The standard is, however, unique in 'leaving the door open' for fire-engineered solutions for buildings which cannot meet its recommendations. An example of this would be the use of smoke control to enable travel distances to exceed those recommended in the document. Another would be the use of an engineered smoke control system to give an equivalent amount of protection to the more traditionally used methods of smoke control such as haystack lanterns over stage areas.

There are numerous other publications produced by other bodies, all of which provide invaluable guidance on various aspects of fire safety in places of public entertainment. However, the Home Office *Guide* and BS 5588: Part 6 should be regarded as essential reading.[7, 9]

Operational precautions

The precautions that need to be taken in places of public entertainment could be divided into those which are necessary to safeguard the customers (the public) and those which are necessary to look after the staff or performers, but such a division would be largely artificial since public, staff and performers are invariably intermingled and at risk simultaneously from a fire.

Nevertheless, a distinction can be made as to how safety is provided for the public on the one hand and for staff and performers on the other. Examples of this would be the type of fastenings provided on exit doors, whether a fire alarm signal was audible or not, and the degree of signposting needed in different parts of the building.

Health and Safety at Work Act 1974

Because of the implications of the Health and Safety at Work Act, it can never be the case that safety can be left to management. It is therefore vital that everybody employed in a place of entertainment understands the implications of his or her actions.

Clearly, different levels of management have specific duties. For example, it would not be necessary for everybody employed in a theatre to know when and at what intervals a sprinkler installation needed to be tested. On the other hand, everybody should be aware that a fire door should not be wedged open and that escape routes should not be used for the storage of scenery, props or anything else. Under the Health and Safety at Work Act, any employee seeing such a situation should immediately rectify it if possible and/or bring it to the attention of his or her superior.

Levels of responsibility can and should be established. Each employee should receive basic training which encompasses familiarization with the building layout and its escape routes, the routine to be followed in the event of an outbreak of fire, and the role he or she is expected to play in such an eventuality. Safe operational conditions can only be provided by the successful interaction of various factors. The main factors are:

• the structural means of escape and fire protection provided
• the active fire protection provided
• the procedures adopted in the day-to-day operation of the building.

Structural means of escape and fire precautions

It is not essential for the licensee or the manager or any of the staff in a place of public entertainment to know to what standard of fire resistance their building is separated from other buildings, or to what standard it is constructed. Neither need they know to what standard of fire resistance various risk areas and the escape routes are enclosed. These matters are only really of interest to the designer and the builder. What *is* important is for everyone to recognize that the building *needs* to be separated from other buildings; that the elements of its construction *need* to be built to have a certain standard of fire resistance; that most if not all areas of ancillary accommodation are a fire risk and therefore *need* to be enclosed with fire resisting construction; and that also all escape routes *need* to be enclosed by fire-resisting construction. If this can be recognized there is a chance that these key separations will not be compromised, although it is extremely rare to walk through a building and not find at least one fire door that is held or wedged open.

Self-closing fire doors can be a hindrance to moving about a building, particularly when goods are being transferred from one location to another. It is always worth identifying doors which constantly cause a problem in this respect and discussing with the relevant authorities whether or not these doors can be held open by means other than permanent wedging, for example by electromagnetic door holders actuated by smoke detectors.

It is equally important that all escape routes are kept unobstructed and final exit doors are not rendered unusable by being locked. These routes are often wide passages and may appear to offer ample space for temporary storage. The temptation should be resisted, however!

Means of escape versus security

The requirements of means of escape and security often conflict. Most final exits from buildings to which large numbers of people resort are required to be fitted with panic bolts only. These afford little security if not adequately maintained, especially if the doors on which they are fitted are not effectively self-closing. It is frequently the practice to lock these bolts with padlocks and chains when a building is closed to the public. If this is the case there must be a routine for removing these fastenings before the public is admitted to the premises. It is not sufficient for this to be done on an *ad hoc* basis. There needs to be some form of quality control by which senior management can be sure that in no circumstances can an escape door be left locked. This has been one of the chief causes of loss of life in the past and must not be allowed to happen in the future. A simple system could be based on the fact that often the exits from a theatre or cinema are numbered, and it would therefore be easy to keep a board in a central position such as the manager's or resident engineer's office on which the locks and chains to each exit door can be hung. What is important, however, is that the checking routine is rigidly adhered to and the public is never admitted until the whereabouts of every lock and chain is known.

The finishes of walls and ceiling linings and the composition of fixed seating, carpets and drapes (curtains) are now all strictly controlled as to their flammability and/or surface spread-of-flame characteristics. It is important that these materials are not changed without consultation with the appropriate authorities.

Whilst maintenance of the structural fire precautions in a place of entertainment is a relatively simple matter in that defects such as holes formed in walls and doors chained shut (or conversely wedged open) are readily visible, maintenance of active measures is not so simple.

Fire protection installations

It would be difficult if not impossible to detect faults in a wide array of active fire protection systems with the proverbial naked eye. However, modern technology is such that systems often monitor themselves for faults, the prime example of this being an addressable smoke detection and fire alarm installation.

Nonetheless, the parts of the equipment such as fire alarm control panels and sprinkler installation display panels which themselves monitor major systems need to be visually examined, often on a daily basis. This means that a sufficient number of staff need to be trained to be competent to interpret what the monitoring equipment is indicating and to take the appropriate action. It is not necessary for every place of entertainment to employ an army of technicians to maintain all the active fire precautionary measures. It is more the case that sufficient personnel are familiar with the functions of the various items of equipment and that maintenance contracts are taken up with installers of the various systems to ensure that they are regularly serviced.

Servicing can mean different things to different people. For example, it would be prudent for the manager of a garage to ensure that a car on which the braking system had been renewed/repaired is test driven. However, after topping up the engine oil it would not be necessary to test drive the car to see if the engine seized up. The same philosophy applies to places of public entertainment. This means to say that the maintenance of fire safety installations can be weighted towards those which achieve the greatest level of fire safety for the public and performers and staff, but this should not lead to neglect of minor items of fire safety equipment.

For example, the continued function of a smoke control system designed to achieve a clear layer below the smoke layer in a fire to facilitate extended means of escape travel distances and, therefore, extended escape times should be considered as being more important in life safety than, say, the maintenance of hand fire appliances. However, fire or licensing authorities and insurance companies will be most unhappy if fire extinguishers are not adequately maintained. At the very least all fire safety systems should be subjected to functional checks wherever possible and full checks as specified in the relevant British Standard.

The most important fire safety systems are as follows:

- fire alarm and smoke detection systems
- smoke control systems
- hose reel installations
- escape lighting systems
- automatic arrangements connected with passive fire protection systems.

The last category might well seem out of place here, but hold-open devices on fire doors and manual releases to safety curtains, haystack lanterns etc. are susceptible to malfunction and therefore need regular functional checks.

Documentation

The importance of keeping records cannot be overemphasized. As a minimum, log books should be kept for all fire systems so that these can be produced to the statutory authorities if required. Alternatively, although not necessarily appropriate for smaller premises, a fire safety manual should be produced for the building which contains all the information relevant to fire safety. This manual can, if properly designed and maintained, form a key part of the effective fire safety management.

It needs to contain most of the following information:

1 a statement about the fire safety strategy for the building
2 management policies for fire safety and how this affects the staff
3 a description of the structural provisions made in the building for means of escape and public safety
4 a description of the compartmentation arrangements and structural fire protection provided
5 a description of the fire safety systems provided in the building including, for example, automatic extinguishing installations, fire alarms including public address systems, escape lighting, signage, communications (e.g. staff telephones or radios) and a complete maintenance record for all fire safety systems
6 the fire brigade access and fire fighting facilities provided including the whereabouts of emergency controls, for example gas shut-off valves, controls for smoke ventilation or ordinary mechanical ventilation installations
7 a detailed breakdown of the building services including electrical and mechanical services and complete maintenance records for these
8 details of the fire evacuation procedures
9 risk management and fire safety auditing covering fire prevention, housekeeping standards and fire safety inspections
10 details of arrangements for differing functions in the building (e.g. extra precautions necessary if the building is used for dancing, boxing, wrestling, exhibitions etc.) and details of conditions contained on various entertainment licences.

Fire safety manuals can, of course, be expanded into safety manuals dealing with all safety matters including safe working procedures for staff, structural safety of the building, lightning protection and general maintenance of the building. Such manuals are extremely beneficial where staff turnover in an organization is high, being a vehicle for new staff to acquaint themselves with fire and other safety matters, especially the routine to be followed in an emergency.

This should not, however, be seen as the only way for new staff to familiarize themselves with the building and its fire safety systems. Fire drills and other rehearsals should be carried out on a regular basis to test whether or not contingency plans are likely to be effective in the event of a real emergency. Even if a building is well managed and has a fire safety strategy which ensures that fire safety systems are maintained and staff know their respective duties in an emergency, things can and do go wrong.

As stated earlier, most licences will specify the numbers of persons that can safely be admitted to a building for a specific function. This is generally arrived at by consideration of the total exit capacity or combined width of exits from the building. In the case of cinemas and theatres where the numbers of persons equate to the number of seats provided, the licence will probably also specify how many people can stand in approved positions.

It is easy for buildings to become overcrowded if a strict check is not kept on the numbers of persons admitted. Whilst overcrowding is not permitted in the rules of management issued by licensing authorities and can lead to prosecution by the latter if this occurs, the consequences of permitting overcrowding can be much more serious in the event of an outbreak of fire, possibly even leading to fatalities. In one of the fires involving numerous casualties mentioned earlier, overcrowding was a factor; in another, inadequate exit widths were cited as a contributing factor, which amounted to the building being overcrowded.

Crowd control

Crowd control is also important, particularly in functions such as pop concerts. In venues where pop concerts are regularly held a public address system is essential. Of equal importance is the provision of attendants in the right ratio to the numbers of persons attending the function. Attendants should be immediately recognizable as such, and the wearing of uniforms tends to lend authority even if the uniform only amounts to sweatshirts of the same colour.

Attendants should be aware of the routine to be followed in an emergency and should ensure that good order is maintained; for example, gangways and exits must be kept clear. At large venues it is desirable that attendants can communicate with each other, for example by radio.

Where performances are arranged specifically for children the number of attendants needs to be increased, particularly if children are to be seated at upper levels. Guidance on the ratio of attendants to public is generally given in rules of management issued by the licensing authorities.

Building works

It is also important that contractors' employees repairing or carrying out structural alterations to buildings are adequately supervised, particularly if the alterations or repairs are being carried out whilst the public is on the premises.

Adequate arrangements need to be made for dealing with an outbreak of fire arising from the carrying out of building works. This is particularly the case if a sprinkler installation has to be turned off to facilitate the works! If hot work is to be carried out, for example using oxy-acetylene cutting equipment or blow torches, extra care needs to be taken.

The use of real flame, pyrotechnics and other special effects and the precautions to be adopted are extensively covered in the Home Office *Guide* and the LDSA Model Rules of Management, and these should be referred to for guidance.

Scenery used on stages

The type of scenery that can be used in theatres depends upon whether or not there is a separated stage. A separated stage is one where the stage tower is separated from the auditorium by a proscenium wall and the opening in the wall is fitted with a safety curtain. The stage area and the accommodation connected to it are protected by an automatic sprinkler installation, and the stage area and any scene dock are provided with haystack lanterns to act as smoke vents.

If a theatre has a separated stage then scenery which has not been durably flameproofed can generally be used. This is particularly useful where theatres take shows which are on tour or come from abroad, where the fire standards may not be as high as in Britain.

If a theatre does not have a separated stage, the scenery which can be used is restricted to that suitable for open stages. This means scenery constructed from any of the following:

- non-combustible material
- inherently non-flammable material
- timber, hardboard or plywood, rendered flame resistant (usually by a process of impregnation)
- durably flameproofed fabric.

Limited amounts of plastic with an acceptable fire performance can also be used.

There is a half-way house where limited amounts of unproofed scenery may be used on stage settings. This would be where the public seating is on one level only at or near to ground level and does not contain more than 500 seats.

The important point to remember with unproofed scenery is that it will burn readily in a fully developed fire. Extra care is needed, therefore, with regard to the maintenance of escape routes form the stage and within scene docks. Smoking must not be allowed on the stage unless it is essential to the performance and adequate precautions are taken. It is also important that only sufficient scenery for the current production is 'flown' or kept on the stage to minimize the fire load.

Escape routes from the grid and fly platforms are invariably provided. It is essential that these are regularly examined as part of a fire safety audit to ensure that they are usable in an emergency.

Sometimes stage settings on a separated stage extend out beyond the proscenium arch on to an apron in front of the stage. In these cases only scenery suitable for use on an open stage should be used on the auditorium side of the proscenium arch, and scenery should not be placed such that the descent of the safety curtain would be impaired. Any problem will automatically be checked if the safety curtain is lowered at least once during a performance, as required by the rules of management issued by some licensing authorities. The safety curtain may be taken out of operation with the agreement of the licensing authority if scenery suitable for use on open stages is used throughout the stage area.

Access for the disabled

Most local authorities have adopted a policy of encouraging licensees of places of entertainment to admit and provide facilities for disabled persons. Often this may involve making special arrangements. Comprehensive guidance on how facilities for the disabled can be provided in new or existing buildings is given in BS 5588: Part 8: 1988 to which reference should be made.[10]

References

1 London District Surveyors Association and Association of London Chief Environmental Health Officers. *Model Rules of Management for Places of Public Entertainment*, LDSA, 1989.
2 Greater London Council. *Places of Public Entertainment: Technical Regulations*, 1972.
3 Greater London Council. *Code of Practice: Means of Escape in Case of Fire*, 1974.
4 London District Surveyors Association and Association of London Chief Environmental Health Officers. *Model Technical Regulations for Places of Public Entertainment*, LDSA, 1991.
5 Department of the Environment and the Welsh Office. *Approved Document B: Fire Safety*, HMSO, 1991.
6 Greater London Council. *Code of Practice for Pop Concerts*, 1978.
7 Home Office and Scottish Home and Health Department. *Guide to Fire Precautions in Existing Places of Entertainment and Like Premises*, HMSO, 1990.
8 Home Office. *Manual of Safety Requirements in Theatres and Other Places of Public Entertainment*, HMSO, 1934.
9 BS 5588: Part 6: 1991. Fire precautions in the design, construction and use of buildings. Part 6: Code of practice for places of assembly.
10 BS 5588: Part 8: 1988. Fire precautions in the design and construction of buildings. Part 8: Code of practice for means of escape for disabled people.

4

Fire safety engineering

Graeme Hansell

Introduction

Most places of public entertainment are governed by statute and licensed, usually by the local authority. The fire safety measures given in guidance documents and codes of practice necessary for the provision of a licence are, as a consequence, essentially prescriptive and are detailed elsewhere (see Chapter 3). These measures include maximum population density, number of fire exits provided, minimum fire resistance of various structural elements, alarm and fire detection arrangements, escape lighting requirements, fire brigade operational requirements, fire safety management and so on.

A new British Standard, BS 5588: Part 6,[1] provides guidance on fire precautions in the design, construction and use of places of assembly, and is applicable to new buildings and to existing buildings undergoing alteration. As in the Home Office *Guide* on existing places of entertainment,[2] the BS provides a commentary for each recommendation: that is, the logic and essential reasoning behind each recommendation are described. This is important, as the BS allows one to go further and provide for a fire-engineered solution to problems which cannot (or ideally should not) be addressed using the recommendations of the standard.

This chapter will not summarize the details contained in the various fire safety guidance documents available, but will examine the fire safety areas which are most readily addressed using a fire-engineering approach. Furthermore, as much of the fire-engineering advice available is applicable to buildings not used for entertainment, and is thus readily available, this chapter will concentrate on the application of fire safety engineering solutions to problems associated with large populations of people concentrated in a single space within a building. Fire safety engineering in this regard can be defined as the application of engineering principles to fire safety problems in order to achieve a level of safety at *least* comparable to that provided by the recommendations embodied in the guidance documentation. Fire safety engineering therefore demands a knowledge of fire processes and their interactions with the building and its occupants, and of the rationale behind the original recommendations of the standard.

Historical development of fire safety engineering

Much has been written on the development of fire safety standards in the entertainments industry, but it is useful to examine this from the perspective of providing an engineering solution to a problem.

In 1881 a fire at the Ring Theatre in Vienna claimed the lives of 441 people. As with many major incidents of this nature, it became the driving force for change. Reacting to this fire the Austrian Society of Engineers examined the problems associated with fires in theatres, particularly those that occur in the stage area. They demonstrated an extremely effective solution to such fires in 1885, which involved the use of a fire safety curtain across the opening between the stage and the auditorium, and haystack ventilators in the roof above the stage. The mechanisms involved in this solution are described later in this chapter.

This system was not present in the Theatre Royal in Exeter in 1887, when 186 people died in a fire. However, this disaster led to a report by Captain Massey Shaw (of the then London Fire Brigade), which described various principles by which access and egress facilities in theatres could be made safer and more efficient, and probably assisted in the passage of Section 36 of the Public Health Act Amendment Act of 1890.

In 1911 fire broke out on the stage in the Palace Theatre, Edinburgh. This theatre had vents fitted above the stage, which operated satisfactorily, and a fire safety curtain which descended but jammed some 3 m above the stage. Despite this mechanical hitch, the system worked as designed, and although the intense blaze caused the death of 9 performers and stage staff, the auditorium remained unaffected by smoke and heat, allowing the audience to evacuate the building without casualty. Thus the success of the first attempt at an engineered solution to a fire safety problem was graphically demonstrated, and the fire safety curtain and above-stage ventilation became an accepted (although at this time not prescriptive) requirement for theatres.

Management of escape

The Palace Theatre fire clearly demonstrated another important feature of fire safety design. If a population does not perceive itself to be at immediate risk, then evacuation of that population may be carried out in an efficient and orderly fashion. The manager of the Palace Theatre was able to request that the audience move to the nearest available exits, without hurrying, thus enabling the safe passage of all, including the few women who fainted.

It is reported that during the evacuation the orchestra played the National Anthem, and the building was cleared in about $2\frac{1}{2}$ minutes.[3] This time became the basis for all subsequent means of escape legislation and guidance to date, and consequently implies a *controlled* and *orderly* evacuation in a situation which is not perceived as posing an *immediate* physical threat.

This can be contrasted with the fire in the Iriquois Theatre in Chicago in 1903, where the vents over the stage were inoperable due to repair work, and the fire safety curtain jammed. As a consequence of this more than 560 people died: some in the highest levels were asphyxiated before they were able to rise from their seats. Similarly, a fire in 1929 in a Paisley cinema, although insignificant, caused around 70 children to be killed due to uncontrolled evacuation (panic). The inability of the audience to identify their escape exits is purported to be the major reason why 124 casualties arose at the 1897 Paris Charity Bazaar fire, which was compounded by a flammable roof lining. This fire has modern counterparts in the Stardust Disco fire in Dublin in 1981, and in the Bradford Football Stadium fire in 1985, where combustible linings contributed to rapid fire spread, and exits were not discernible or not available.

It would appear, therefore, that the major ingredients for catastrophe are: rapid fire spread and/or smoke production; the *perception* of immediate risk to safety; the inability to quickly discern exit routes or use them; and lack of direction by people familiar with the building, i.e. management and staff.

Modern fire safety principles attempt to reduce the potential for fire and fire spread and to control the movement of smoke, thus improving the perception of the risks to safety. Thereafter, escape routes are clearly marked to adequate exit points, and management and staff are able to direct and assist in the efficient evacuation of the building. These principles are outlined in References 1 and 2. As a total package, engineered alternative solutions to specific problems can be submitted to the approving authorities for consideration.

Fire spread and smoke production

In order to be able to engineer an alternative solution to that recommended or prescribed in the available guidance,[1,2] a basic knowledge of the physical processes involved is required. These will be addressed in terms of the growth rate and the smoke production of a fire.

Growth rate

The rate of burning of a fire typifies how fast the fire will spread. Figure 4.1 shows three fire growth conditions which may be encountered. Curve A represents the fire growth condition that most people are familiar with, i.e. a fire in the open atmosphere. This is the fire that can be related to: the garden bonfire that can be managed and controlled. People are, however, unfamiliar with the rapidity of fire spread in an enclosed or semi-enclosed space. In a partially enclosed space such as an auditorium, a fire will grow faster, as shown in curve B, and the mechanisms that dictate this growth rate are discussed below. In a totally enclosed space, such as in a dressing room, an office or a theatre box or on a stage, the burning rate will be significantly faster, as shown in curve C.

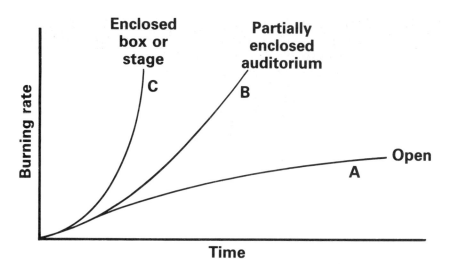

Figure 4.1   *Fire growth rates for various enclosure conditions*

The difference between growth rates B and C and the open fire growth curve A is what creates a problem in terms of people perceiving that there is a risk due to a fire. Anecdotal evidence suggests that if there is a bomb alert in an assembly building then people are likely to evacuate much faster, as they recognize the risk of injury or death due to an explosion. However, perception of fire is such that most people do not actually recognize the risk and, as a result, they react inappropriately. The Bradford Football Stadium fire was an example of how people did not really perceive the risk to their lives. This fire probably followed growth curve B, at least initially, and then developed into growth curve C at some later stage as it really took hold.

In fire growth curve A, heat is being radiated both from the column of smoke rising above the fire, and from the fire itself (Figure 4.2). This radiation in turn causes volatile gases to be released from the combustible material around the fire and these gases, with the ignition source adjacent, ignite and spread the fire. This fire spread mechanism is dependent upon, firstly, having a sufficiently hot source to generate enough radiation to cause volatilization of the uninvolved combustible material around the fire, and secondly, having sufficient material surrounding the fire to enable it to spread. Remove the materials and the fire cannot spread: it will eventually burn out.

Fire growth curve B is for a partially enclosed fire, which grows faster. This could be considered to be analogous to the tiered seating arrangement in a theatre or a stadium. In these situations radiation is impacting not only on the combustibles immediately adjacent to the fire, but also on the tiered levels *above* the fire, with volatile gases being released beyond the immediate vicinity of the fire (Figure 4.3). Hence fire spread is not only horizontal, radially away from the fire,

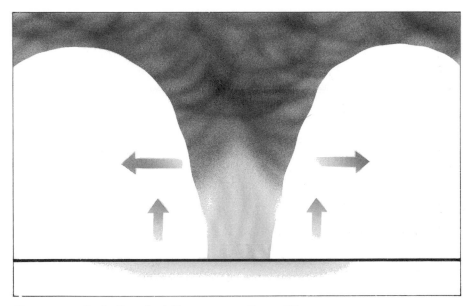

Figure 4.2   *Production of volatile gases: open fire condition*

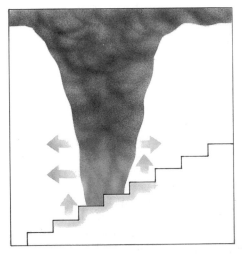

Figure 4.3   *Production of volatile gases: partially enclosed condition*

but also vertical. In addition, more gases are being released from combustibles above the fire than adjacent to it and so the condition arises where the fire is likely to spread faster in the vertical plane. Figure 4.4 shows the results of a partially enclosed fire in a theatre.

Figure 4.4   *Aftermath of a partially enclosed fire in a theatre*

Fire growth curve C is for an enclosed fire. This is where an enclosure, which does not need to be complete but has a ceiling and three walls, surrounds the fire. In this situation there is radiation not only from the plume and fire spreading outwards, but also from the smoke layer forming in the ceiling space above. This smoke layer will get hotter as the fire grows and, when it reaches a temperature of around 500–600 °C, there will be sufficient downwards radiation to spontaneously ignite all other combustible material adjacent to the fire and beyond the immediate impact of the fire (Figure 4.5). This 500–600 °C range is approximate only, and relates to a received radiation intensity of about 20 kW/m². Anecdotal evidence of the Bradford Football Stadium fire[4] suggested that the incident radiation was about 60 kW/m². Once this mechanism of fire spread occurs, spontaneous ignition of the combustibles can follow very rapidly, producing a condition known as flashover. When flashover occurs the whole space becomes engulfed in fire.

Two fire conditions can arise from flashover. The first is known as fully involved large opening (Figure 4.6) where, with an opening which is large relative to the fire

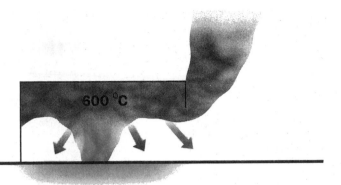

Figure 4.5 *Production of volatile gases: fully enclosed condition*

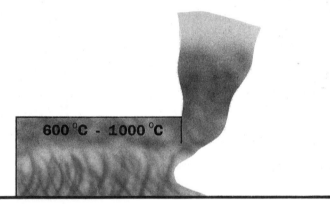

Figure 4.6 *Fully involved, large-opening fire*

area, there is usually a considerable body of flame with temperatures of 600–1000 °C inside the room, and an amount of unburnt gases leaving the room opening which, when mixed with the oxygen-rich atmosphere outside, will produce a flame. The second and more severe condition arising from flashover is known as ventilation control (Figure 4.7). A ventilation controlled fire is not, as the name might suggest, controlled by a ventilation system. Rather, the fire inside the room is so large relative to the opening that the fire is deprived of oxygen, and therefore a great deal of inefficient combustion takes place. The usual consequences of this are that a large body of flame develops inside the room with internal temperatures of at least 1000 °C, and a substantial quantity of unburnt gases leaves the room opening. This will result in flames of considerable length leaving the room, depending upon the nature of the fuel inside. The damage and fire spread potential of this type of fire is very high indeed.

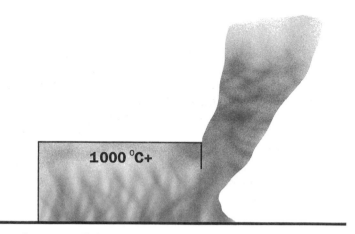

Figure 4.7   *Ventilation-controlled fire*

In the absence of suppression devices such as sprinklers, flashed-over fires can spread very rapidly and may then start to extend beyond the room of origin if uncontrolled. The devastation in Figure 4.8 could be the consequence of such a situation, with complete burn out of this part of the building.

Figure 4.8   *Results of an uncontrolled fire*

Smoke production

Having looked at the mechanisms of the spread of fire and how they can be affected by various factors, it is important to examine the mechanisms of smoke production and why it is so necessary to ensure that the means of escape is protected. Figure 4.9 shows the simple situation of an unenclosed fire. Air is taken in for the combustion process and then discharged upwards as a very hot stream of gas above the axis of the fire. This hot stream of gas will draw the surrounding air into the rising stream in a process of entrainment. Consequently, the mixing of that air with the fire gases results in the column or plume of smoke, and the amount of air that is entrained into the rising plume is very large.

As the plume rises further the amount of smoke produced increases, owing to entrainment. Hence smoke plumes in tall buildings will result in very large quantities of smoke being produced. Obviously, if the building was sufficiently tall and the entrainment rates were sufficiently great then, as with the garden bonfire, there would be sufficient dilution to reduce the smoke to a safe level. However, for all but small fires in the very largest buildings, the rates of entrainment are too slow to render the smoke sufficiently dilute for safe evacuation within it. A fire can be considered as a pump, drawing air in for combustion and entrainment, contaminating and heating it, and pumping it back into the building. There is no way to prevent this from occurring, other of course than to extinguish the fire.

Figure 4.10 shows the formation of a simple plume which has been intercepted by an obstruction, such as a balcony projection above the fire. In this situation some of the smoke will flow towards the rear of the balcony, and some of it will

Figure 4.9 *Entrainment into a simple plume*

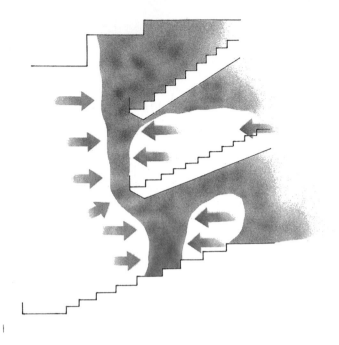

Figure 4.10   *Complex entrainment mechanisms in an auditorium fire*

spill beyond the balcony edge. That which moves towards the rear is very likely to be eventually entrained into the fire, as the incoming air is being pulled in from the local environment from all directions, and after a period the area between the fire and the escape route can become smoke-logged. If the smoke layer under the balcony is able to deepen sufficiently, then smoke will spill beyond the balcony front across its entire width in what is known as a spill plume. The mechanisms of entrainment for a spill plume cause large quantities of air to be drawn into the plume. If this plume is intercepted by a higher balcony level, then the now very cool smoke will tend to spread towards the rear of that level and smoke-log the upper reaches of the higher balcony. Eventually, of course, the smoke will reach the roof where it will be extremely cool, and it is likely to smoke-log the top levels very quickly.

A stage environment is a partially enclosed situation, with the smoke from a fire being produced initially by a simple plume. Eventually, if the fire is unsuppressed and the proscenium opening is unprotected, smoke will fill down to beneath the arch of the proscenium and then pass out into the auditorium as a spill plume (Figure 4.11), causing extremely large quantities of smoke to be produced in the auditorium beyond the proscenium. Hence, auditoriums without protection

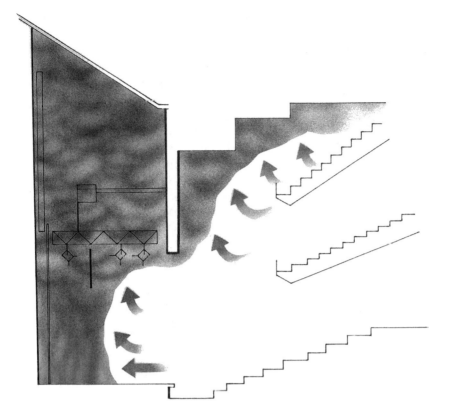

Figure 4.11   *Complex entrainment mechanisms in a stage fire*

against this smoke movement will eventually have large quantities of smoke at a high level: the smoke will be fairly cool but may still be highly toxic.

In many leisure buildings there are also storage facilities, some of which, particularly in theatres, are fairly substantial. The major problem in the storage environment concerns access and protection for firemen who are faced with trying to tackle fires in these situations. In the enclosed space of a large storage environment a simple plume will be produced by the fire source. With no means of controlling or removing the smoke, the smoke layer will fill the space from the ceiling downwards in a short period (perhaps only minutes). At some point the filling mechanism will change so that smoke will be dragged down to floor level fairly rapidly. The mechanisms causing this phenomenon are as yet unclear, but anecdotal evidence suggests that it will occur when the smoke is about 2–4 m above the floor. Fire-fighting crews may be faced with the situation where smoke at the critical level can suddenly descend to the floor, perhaps behind them, and create a completely smoke-logged space. There is no way of clearly indicating to the fire crews where the fire is, and no safe way of tackling it. The usual consequences are the withdrawal of fire fighters from the space, and attempts are then made to tackle the fire from outside.

It can be deduced from the foregoing that various fire and smoke control techniques need to be present or made available to minimize these problems, in order that the means of escape can be protected and thus life safety enhanced, and fire fighting activities effected more quickly and efficiently.

Fire control and suppression

Historically, the prevention of fire spread within (or to other) buildings has been by the containment of the fire and its products, which is achieved by compartmentation and separation. Dividing the building into fire-resistant cells with a maximum limiting volume has, in the past, isolated the fire from the majority of the building users, thus allowing orderly evacuation. The design of structural compartmentation and separation has been largely empirical, and the concepts have been gradually refined and enhanced in such a way that the Building Regulations now cover primarily life safety and the protection of the means of escape.

Live entertainment often demands venues which have a large space included in their design within which the majority of the building users are situated, e.g. theatre auditoriums and stadiums. Thus most of the building's population are exposed to the effects of a fire entering that space, giving rise to the considerable loss of life in the theatre fires described previously.

In situations where passive compartmentation (e.g. walls and floors) cannot be employed, the use of alternative solutions producing the same level of performance needs to be considered. The major fire hazards in (early) theatres – the stage and associated scene dock – were therefore isolated from the auditorium in the event of a fire by the action of the fire safety curtain, the first example of an engineered containment system. As with many similar situations, with constant use the system became the norm and was embodied in guidance documentation, and eventually the original rationale behind its development was forgotten.

At some time following its introduction, the fire safety curtain came to be considered inadequate for the purpose for which it was originally designed, without some additional form of protection. This was to ensure that it would descend freely and remain unaffected by the intense fire which could develop on the stage, and may well have arisen from experience of theatre fires and the curtains' performance. Improvement upon the original performance of the curtain was afforded by the provision of drenchers, to cool the curtain fabric and guide rails. With a water supply available on the stage for drencher activity, it was a simple matter to extend this to include a fully automatic sprinkler system over the stage and associated areas. Hence in proscenium arch theatres, the major fire risk (historically) can be contained, and the fire suppressed.

Sprinklers are, however, of limited use in the auditorium owing to their installed height above the likely fire source. As was shown earlier, tall spaces such as auditoriums and stadiums will have tall smoke plumes, and the dilution created by the large rates of air entrained will cause the smoke temperature often to be too low to activate ceiling mounted sprinklers during the evacuation of the building. Furthermore, it is recommended that sprinkldrs should not be installed above a closely seated audience, in case of accidental discharge.[1] Hence, in the absence of effective sprinkler activity, a fire in an auditorium or stadium can best be prevented from affecting an escaping audience by minimizing the fire load available in the space, and ensuring that the means of escape are adequate.[1]

However, even when these conditions are complied with, it may still be necessary to employ additional protection to the means of escape. For example, a stadium may have fire exits situated at the highest points of the seating levels, and may need to utilize a smoke control system to delay the descent of the smoke layer to these points until the stadium is entirely evacuated.

When the fire occurs in a room adjoining a large open space within the building, hot and toxic smoke can flow from the room into the space where it will accumulate, filling the space, and spread throughout the building, even when there has been no appreciable flame spread from the room into the space itself. The use of sprinklers in such buildings can prevent excessive fire growth or the passage of fire from the room of fire origin into the space, whilst containment principles such as doors can prevent the passage of smoke from the room into the space. This approach cannot, however, be adopted for fires within audience spaces, other than proscenium arch theatres (where the stage is regarded as part of the space).

The major hazard to safe and efficient escape in these environments appears to be the accumulation of smoke within the escape routes. Enclosed spaces will confine smoke, the quantity and density of which can impair visibility to an extent that renders escape or rescue difficult. The toxic characteristics of the smoke will be a danger to people trapped or hindered within the space. Smoke is a complex mixture of highly toxic and irritant fire gases, suspended particulate matter and air. It is the quantity of the gases and particles contained in the air that will determine whether an escape route is tenable.

This makes deviations from the fire safety requirements embodied within the various guidance documents difficult, without resorting to the use of a smoke control system. It is therefore worthwhile briefly examining the nature of smoke and the measures employed in its control.

Smoke density

The particulate matter contained within smoke will determine its ability to scatter or absorb light, which will limit visibility for people trying to pass through it. The properties of smoke which control visibility are the colour, size and density (number) of particulates, the level of irritancy, and the dispersal ventilation levels. A detailed study on the relationship between visibility and smoke density has shown that large variations in perceived visibility could be expected when the brightness and position of the illumination changed, or even if the observer's mental state varied.[5]

Lack of visibility was the main reported hazard to escape in the fire in April 1973 at the Hyatt Regency O'Hare Hotel, Chicago, where the visibility in the atrium of the hotel was reduced to less than 3 m.[6] Escape exits could not be located because they were the same colour as the walls. It has been suggested that, depending on how familiar the escaping occupants are with their environment, a 'safe' escape visibility may vary from 3 m to 20 m.[5] In a theatre or disco, where the public will be unfamiliar with the layout, the upper limit (20 m) will be applicable.

Smoke toxicity

All fires produce gases and vapours which may be toxic and irritant and which, if inhaled, may cause debilitation, unconsciousness and possibly death. It has been indicated that very small quantities of the toxic products of combustion are required to produce lethal conditions, even for a short exposure.[7]

Carbon monoxide (CO) is present in all fires and is often produced in very large quantities. CO is a narcotic gas which causes confusion and loss of consciousness, impairing or preventing escape, and it is the major cause of death in fires.[7] Levels of CO above 5% will cause incapacitation, and it has been shown that concentrations of up to 10% can be produced in some experimental fires.[8] Further complications can arise due to the possible synergistic effects of the evolved fire gases,[7] which may increase the rate of respiration and thus the rate of inhalation of the gases.

Smoke movement and control methods

The usual requirement for smoke control in buildings is to protect the means of escape and facilitate fire brigade operations. The form and distribution of the escape routes, the presence and nature of fire suppression devices and the building use will determine the passive and/or active control techniques to be employed. The techniques will include the use of containment, ventilated lobbies, dispersal, pressurization, throughflow or depressurization ventilation: all of these will be explained below.

Containment usually means the confinement of fire products, typically involving the use of smoke stop doors at predetermined intervals along fire protected escape corridors, and of lobbied protection of escape stairwells. A ventilated lobby is designed to relieve to atmosphere the excess pressure resulting from the accumulation of fire gases. In situations where containment cannot be used, a fire brigade operated smoke dispersal or cross-ventilation system may be employed in the fire room, although this will rarely aid the means of escape.

Pressurization systems are employed as an alternative to the naturally ventilated stairwells and lobbies. Fans pump clean external air into the stairwell to raise the pressure difference between the stairwell and the fire room to a level sufficient to prevent the passage of hot smoke through the potential leakage paths.[9] Furthermore, fire safety design of the means of escape in public buildings requires an additional protected stairway to be provided, in case one becomes unusable owing to smoke and heat contamination. Where pressurization systems are used, the requirement for this additional staircase may be considered unnecessary by the approving authority. Pressurization systems may also be used to provide fire fighting access into the building.[10]

Control by throughflow or smoke exhaust ventilation is designed to prevent smoke from descending within a space to a level that would compromise the safety of an open escape route passing through that space, i.e. a thermally buoyant smoke layer is maintained at a high level. Where the space is an auditorium or stadium, the smoke layer must be above the highest open escape route. In the case of a separated stage, the concept of depressurization ventilation may be used (see the section 'The separated stage' to follow). Empirical evidence suggests that in most instances, providing there is a limited fire risk (e.g. a separated stage) and the unprotected travel distance is sufficiently short, entertainment buildings do not need smoke exhaust ventilation to protect the means of escape.

There may be cases where the building design is such that it cannot comply with the guidance recommendations. For example, it may be desirable to extend the unprotected travel distances in order to make the space more flexible in use, e.g. stadiums. Many buildings have the flexibility to accommodate different forms of entertainment, and fixed escape routes within the unprotected space may drastically limit this flexibility in some instances.

There is no reason why an existing ventilation or air conditioning system should not be used for smoke removal, providing the system is designed to do so. Furthermore, smoke removal systems installed for fire brigade operations may similarly be used to advantage during escape, providing their operation will not compromise the integrity of any escape route. In many instances, however, it is necessary to provide an engineered smoke control solution. The most commonly used and understood method of smoke control is that known as steady-state or smoke exhaust ventilation.

Steady-state flow ventilation, as the name suggests, is simply equating the quantity of smoke being produced by the fire to the level of ventilation required to remove that quantity, for a smoke layer to be established at a given level in the building. Figure 4.10 shows a smoke movement situation which is fairly complex, and smoke control will be very difficult to achieve owing to the interruptions to the vertical flow of the smoke, causing significant quantities of smoke to be produced at and beyond the interception points. A degree of control can be achieved by removing some of the smoke, preferably at the points where means of escape is to be effected, and replacing it by the same quantity of fresh air coming into the ventilated space. No ventilation system can function efficiently without a replacement air supply, whether powered or natural, and this necessary supply may be provided by opening doors and windows, or by inlet ventilators designed for that purpose. Figure 4.12 shows how an existing ventilation system may be of benefit, by extracting the air from underneath balconies and thus preventing localized smoke-logging at the exit points from the aisles. Similarly, in the ceiling space it is possible to extract some smoke through the ventilation system in the roof and provide replacement air at lower points in the building, to keep the affected areas relatively clear of smoke, at least during the initial escape phase.

Clearly, providing the design of the system is adequate, the existing ventilation systems in entertainment buildings can be used to provide a means of smoke control during the early growth phases of the fire. If however the design is inappropriate, and the ventilation system is left operating, then its use may be detrimental to safe escape. If it operates such that air is discharged from ceiling level towards the floor, and perhaps even extracted at floor level, smoke flow patterns may be created which are highly undesirable (Figure 4.13). Clean air will

Figure 4.12   *Control of smoke using existing ventilation systems*

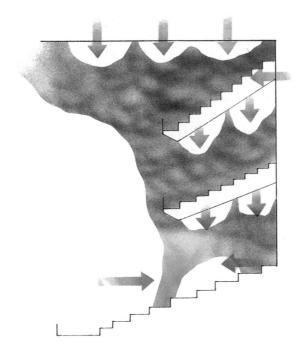

Figure 4.13   *Detrimental smoke movement due to improperly used ventilation system*

be introduced into the top of the relatively cool smoke layer, cooling it further and causing it to lose buoyancy and perhaps descend to floor level. Cool smoke may also be caught up by the entrainment process of the fire, and will quickly cause smoke-logging to occur, possibly in places where it is least desirable. It is therefore advisable that ventilation systems that operate contrary to the buoyancy of the smoke should cease to operate in the fire condition, or switch to a mode of operation compatible with the safe control of the smoke.

For instances where a fire can occur beneath a balcony in a multi-level auditorium, it is possible to provide a properly designed ventilation slot across the front of the balconies to prevent any smoke from discharging beneath the balcony (Figure 4.14).

The separated stage

The protection of the auditorium of a theatre with a separated stage is achieved using a subtly different form of smoke control in the stage area, known as

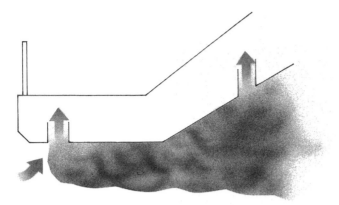

Figure 4.14   *Slot exhaust system*

depressurization. The concepts employed in the successful design of such a system are relatively simple, but are generally contrary to the principles employed in successful throughflow ventilation systems. It is therefore necessary to examine these concepts.

In any space where there is an accumulation of heat energy for any reason, openings to the outside at the top and bottom of the space will create a ventilation flow due to the stack effect, i.e. thermal buoyancy (Figure 4.15). For air to pass through the upper opening, the pressure under the ceiling must be higher than the pressure outside. Similarly, for air to come through the bottom opening, the pressure in the lower portion of the space must be lower than that outside. It follows therefore that at some point in the space there is a pressure equal to that outside, and this is known as the neutral pressure plane. Air in the space above this neutral plane is at a positive pressure relative to the external ambient, and that below is at a negative pressure relative to ambient.

If the inlet system to the space was closed off, the ventilation rate would stop or slow down significantly. The amount of ventilation provided by the upper opening is a function of the depth of the neutral pressure plane beneath that opening. The deeper the neutral pressure plane, the more ventilation actually occurs. Reducing the inlet ventilation in the lower part of the space causes the neutral pressure plane to rise in the space. Since the rate of ventilation is dependent upon the depth of the neutral pressure plane, then if the ventilation rate has been significantly reduced, or has ceased, the neutral pressure plane will eventually rise to close underneath the roof (Figure 4.16). However, there is now a situation where there is a negative pressure acting across the entire façade of the enclosed space, trying to draw air in through all the cracks and interstices in the enclosure. This is an effective way of controlling smoke.

The concept of the separated stage was originally developed by the Austrian Society of Engineers following the Ring Theatre fire. They probably recognized

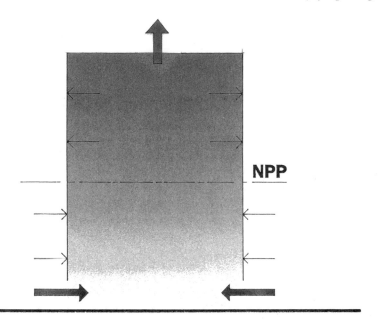

Figure 4.15   *Position of the neutral pressure plane: inlet area equal to vent area*

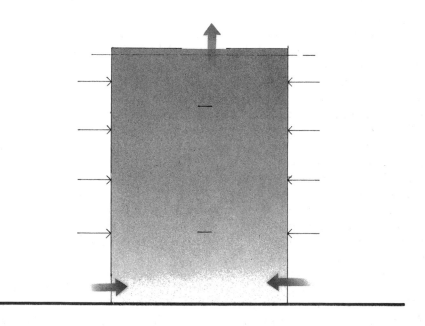

Figure 4.16   *Position of the neutral pressure plane: vent area much greater than inlet area*

that due to the severity of fires on stages it would be extremely difficult to actually control the fire and remove the smoke at the rate it was produced. Their solution was the provision of a substantial quantity of ventilation over the stage and a fire safety curtain (Figure 4.17). The consequence of this is the almost total enclosure of the stage area, apart from the small doors around the base of the stage area which open on to closed corridors and rooms. With the inlet facility removed to the enclosure, but with a large area of ventilation at the top, the neutral pressure plane in the stage area will ascend towards the roof, above the arch of the proscenium. As a result, a negative pressure develops beneath the neutral pressure plane in the stage area, drawing air in from all possible leakage points, including all the cracks

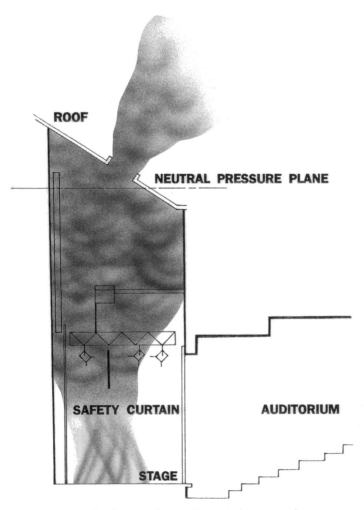

Figure 4.17   *Smoke control using the neutral pressure plane*

and leakage areas around the safety curtain. The net effect is the suction of air into the stage area from the auditorium, rather than a flow of smoke in the opposite direction. The consequence of this approach is that a powerful pressure differential develops across the safety curtain. Following the fire at the Theatre Royal in Portsmouth in 1972, anecdotal evidence from fire officers attending the fire, who were in the auditorium at the time of the fire, was that the fire safety curtain was bowing inwards towards the fire, indicating the nature of the pressure being developed across the fire safety curtain (Figure 4.18).

This form of smoke control must not be misinterpreted. It is not a ventilation system in the accepted sense, and will not remove smoke from the stage in any great quantity. It is a system that creates a pressure differential across the safety curtain, lowering the air pressure in the stage area to less than that in the auditorium, thus holding the smoke back and rendering the auditorium safe. Even in a situation where the safety curtain does not come down completely, as

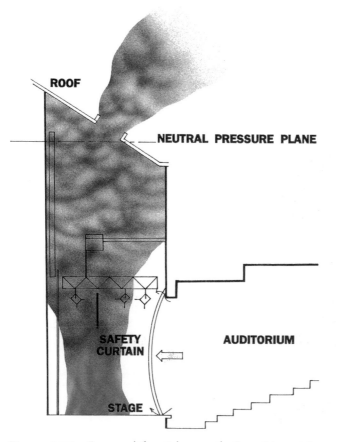

Figure 4.18 *Pressure differential across the fire safety curtain*

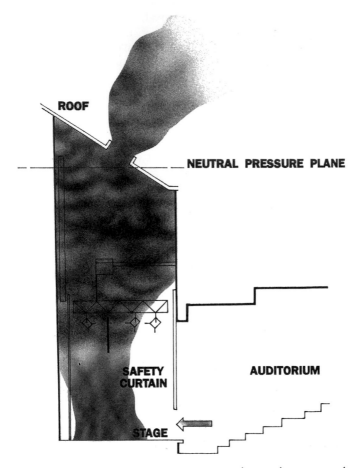

Figure 4.19   *Direction of air movement with partial opening to the safety curtain*

happened in the 1911 Palace Theatre fire, the auditorium may still remain protected and clear of smoke (see Figure 4.19). The design parameters for this form of smoke control system (Figure 4.20) are:

the effective leakage area around the curtain and stage, A_iC_i (m²)

where A_i is the inlet leakage area
where C_i is the inlet flow coefficient,

the effective ventilator area, A_vC_v (m²)

where A_v is the ventilator area
where C_v is the ventilator flow coefficient,

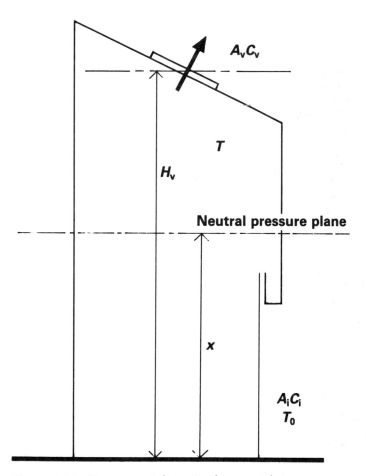

Figure 4.20   *Parameters of design for the separated stage*

the height to the ventilators, H_v (m),
the position of the neutral pressure plane, X (m),
the smoke temperature, T (K),
the ambient temperature, T_0 (K).

$$\left[\frac{A_v C_v}{A_i C_i}\right]^2 = \frac{T}{T_0\left[\dfrac{H_v}{X}-1\right]}$$

These parameters are usually more than adequately catered for by the ventilation areas recommended in the available guidance documents. It should be remembered, however, that the stage area will become completely smoke-logged, as their will be no smoke *ventilation* as such.

Fire on a stage where there are no sprinklers will generate very high temperatures, maybe 1000 °C or higher. In this instance, if the neutral pressure plane is set at just above the proscenium arch, sprinkler activity will result in a reduction of the smoke temperature, causing the neutral pressure plane to rise higher. Hence the use of sprinklers in the stage area, which was designed to be protected in their absence, will actually enhance the level of protection even further, not only by suppressing the fire and perhaps even extinguishing it, but by causing the neutral pressure plane to rise further in the stage area.

On an unsprinklered stage the smoke temperature may be regarded as being that of flame temperature at peak burning, i.e. approximately 1000 °C. Where sprinklers are present it is unlikely that the smoke temperature will exceed about 300 °C prior to sprinkler operation, and should be lower than this value subsequently. This suggests that the level of protection against smoke movement which is afforded in the absence of sprinklers can be provided when they are present by using two-thirds of the prescribed ventilation area above the stage.

There are other effects associated with sprinklers. If no safety curtain is installed

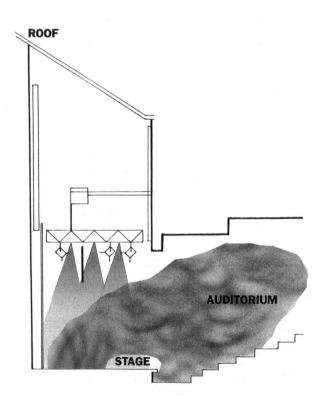

Figure 4.21   *Smoke movement with sprinklers but no safety curtain*

then there is the potential for a large quantity of cool dense smoke to underspill into the auditorium, assisted by the downward drag of the sprinkler sprays (Figure 4.21). This in itself is undesirable, and in the absence of a safety curtain a sprinklered stage will need a smoke ventilation system that will prevent smoke from underspilling into the auditorium, unless there is sufficient capacity to maintain the base of the layer above the proscenium arch. This ventilation requirement is unlikely to be achieved by a system designed for depressurization, and would require a system based on the principles of throughflow ventilation.

The use of sprinklers is highly desirable for the suppression of a fire. However, sprinklers sited over a stage may take some while to operate owing to their installed height, resulting in a strong probability that smoke will be underspilling the proscenium arch prior to activation. Furthermore, sprinklers usually reduce smoke production by suppressing the fire, but even in the presence of sprinklers very large quantities of smoke can be produced, which must be taken into account. Figure 4.22 shows an experimental rig used at the Fire Research Station, Borehamwood, Herts, to simulate a small sprinklered fire in a retail environment,

Figure 4.22   *Simulation of a small sprinklered fire, Fire Research Station*

using a rack $2\,m^2$ in area, with typical materials found in everyday use. This fire generated about 1 megawatt of energy, not very significant in fire terms: nevertheless, it produced the smoke shown in Figure 4.23. The smoke produced by this small sprinklered fire may be considered analogous to that which could occur on a stage before the fire safety curtain came down, or if there were no curtain installed. The quality of the smoke is very poor and it would adversely affect the means of escape if uncontrolled.

It is reasonable to suggest that the presence of sprinklers above the stage can allow the present prescriptive requirements for the stage to be relaxed to perhaps include the following arrangements. The first is to provide no fire safety curtain, and to use a throughflow smoke control system above the stage, designed to keep the smoke layer above the proscenium arch. This will require a sizeable inlet to the auditorium. The fire size used in the design should acknowledge the sprinkler activity, but be reasonably pessimistic and meet with the approval of the regulatory authorities.

A second possibility is to install a fire safety curtain which has a reduced material

Figure 4.23   *Smoke from simulated fire, Fire Research Station*

specification. The presence of sprinklers implies that the curtain need not withstand the temperatures produced by an intense fire. A material able to withstand the test requirements of BS 7346 Part 3 should be adequate for this purpose.[11] It will still need to meet the mechanical requirements of current curtain specifications, but in theory can be lighter.

A third arrangement might use powered extraction as an alternative to natural ventilation. The average smoke temperature is not likely to rise above about 300 °C prior to sprinkler operation, and should be considerably lower subsequently. With appropriate assumptions for the ambient temperature (e.g. 15 °C) and the inlet flow coefficient (e.g. 0.65), the volumetric rate of exhaust required V_1 may be found from the relation

$$V_1 = 4.2 A_i x^{1/2} \quad m^3/s$$

where, as before, x is the height of the neutral pressure plane above the stage (m) and A_i is the inlet leakage area (m^2). Note that A_i should be calculated on the worst leakage condition: where doors from the stage area can open to the outside, these should be assumed to be open. The height x *must* be above the proscenium arch for successful operation of the system.

Fire resistance and sprinklers

The guidance documentation mentioned previously indicates where sprinkler systems are recommended for both property protection and life safety.[1, 2] Where these recommendations are made, the fire resistance of the elements of the structure should already take into account the presence of sprinklers.

Where there are no recommendations for sprinklers in a space, it is possible that agreement may be reached with the regulatory authorities that the level of fire resistance of the structural elements bounding the space may be reduced if a properly designed sprinkler system is installed, on *both* sides of the bounding element, unless one side (i.e. that which can remain unsprinklered) presents a substantially lower fire hazard. It is also possible that calculations may be produced to justify the use of non-traditional materials for fire resisting construction, or to indicate that a particular guidance requirement may be overly severe.

Detection and alarm

In entertainments venues, the rapid detection of the fire and raising of the alarm is extremely important. It is easy to see how so many people died in the early theatre fires, as large crowds of people gathered together, often in darkness and totally oblivious of fire precautions, created the ideal situation for loss of life. Modern entertainment facilities will have many of the life safety features discussed above. However, probably one of the most important is the communications system.

The fire must be detected rapidly if large crowds of people are to be evacuated safely. Smoke detection systems are highly recommended by most guidance documentation, although it is recognized that however the alarm is raised, it need not be raised in the *public* spaces, but in staff areas, to enable the evacuation of the building to follow a predetermined plan. The performance will need to be stopped before the evacuation starts, and a general announcement should be made. Thereafter, evacuation can be enhanced by the use of pre-recorded announcements using the public address system, designed to aid efficient evacuation.

Detectors may be extremely useful in buildings with operating plant such as ventilation systems which may adversely affect the passage of smoke. The detection system can initiate a variety of functions, e.g. the releasing of doors that close automatically, and the opening of ventilators or the starting of fans for the removal of smoke.

The future

Fire safety engineering is still in its infancy. The knowledge base is expanding through continued research. The fire safety products available are increasing as a consequence of legislation that permits an engineered solution. The use of computer technology is also increasing, allowing fire safety designs to be created which do not depend upon a historical perspective, or rely solely upon test data. It is likely that buildings in the not too distant future will be designed to be fire safe without recourse to prescriptive guidance, and hence be more flexible and innovative in design.

References

1 BS 5588: Part 6: 1991. Fire precautions in the design, construction and use of buildings. Part 6: Code of practice for places of assembly.
2 Home Office and Scottish Home and Health Department. *Guide to Fire Precautions in Existing Places of Entertainment and Like Premises*, HMSO, 1990.
3 Home Office. *Manual of Safety Requirements in Theatres and Other Places of Public Entertainment*, HMSO, 1934.
4 Hinkley, P.L. Private communication.
5 Jin, T. *Visibility Through Fire Smoke*, Building Research Institute, Tokyo, Report No. 30 (March 1970) and Report No. 33 (February 1971).
6 Sharry, J.A. 'An atrium fire', *Fire Journal*, vol. 67, no. 6, 1973, p. 39.
7 Purser, D.A. 'Toxicity assessment of combustion products', in *SFPE Handbook of Fire*, Engineering Society of Fire Protection Engineers, National Fire Protection Association, USA, 1988, pp. 1–200.
8 Rasbash, D.J. 'Smoke and toxic products in fires', *Journal of Plastics Institute*, trans. conference supplement no. 2, January 1967, p. 55.

9 BS 5588: Part 4: 1978. Fire precautions in the design of buildings. Part 4: Smoke control in protected escape routes using pressurisation.
10 BS 5588: Part 5: 1991. Fire precautions in the design, construction and use of buildings. Part 5: Code of practice for fire fighting stairways and lifts.
11 BS 7346: Part 3: 1990. Components for smoke and heat control systems. Part 3: Specification for smoke curtains.

5
Electrical safety

Bob Anderson

Introduction

Everybody uses electricity: for heat and light, for transport, for all manner of labour saving gadgets, for communications and for entertainment. Our civilization depends on electricity and, by and large, it is a docile and obedient servant. This is not, of course, a matter of chance, but the result of nearly two centuries of intelligent experiment and investigation that have produced a great mass of theory, data and techniques to help scientist, engineer and technician predict and control this potent but invisible force. As a result, the general public can purchase safe, reliable and convenient products that can be used without fear of disaster or accident provided that a few elementary precautions are observed. These amount to little more than using the product only for the purpose and circumstances for which it was designed, taking care to check regularly for damage, and then, if damage is suspected, taking competent advice on the options of repair or replacement. Competent, conscientious manufacturers take great care to ensure that their customers can depend on this security, influenced of course to an increasing degree by legislation. Danger, accident and injury then, when they happen, must come from incompetence, with or without the added factor of negligence. This chapter cannot offer a remedy for either of these human defects but it will discuss some of the more common fields of ignorance and carelessness that have been observed to prejudice electrical safety.

The hazards

Electrocution and fire must be the main risks to be expected from misuse of electricity. Human death by electrocution can result from contact with a mere 50 volts, and a fire can be starting by sparking or overheated wiring carrying only a few amperes. A few hundred amperes can produce a major explosion. Consequently, shock and fire risks are strictly controlled by legislation and professional codes of practice, but misuse of electricity can cause injury in other ways. Reflex withdrawal from a minor shock may result in falling off a ladder or high platform with potentially fatal results, or merely bruising if the reacting hand only collides with a wall. Electric motors, if not properly controlled, can move their loads beyond safe limits, or at dangerous speeds, or continue to move when they should be at rest. Loss of control may be the result of a basic circuit error or damage or misuse. Designers are, of course, expected to check their work thoroughly, but they must also try to arrange their design to minimize the consequences of foreseeable damage and misuse. Stray electric and magnetic fields, particularly from high-frequency circuits, can induce voltages and currents outside the basic circuit wiring and thereby cause shock from apparently intrinsically safe parts; or may cause overheating, perhaps leading to fire. Stray fields can also affect sensitive electronic equipment and prevent correct operation, again with potentially disastrous results if the electronics are being used for navigation, safety communications, or as control circuits for other dangerous systems. Stray fields may also, perhaps, have a direct physiological effect on human health. Loss of power at an inopportune moment can, by blacking out essential safety lighting for example, be another risk.

Competence

A competent electrical engineer or technician will take steps to avoid foreseeable hazards in accordance with the latest appropriate techniques and codes of practice. An incompetent dabbler may not even be aware that the risks exist. The introduction to the *Memorandum of Guidance on the Electricity at Work Regulations 1989* puts the problem clearly: 'A little knowledge is often sufficient to make electrical equipment function but a much higher level of knowledge and experience is usually needed to ensure safety.' Entertainers, managers and all technical staff involved in the use of electricity must, therefore, take care that the 'experts' they rely on to provide electrical safety are, in fact, sufficiently competent. This has especial importance for those employed as engineers, electricians or electrical technicians who must themselves decide on the limits of their own ability and admit these limits if asked to carry out work beyond their competence. If they fail to do so, this in itself could be a criminal offence.

Legislation

The UK Health and Safety at Work Act 1974 and the Electricity at Work Regulations 1989 have now laid very clear and far-reaching duties and responsibilities on both employer and employee in the field of general electrical safety in Britain. In addition European Community legislation, expressed as Directives, reinforces the UK laws and adds other requirements, often more detailed and restrictive. The main points that affect the entertainment industry are summarized below, but it must be emphasized that everybody with duties involving the safety of others or their own safety should read and take steps to understand the full texts. Failure to comply with the requirements of this legislation is, in general, a criminal offence whether or not an accident ensues. Managements, with the help of their technical advisers, are expected to be self-policing to ensure safety without external supervision. Electricity supply company engineers, health and safety inspectors and local government officials may all have powers to draw attention to defects and probably to initiate preventive action, but failure by any such official to object to an unsafe situation cannot be assumed to imply approval. Every employer and every employee must ensure that the foreseeable consequences of their own actions are safe.

A somewhat different special form of legislation applies to many types of entertainment venue – the local government licence. This is purely local legislation prepared by the licensing authority's own staff, listing the conditions to be complied with by the licensed venue. Usually they include many clauses dealing with the use of electricity, though many of these merely repeat requirements contained in the *IEE Regulations* or the Home Office *Guide* (see below). In the past the GLC *Rules of Management* and the GLC *Technical Regulations* have been held to be among the better examples of such local government conditions, and the replacement document prepared by the London District Surveyors Association may, in time, achieve equal acceptance. However, each licensing authority values its freedom to decide on its own controls and a standard approach throughout the country seems remote. Failure to comply with a condition not required by national legislation or EC Directive, once discovered by the council's inspector, leads only to threatened or actual loss of licence rather than criminal proceedings.

Principal UK electrical safety legislation

Health and Safety at Work Act 1974
The foundation for today's law on safety in the workplace. Sets up the Health and Safety Executive and defines its powers. Too much has happened since 1974 for any layman to even begin to summarize the law in general, though the principle of joint employer/employee accountability is still clear.

Electricity at Work Regulations 1989 SI no. 635
Thirteen short regulations with general application plus another twelve relating only to mines and a few explanatory paragraphs. The main headings are:

- systems, work activities and protective equipment
- strength and capability of electrical equipment
- adverse or hazardous environments
- installation, protection and placing of conductors
- earthing or other suitable precautions

- integrity of reference conductors
- connections
- means for protecting from excess current
- means for cutting off the supply and for isolation
- precautions for work on equipment made dead
- work on or near live conductors
- working space, access and lighting
- persons to be competent to prevent danger and injury.

Failure to comply with any of these regulations is a criminal offence, but Regulation 29 states that in certain cases 'it shall be a defence for any person to prove that he took all reasonable steps and exercised all due diligence to avoid the commission of that offence.'

Memorandum of Guidance on the Electricity at Work Regulations 1989
Well written and helpful explanatory notes on the Regulations. Not strictly part of the law, but expected to be taken into account in court when considering charges and defence under the Regulations. Every electrician should own and read a copy.

Three ideas not always appreciated by entertainment electricians are emphasized in the Regulations. These are that work on live equipment is illegal if danger might arise; that the management shall set up a safe system of work; and that all work shall be done by competent persons. The *Memorandum of Guidance* goes a long way towards explaining what these and the other requirements mean. It is also clear that, since the Regulations are intended to be enforced, some unfortunate people will find themselves in court charged with an offence. Lawyers, being lawyers, will want documentary evidence to support defence claims that design, installation, maintenance and use were sufficiently safe. Comprehensive record keeping is now essential.

EEC Low Voltage Directive 1973 (73/23/EEC)
The Low Voltage Directive states principles to be observed by all members states to ensure electrical safety. Like most other European countries, the UK has had to introduce new legislation to ensure compliance. The Electricity at Work Regulations 1989 are the main instrument, supported by the Low Voltage Electrical Equipment (Safety) Regulations 1989. The more recent editions of the *IEE Regulations* provide detailed support. 'Low voltage' means 50–1000 V AC or 75–1500 V DC.

The key statement is probably in Article 2: 'The member states shall take all appropriate measures to ensure that electricical equipment may be placed on the market only if, having been constructed in accordance with good engineering practice in safety matters in force in the Community, it does not endanger the safety of persons, domestic animals or property when properly installed and maintained and used in applications for which it was made.' The rest of the Directive explains at length the methods to be adopted to bring this requirement into use – in short, the new rôle of British Standards and the harmonized European Standard and other European national standards.

Low Voltage Electrical Equipment (Safety) Regulations 1989 SI no. 728
This is the UK legislation following from the EEC Low Voltage Directive. In the future, if a harmonized standard for a particular product exists, everything sold for use in Europe must comply with the standard and be marked accordingly. By the end of 1992 there should be harmonized standards for the great majority of electric devices, though many more will still be in preparation. If there is no appropriate standard the designer and manufacturer must take full responsibility and be prepared to demonstrate with full documentation how the safety aspects of the design are achieved. Major manufacturers should have faced up to this legislation in the early 1990s, but purchasers and smaller manufacturers may not yet realize that they no longer have the freedom to purchase or to offer for sale products that cannot be confidently declared safe.

Electromagnetic Compatibility (EMC) Directive (89/336/EEC)
This recent piece of European legislation will attempt to define and control the acceptable electromagnetic radiation (interference) that may be emitted or received by all types of electrical equipment. All radiation generated will have to be limited, as also will the vulnerability of sensitive control devices. Sound and lighting control boards, thyristor dimmers, fluorescent and discharge lamps and some electric motors are among the devices and systems that will be affected in live entertainment. User and manufacturer alike are working hard in committees and lobbying to try to ensure that the implementation makes practical and economic sense. Obviously, one main result of this work will be to minimize the risk of danger arising when interference from one piece of equipment influences another, so there can be no objection to the idea. However, since all equipment will have to be tested and certified, there will be another burden on manufacturers and on the user's pocket.

Codes of practice

In Britain, until recently, electrical safety was dealt with by rather simplistic general legislation supported by voluntary codes of practice. The most comprehensive and well known of these was, and continues to be, the *IEE Wiring Regulations* which deals with wiring for domestic, commercial and industrial buildings at mains voltages. In addition, the British Standards Institution has published many codes of practice relating to electrical safety, and the standards themselves can also be included under this heading. While not recognized directly in UK criminal legislation, compliance with the *IEE Regulations* and appropriate BSI codes and standards could usually be relied on to show that proper care had been taken as a defence against charges of negligence or incompetence. This will continue under the new European legislation, with the added advantage that one of the defined methods of complying with the Low Voltage Directive will be to comply with BSI or other European harmonized standards.

Codes of practice, in general, give proven practicable solutions to standard problems with reliable methods for calculating loads, safety factors etc. and fully verified tables to assist selection of component products from a defined range, usually standardized elsewhere. Equipment or installations designed using codes of practice should need no further supporting experimental or theoretical justification, whereas equipment or installations using novel or unorthodox techniques would have to be carefully justified by somebody competent to evaluate the problem and test results, and willing to undertake the concomitant responsibility.

The following list of codes of practice and British Standards may be helpful and relevant for solving problems in the entertainment industry. Manufacturers, equipment installers and technicians modifying or repairing existing equipment or installations should take care to comply with the recommendations of the appropriate codes and standards unless there are exceptional reasons to do otherwise.

Principal UK electrical safety codes of practice and standards

IEE Regulations for Electrical Installations (IEE Wiring Regulations)
(BS 7671: 1992)
Prepared by expert committees of professional engineers, this is the industry's leading work on good installation practice. Although it has no legal status, compliance is generally required by contract and local government by-laws. The 16th edition came into force on 1 January 1993, and takes account of EEC Directives. The chapter headings include:

scope, object and fundamental requirements for safety
assessment of general characteristics
protection for safety
selection and erection of equipment
inspection and testing.

Appendices include comprehensive data for the selection of cable sizes.
A number of explanatory handbooks are also available to assist the professional designer and the site electrician to understand the significance of the *IEE Regulations*.

Guide to Fire Precautions in Existing Places of Entertainment and Like Premises
(1990)
This Home Office/Scottish Home and Health Department *Guide* gives up-to-date and authoritative advice on all aspects of fire prevention in existing entertainment buildings.

Protection Against Electric Shock (HSE guidance note GS 27, 1984)

Electrical Test Equipment for Electricians (HSE guidance note GS 38, 1986)

Electrical Safety at Places of Entertainment (HSE guidance note GS 50, 1991)
A rather inadequate rag-bag of advice. Not to be ignored, but with insufficient technical justification to satisfy real electricians.

Electrical Safety for Entertainers (1991)
An HSE publication aimed at non-technical performers and musicians. Good, well-illustrated rule-of-thumb advice to help improve safety awareness.

Electrical Safety – A Practical Guide
Published by the Musicians' Union about 1980. Still relevant and still available.

Safe Sound – A Guide to Electrical Safety for Musicians
Published by the Association of British Theatre Technicians, also about 1980. Still relevant and still available.

British Standards and codes of practice

BS CP 1013: 1965 Earthing
Methods for earthing electrical supply systems and equipment. Helpful advice on minimum impedance values and testing.

BS CP 1017 Distribution of electricity on construction and building sites
Details of the well-known 'yellow' 100 V centre tapped earthed system now mandatory on all building sites, plus further information on general site power distribution.

BS 5550: 7.5.1 Code of practice for distribution of AC electricity for location lighting
Details of the equipment and method of use recommended for distributing power for lighting on film and television location sites.

BS 5266: Part 1: 1988 Emergency lighting
A code of practice for the emergency lighting of premises other than cinemas and certain other specified premises used for entertainment. It gives minimum light values plus many other safety details.

BS 1007: 1955 Maintained lighting for cinemas
Left-over legislation. It was hoped that this would be withdrawn and replaced by a revised BS 5266: Part 2. So far this has not happened. Its main special requirement is for general maintained lighting in the auditorium throughout the performance.

BS 4533: Part 101: 1990 Luminaires – specification for general requirements and tests (equivalent to EN 60 598: Part 1)
Basic safety requirements applicable to all types of luminaire unless exempted in the appropriate Part 102.
   There are many Part 102 standards for specific types of luminaire (see below).

BS 4533: 102.17: 1990 Particular requirements for luminaires for stage lighting, television, film and photographic studios (outdoor and indoor) (equivalent to EN 60 598-2-17)
Clearly applicable to most of live entertainment and probably applicable to discos etc. in the absence of anything else.

BS 6651: 1990 Code of practice for protection of structures against lightning
Worth reading for dreadful warnings and more advice on earthing.

BS 5588 Fire precautions in the design, construction and use of buildings
Various parts dealing with different types of building and construction problem. In particular Part 6: 1991 'Code of practice for places of assembly' deals with buildings used for live entertainment.

BS 3535: 1990 Specification for safety isolating transformers for industrial and domestic purposes
Used to make single items of portable equipment earth-free to minimize the effects of poor insulation or damage.

BS 4293: 1983 Specification for residual-current-operated circuit breakers

Permanent installations

The design of a safe permanent electrical installation for a live entertainment venue such as a theatre, multi-purpose hall or disco presents few special problems. The *IEE Regulations* provide satisfactory guidance once requirements for power and location of distribution boards have been decided. However, special problems of earthing and segregation may have to be resolved to the satisfaction of the audio and control systems suppliers.

Power requirement

The *IEE Regulations* give guidance for diversity allowances for most conventional power requirements, but stage lighting needs special consideration. For long-term flexibility it is usual to install much more dimmer capacity than will ever be used on any one show. Consequently, the apparent power requirement calculated by summing all installed dimmer capacity can be grossly excessive, and an experienced theatre contractor or consultant can confidently confirm a far lower figure and consequent cost saving. However, if the installation is sized for this lower figure, overload protection devices on feeder cables must, of course, protect the cables and other switchgear, with the possible consequence that an unusually large or unbalanced load will trip the protection. To avoid this and the consequent possible hazard of an unexpected blackout, ammeters should be provided for each phase of the dimmer system at a position where the show electrician can check loading during rehearsal.

Wire sizes

The *IEE Regulations* are clear but tend to produce excessively expensive solutions. Consequently the voltage drop and grouping factor calculations need some thought. For the long runs between a central dimmer room and remote sockets in a big theatre, cable size calculated for the specified maximum voltage drop of 2.5% required in the 15th and earlier editions of the *Regulations* could be several sizes larger than needed for current carrying and fault clearance considerations. Although the light output from an incandescent lamp is very sensitive to voltage, the universal use of dimmers to balance lighting effects makes the need to achieve full voltage uncommon, and so it may sometimes be reasonable for the designer to allow a greater full load drop. Safety will not be impaired if current capacity limits are not exceeded. The relaxation to 4% in the 16th edition should therefore be very welcome.

Nominal current capacity of wires grouped in common conduit or trunking must be reduced according to *IEE Regulations* Table 4B1 (16th edition). This can reduce current capacity by up to two-thirds and is most significant for wiring in trunking leaving the dimmer room where hundreds of circuit pairs may be routed. Without derating, serious overheating would be certain but, as noted above, there may be a large diversity factor to be taken into account as only part of the installation will be used at any one time. Determination of a limited derating scheme, that is both safe and economic, taking account of grouping and ambient temperature and other relevant factors, is a matter for expert advice. Full derating should be applied if this is not available.

Earthing

Audio technicians and artistes often, unfortunately, fail to appreciate the function of good earthing for limiting the potential shock voltage from a power leakage fault and for ensuring disconnection of the circuit by blowing the fuse or circuit breaker in serious cases. They see 'ground' only as an audio screen or reference point. Manufacturers may aggravate the problem by connecting internal 'grounding' conductors, which do not need safety earthing, to the exposed external chassis, which usually does. The consequence has often been that earths have been disconnected to cure audio interference problems, ignoring the loss of essential safety protection. The result has more than once been a fatal electrocution. The safety functions of earthing and bonding must, then, be continually stressed and connections verified as frequently as possible.

To help with this problem, audio engineers, and to a lesser extent dimmer and stage machinery suppliers, may want a 'clean earth' for all their sensitive electronic hardware. If this is purely for signal screening purposes then an insulated connection to the building earthing terminal can easily be provided without regard to fault clearance calculations. If, as is more usual, the clean earth also has to provide safety earthing, then all relevant power sockets have to have an earth conductor system which is sized and connected to provide earth loop impedance values to give satisfactory disconnection times for faults on the power system but which is immune, as far as practicable, from carrying standing earth fault currents which disturb the operation of the electronics. The solution is usually to insulate all protective conductors serving the audio systems except at the essential single connection to the building ground point. This will limit standing earth fault currents to those produced by the sound system itself which are usually small enough to keep noise voltages low. However, fortuitous interconnections of power and clean earth systems at a later date, usually through use of unsuitable portable equipment, cannot be prevented and means may be requested to test for such connections by a removable link at the earth point. While reasonable under proper supervision, such a link can be highly dangerous if misused and should not be provided except at a secure location, such as within the main switch room, accessible only to competent staff.

All new mains powered electrical equipment for entertainment use offered for sale within the EC, wherever made, should in future comply with one or more British and European safety standards and will be either properly earthed or double insulated. Old equipment and some American and other foreign items designed for sale outside the EC may not comply. Damaged equipment may not comply. These items must not be used until brought to present-day British safety standards.

Segregation

Separate ducting systems are required by *IEE Regulations* for fire alarm and emergency lighting wiring to ensure that these safety circuits are not damaged by faults on the general wiring. Segregation may also be required to separate other wiring systems with incompatible voltages and insulation. The installation designer must also consider separating power circuits and control data wiring, especially that controlling moving items, to prevent dangerous or inconvenient interaction. Thyristor or triac dimmers produce exceptionally high noise levels unless fitted with inductive filters. Good quality dimmers intended for theatre or television studio use will have such protection but low-cost designs for the disco market may have only minimal filtering. Segregation of circuits from any quality of dimmer into separate metal trunking or conduit will do much to avoid interference with audio and data circuits.

Switching and isolation

Theatres and other entertainment venues are often large buildings with few permanent staff. Consequently it is helpful for both safety and convenience if means to switch off lighting and sound and other entertainment systems are grouped together centrally at locations to which only responsible staff have access. Direct or remote contactor control from control rooms or the stage will be valued. It is important to note that the semiconductor dimmers invariably used to control entertainment lighting do not provide safe subcircuit isolation even though appearing to extinguish the circuit, and provision of a switch at each load socket is unwelcome as being a known cause of operating error. Isolation for safe relamping is traditionally done by unplugging at the luminaire.

RCD protection

An RCD is a circuit breaker operated by a residual current detector, as explained in Chapter 6. RCD protection for circuits supplying portable sections of the audio system is now considered beneficial especially where hand-held microphones and instruments are to be used. For maximum benefit all sockets on stage provided for use by the entertainers should be individually protected by 30 mA double-pole devices; alternatively, where individual protection is deemed to be too expensive, a minimum of two RCD protected circuits should be used, each feeding small groups of sockets. There is less agreement on the merits of RCD protection for central audio systems or for lighting and machinery systems. If fitted at all, RCD protection on such permanently installed equipment should be on the basis of one RCD per maximum six or eight final subcircuits. The objection to RCDs in live entertainment is that nuisance tripping from trivial direct phase-to-earth or neutral-to-earth leakage, not involving human contact, can itself result in danger from unexpected loss of lighting or machine response. The problem of discovering and remedying small neutral-to-earth faults is great and itself argues for subdivision of RCD protection. Section 607 of the 16th edition of the *IEE Regulations* gives useful additional advice for dimmers and other electronic devices with inherent earth leakage currents.

Records and testing

IEE Regulations put great emphasis on the need to prepare and keep proper up-to-date records of the electrical installation, and the new Electricity at Work Regulations make this a legal obligation. Because modifications are often demanded at short notice in theatres to suit the needs of new productions, it is doubly important that full records and drawings are obtained from the original installer and are then kept up to date and available for ready reference by house staff. The completed installation should be tested to confirm, among other things, correct polarity, satisfactory insulation, and earth loop impedance, and these records should be kept for future reference. Retesting of the fixed installation should be carried out at yearly intervals and may be demanded by the licensing authority as a condition of the licence. In small venues this may be outside the competence of the house electricians and should be done under contract by a suitable electrical firm who may also be able to offer a maintenance and repair service. Portable items, including all stage lighting, must also be tested and records kept. Consequently every lantern and possibly every extension cable must, in future, have a serial number or some other unambiguous identifying mark.

Temporary installations

Live entertainment is, by nature, transient. Audiences rarely want to see a show twice, playwrights and directors think up new and more pressing topical messages, artistes get stale and look for new challenges, and technical fashions change. So, even in the best equipped performance building there will be occasional pressure to do something new — something that will stretch the existing facilities beyond the expectations of their original designers and which will necessitate alteration of the old design. In a building or at a temporary site where the facilities are less than adequate or are non-existent, the need for new work is self-evident. The means to satisfy these needs may be a permanent requirement justifying normal installation standards or, just as clearly, may be short term when the argument to use temporary techniques on grounds of speed, cost and convenience will be strong.

It must be expected that temporary electrical installation methods are likely to be somewhat less safe than established permanent installation methods, but the lower standard can sometimes be justified. A decision to use a suitable sheathed flexible multicore cable system rather than a trunking and conduit installation for a touring pop concert lighting rig is a familiar example. The relaxation will be made on the grounds that the work will be removed before it has time to wear out or to suffer significant damage. Also, the users will remain fully aware of any peculiarities or potential danger problems, whereas over a longer term, staff will change and the risks and necessary precautions may be forgotten.

Temporary electrical installation techniques, then, can be accepted when properly justifiable, provided proven methods are used and the installation is designed and supervised by competent persons. Local authority licensing rules usually acknowledge this but stipulate that the temporary work must be replaced by a permanent installation if kept in use for longer than the approved period. The problem is that there is less guidance and agreement on the standards necessary for temporary work.

Temporary power

There are three ways of obtaining power for temporary entertainment use. Spare capacity from the existing supply may be available; the supply company may be able to provide power from elsewhere in their system; or a generator may be necessary.

The first option requires installation of a suitable take-off switch with proper circuit breaker or fuse protection and fully enclosed phase, neutral and earth terminals for the outgoing load. Connection of the new switchgear must, under the Electricity Regulations 1989, be made without working on live conductors, so a time must be scheduled for the main system to be switched off. Connection of the temporary wiring must also be made without working live, and access to the terminals should be interlocked to ensure this. The temporary connection point should therefore be designed carefully to take account of possible future needs and installed by qualified staff. For security, means to lock the switch and terminal chamber and to monitor loads may be worthwhile.

Provision of power by the supply authority must also be arranged to result in provision of switchgear, protection and a terminal chamber and, probably, additional energy (kW h) metering. The supply authority will usually provide a suitable earthing connection though, if the venue is in a rural area, additional earthing rods may be stipulated.

If power has to be obtained from a generator it is advisable to employ a specialist contractor who will guarantee the safety of the complete power system. The generator must be specified to provide the necessary power with the correct voltage and frequency control and to remain stable with unbalanced loads and sudden switching from full load to no load or vice versa. The wiring system will usually use a protective conductor to link all system metalwork as is done by the usual permanent earth wire and conduit system, and the generator neutral will be connected to this protective system. Additionally, connections between the protective conductor and ground must be made using an earth spike or similar method. Multiple connection points between the protective system and ground and to other unearthed metalwork may be required to achieve equipotential bonding. The contractor must be competent to measure the quality of the earthing provided and to guarantee its suitability. RCDs may be used to protect portable equipment if a fully earthed generator system is used, providing care is taken to protect the RCD from vibration from the generator.

Very small 'domestic' generators are sometimes supplied without provision for earthing. This may be safe if only a single item of equipment is connected or if only double-insulated equipment is used. It is important to remember that RCDs cannot provide any worthwhile protection if earthing is not used.

For all sources of power it is important that the temporary switchgear is able to withstand and safely disconnect the prospective (worst case) short circuit fault current.

Cables

Normal 13 A or 15 A sheathed three-core cables as used for portable equipment in permanent installations should be satisfactory for temporary installation use. However, if the use is outdoor, care must be taken that plug and socket connections are protected from the weather. Care must also be taken that the many cables that connect to dimmer cubicles and other switchgear are not coiled, stacked or bundled together to reduce ventilation and thus overheat the insulation. Multicore cables with multipin plug systems are often used for dimmed lighting circuits. The cables and plugs must be confirmed to be correctly insulated for the system voltage to be used as well as having sufficient current capacity. Preferably, every circuit should have a live, neutral and earth conductor, though reduction of earth wire count may be permissible down to a cross-section comfortably exceeding that required by the highest subcircuit protection *and* providing the plug system cannot connect power without first connecting earth. Conductor current capacity may require derating for grouping, especially as these cables often remain partly coiled when in use.

Single-core cables of the type supplied for installation inside conduit or trunking are not suitable for unprotected use. All temporary unprotected cables used for main power connections between dimmer racks, switchgear, sound power units etc. must be insulated for the correct phase-to-phase or phase-to-neutral voltage and be double sheathed. All cables must be protected by a correctly rated fuse or circuit breaker on the supply side.

Although it is always preferable to feed entertainment lighting and sound equipment from a single-phase supply, it is often necessary to accept a 415/240 volts star (Y) connected three-phase supply. This gives three more or less independent single-phase supplies, though if the loads are not balanced then the full capacity of the supply cannot be used and the neutral-to-earth voltage may be higher than normal. It is important to accept that entertainment loads cannot be balanced and may, for short periods, be totally out of balance owing mainly to the uncontrollable flow of lighting effects. A full size neutral is therefore essential.

Traditionally, it has always been thought to be good practice to separate equipment and wiring fed from different phases by 2 m or more, and many electricians will still take trouble to do this. Nowadays, however, separating phases cannot be a major contribution to safety when so much emphasis is placed on ensuring that 240 volt phase-to-earth shocks are prevented. Indeed, many portable dimmer packs are designed in multiples of three dimmers specifically for three-phase operation. However, labels declaring the presence of 415 volts should always be provided wherever more than one phase is present.

Connectors

Connectors used for final power circuits should be industry standard two-pole and earth devices, rated at 32 A or 16 A to BS 4343, 15 A or 5 A to BS 546, or 13 A to BS 1363. The fused 13 A connector is not considered suitable for dimmed lighting circuits because of the unreliability of the fuse when fully loaded and the difficulty of access for replacement in suspended rigs. Dimmed lighting circuits are always wired radially with only one or two outlets. These can be properly protected by the circuit fuse at the dimmer rack.

The larger sizes of BS 4343 (Ceeform) connector offer single- and three-phase connectors in 32 A, 64 A and 120 A sizes. When a temporary system is to be transported or connected and disconnected frequently, these connectors offer convenience and security against poor quality site workmanship and circuit errors. Note that the colour code and pin connections are defined in the standard and must not be changed. Blue is always 220/240 volt, red 400/415 volt and yellow 110/120 volt.

Whether or not connectors are used for temporary power distribution, the technician in charge of the installation must take particular care to ensure that earth and neutral connections are correct before applying power.

Very large portable temporary installations may need to use single-core cables and single-pin connectors such as the American Cam-lok design or the design recommended by BS 5550: 7.5.4. These may provide little or no inherent protection either mechanically or by colour coding against connection errors and must be treated with the greatest care by the installers and electrical supervisor. In particular, the connection sequence – earth first, then neutral and finally phases – should be observed to ensure that safety components are firmly in place before power can be applied. Inspection and testing by the senior qualified electrical person in charge of the installation should be mandatory before switching on. If three-phase motors are to be supplied then the correct phase sequence must be double checked or the motors will turn the wrong way and not respond properly to limit switch control.

Earthing

The two purposes of earthing on a temporary entertainment power installation are the same as for permanent installations: to ensure that a fault which might make exposed metalwork dangerously live trips the protective device and disconnects the supply, and to keep all pieces of exposed metalwork at near-zero potential to one another and to earth. Earthing to *IEE Regulations* and British Standards requirements will ensure this. The special problems of temporary installations are to maintain a sufficiently low value of resistance for the protective earth conductors throughout the installation and to ensure that the seemingly useless equipotential bonding is fitted.

Acceptable values for the protective earth conductor impedance are related to the type of fuse or circuit breaker used and the desired fault clearance time. In permanent installations, 5 seconds is the maximum time allowed for fixed equipment and (except in special circumstances) 0.4 seconds for socket outlets. It seems obvious that temporary entertainment installations should always be designed to achieve the faster 0.4 seconds criterion. However, if the installation is outdoors it might be even wiser to use the 0.2 seconds time limit recommended for building sites and agricultural premises.

To check that the protective device will trip, the earth loop circuit between every probable fault location and system earth must be calculated and then measured and confirmed to be satisfactory when the installation is complete. The 16th edition of the *IEE Regulations* gives full information about these tests. Hand-held test meters are available for quick and reliable checking. The person in charge of the installation must be supplied with the design data and be competent to do the tests. The measurements should be recorded.

Equipotential bonding is required when exposed metalwork such as water pipes, structural steelwork, scaffolding etc. are within reach (2 metres) of mains powered equipment. In practice this means every installation. All such extraneous conductive parts have to be positively connected to the earthing conductor system. Equipotential bonding is needed only while an earth fault is clearing and ensures that the touch potential between the protective conductors carrying the fault and the extraneous conductive parts is kept at a safe low value. Exposed metal parts of a building structure may or may not be well earthed and must be tested. Additional supplementary bonding may be necessary. Temporary scaffolding will probably not be well earthed and must be bonded. Dimmer racks and sound bays should be well earthed through the incoming earth wire in their mains power cable, as should luminaires and other lighting equipment. Stands, booms and hanging pipes may be unearthed until luminaires are fitted, when there should be sufficient earthing from the luminaire through the hanging clamp. To comply with safety requirements, all cases must be considered and must be tested if there is doubt, and supplementary bonding must be fitted if necessary. Because entertainment electricians are often unclear about what is needed and how to carry out proper tests, it may be that house rules have to be devised by supervisory engineers with kits of bonding leads provided to deal with all normal conditions.

Residual current devices

Residual current devices have already been mentioned in this chapter, and they are also recommended in several other chapters of this book for protecting portable equipment, especially electronic musical equipment plugged into domestic-type sockets. RCDs can also play an important part in ensuring the safety of a temporary installation if fitted at the point of supply or to protect major subcircuits. Such protection should be less sensitive than the 30 mA devices recommended for final subcircuits in order to ensure discrimination and to give a wider safety margin against nuisance tripping. In such cases 300 mA devices are usually used. These provide protection against leakage currents which might cause fire and will be necessary to protect against the risk of electrocution if earth fault loop impedance cannot be reduced to give suitable tripping times from the circuit breakers or fuses. If the temporary installation is to be operated in the charge of a competent person, it may be sufficient to use the RCD as an indicator rather than an automatic trip. A suitably connected monitoring coil and milliammeter can be provided as part of the switchgear, with the option of an audible or visual alarm set to operate at say 30 mA, plus provision for a 300 mA fault to trip the circuit breaker. Provision of a monitoring circuit rather than automatic tripping is essential if rapid diagnosis and elimination of earth leakage faults is to be ensured. The final connection to the trip coil may be through a key-operated switch so that automatic disconnection can be inhibited during fault finding or during a public performance when the result of power loss is judged to be a greater danger than allowing a fault to persist. BS 5550: 7.5.2 gives recommendations for such a system for use with film and television location lighting installations.

It is important to remember that RCDs cannot be totally reliable and that they only protect against shock to earth. Direct shock between phase and neutral or between phase and phase will not necessarily produce a residual current and the device cannot be expected to trip. Insulation and proper enclosure of all live parts remains the essential primary means of protection.

Alterations

Alterations to electrical work require special care as it may be necessary to know about the original design in great detail to be able to correctly predict the full consequences of an alteration. This may be beyond the ability of an inexperienced or partially qualified electrician who is instructed to make a seemingly minor change. Managements and technical staff must take care to ensure that the necessary competence is provided.

To ensure that changes and fault finding can be done easily and safely it is important that full records are maintained of the original design calculations, the wiring and equipment 'as installed', the results of tests carried out during commissioning, the results of routine tests, and details of all previous alterations. These records may also be needed if, in the case of an accident, investigating officials need to confirm that proper safety precautions have been taken.

Portable equipment

The safety of specialized lighting equipment used in live entertainment is fully dealt with in Chapter 7. The construction standards and maintenance techniques required are also appropriate for most other portable and fixed equipment used in the entertainment environment. Lower standards should not be accepted.

Particular care must be taken with power-driven moving machinery where the hazard of loss of control must be added to the risks of electrocution and electrical fire. Control circuit connectors, position limits and overrun switches, relays and contactors and control logic are all subject to added stress on portable equipment and may not function correctly after heavy use. Circuits should be designed to fail safe, and protective circuits should, as far as possible, be fully independent of the main control circuit, not merely contain a few duplicated components. Provision and location of emergency stop switches should be given particular attention and, where remote starting is essential, permissive switches should be included that have to be reset before each operation.

Portable audio equipment, including electrically powered musical instruments, must be well earthed or double insulated, and manufacturers' data and marking should confirm that this is to the appropriate British or European Standard. As noted elsewhere, this class of equipment has been the cause of serious accidents in the past, sometimes because the original design was unsatisfactory, but more commonly because the equipment had been modified or damaged. Owners and users of such equipment must be encouraged to obtain proper advice to check that it is safe and remains safe. Technical staff required to provide power for or to handle musical and audio equipment should be encouraged to make their own checks, where possible without damaging the property of others, and to report faults and to press for immediate repair if defects are discovered. This condition might be a part of every management/artist contract. Provision of 30 mA RCDs should be an automatic safety precaution, but these are not entirely reliable and do not protect against direct line-to-neutral contact.

Audio equipment designed for 120 volt North American power supplies is in common use by professional pop musicians. Conversion to use UK 240 V supplies requires the addition of an internal double-wound transformer or a separate portable transformer. If the portable transformer is a safety isolating transformer to BS 3535 it may be used with its secondary winding unearthed to supply one instrument only. Any other transformer must have the secondary earthed, either at a centre tap or on one pole to be treated as the neutral of the 120 V output. The unearthed output must be fused. Earthing should be by direct connection to the incoming 240 V earth wire system. The 120 V wiring must use plug and socket connectors (usually American types) that will not connect to the 240 V system. RCD protection may be fitted on the 120 V wiring but will only work if the 120 V wiring is earthed.

Safety aids

Artistes, electricians and venues likely to have problems with badly insulated or poorly maintained portable equipment should carry their own portable domestic-type RCDs ready fitted with suitable plugs and sockets. For musical and audio equipment these should be a robust 13 A design satisfying BS 4293. The RCD should be tested before each and every use. A set of ready wired and tested connection leads offering alternative input plugs is recommended to ensure that plugs do not have to be hastily rewired to suit the supply. A full kit of spare fuses should be carried.

An alternative to using an RCD is to use a BS 3535 240/240 V isolating transformer for each instrument or amplifier. This makes the equipment earth free and much safer provided internal 'live' and 'neutral' connections are not accessible to touch.

Isolating transformers and RCDs must be strongly made to withstand the damage commonly encountered during transport and rigging.

Testing and maintenance

Anybody having responsibility for electrical equipment of any kind must take all reasonable steps to ensure that it is safe. New equipment should be warranted safe for its intended purpose by the manufacturer and should be labelled with a BS or European safety mark. The equipment must also have instructions to tell the user how to use the equipment safely and, if necessary, what the equipment is and is not designed to do. These instructions must be passed to everybody who may need to know about their message.

Once in use equipment will, in time, wear out and is likely to suffer damage. The owner, the user or a competent maintenance technician must therefore keep a regular check on the state of repair of every piece of electrical equipment to be able to anticipate when a potentially dangerous fault may occur. In practice, this needs constant vigilance on the part of the day-to-day user plus a considered scheme of testing and records operated by the owner and maintenance staff. Records require that every piece of equipment can be separately identified.

The tests appropriate to fixed or portable equipment must be decided by competent electrical staff. Inspection for damage, an insulation test, a check of polarity and an earth continuity or earth loop impedance test must all be considered. The electrical tests must be proper measurements using reliable test gear and the results must be logged for future reference. They will be needed to check if there has been any change in value between routine tests (an important early warning of developing faults) and they may be needed to convince an inspector or court official that there has not been negligence. Failure to use electrical equipment safely is now clearly a criminal offence and civil damage actions can also be expected in most cases. The HSE guidance note GS 50 offers suggestions about the appropriate test frequency for electrical audio equipment and these suggestions should also be appropriate for other electrical items. For the installation as a whole the *IEE Regulations* recommend suitable test intervals and the types of test and certification.

Larger theatres may have the competence and the time and money to organize proper safety testing using their own staff. Smaller companies may prefer to place contracts for such work. Whoever organizes and carries out the testing must be demonstrably competent and be prepared to take the responsibility incurred.

Testers, like repair and maintenance staff and installers of new or modified electrical systems, must remember that work on exposed live systems is nearly always illegal if danger can arise, and must devise ways to carry out their work without taking such risks. Equipment manufacturers must, in turn, now offer equipment that can be tested by competent users without removing safety covers.

6

Residual current devices

Tony Brown

Introduction

Changes in European legislation throughout the 1980s in the areas of health and safety, product liability and consumer protection, combined with increased public awareness of safety, have led to an upsurge in the use of residual current devices (RCDs). These are special items of switchgear which automatically disconnect the supply if current is detected to be flowing outside the main live-load-neutral circuit. The assumption is that if current is flowing outside its prescribed path it may be flowing to earth via a partial short circuit (with the risk of overheating and fire) or it may be flowing through a person (with the risk of electrocution). The live entertainment industry, with its widespread use of temporary electrical equipment, electronic musical instruments and frequent jury-rigged fit-ups, was quick to embrace these devices as a means of improving the safety of performers.

The physiological effects of electric current on the human body are extremely complex and are well documented in IEC report 479.[1] In simplistic terms, the severity of the effect of an electric shock on a human body is a factor of:

- the current path through the body and the muscles and organs
- the magnitude of the current flowing through the body
- the time for which the current flows.

Death by electrocution is usually the result of current passing through the heart, causing it to fibrillate and cease normal beating. The purpose of earth leakage protection equipment in the context of personnel safety is to detect the fault current and disconnect the supply before irreversible harm occurs to the victim. It should be noted, however, that many more accidents involving electricity result in burns, falls and injuries due to explosion rather than electrocution. It is essential for users to be aware that there are many circumstances where earth leakage protection devices may not necessarily provide immunity against these dangers.

Earth leakage protection equipment has been available for many years, although in the UK the 15th edition of the *IEE Wiring Regulations* was needed to act as the catalyst which promoted common usage (the 16th edition is now in force).[2] There can be no doubt that RCDs have significantly reduced the incidence of fatal electric shock. Similarly, their installation is a way in which an employer can demonstrate that he has taken 'reasonably practicable precautions' to protect against accidents – a term favoured by the new generation of legislators and given legal status in the HSE *Memorandum of Guidance on the Electricity at Work Regulations 1989*.[3]

However, as with many apparently simple panaceas, there is a risk that the solution is embraced without full understanding of the technical limitations and constraints. In particular, the effect on the operation of these devices in conjunction with the phase-controlled dimmers used in stage lighting, or their use in conjunction with electronic equipment which may include switch-mode power supplies, need careful consideration. The use of residual current devices should not be denigrated, but caution and an understanding of their limitations are required by those responsible for specifying, designing and installing electrical services in a live performance area. Some of the pitfalls are revealed in the rest of this chapter.

Types of earth leakage protection

The first problem is one of nomenclature: there is an abundance of mysterious initials, many similar but not quite interchangeable (Figure 6.1). The generic title 'earth leakage circuit breaker' (ELCB) has fallen from common usage in recent years and is no longer used by the IEE. This is because the term covers two different operating principles: the voltage-operated ELCB, as defined by BS 842,[4] and the current balance ELCB, also known as the residual-current-operated circuit breaker (RCCB or RCB) as defined by BS 4293,[5] and also referred to as the residual current device (RCD).

Voltage-operated ELCBs (Figure 6.2) require the earthed metalwork of all the equipment being protected to be electrically isolated from the structure of the building. Separate earth continuity conductors are fed back to the ELCB which, in turn, has a connection to an earth electrode of defined impedance.

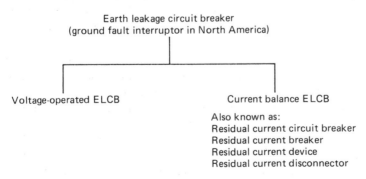

Figure 6.1   *Earth leakage protection terminology (courtesy of Strand Lighting Ltd)*

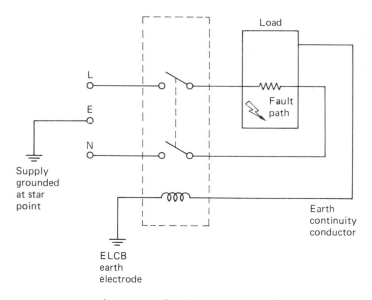

Figure 6.2   *Voltage-operated ELCB (courtesy of Strand Lighting Ltd)*

This concept has several serious disadvantages as the breaker may fail to operate under certain conditions:

- if the earth electrode impedance is too high
- if there is a short circuit between the equipment and the building structure (e.g. luminaires hung from a metal roof truss)
- if the fault current is flowing from the line conductor to earth rather than to the earth continuity conductor.

For the above reasons the 16th edition of the *IEE Regulations* does not allow the use of voltage-operated ELCBs in new installations in the UK. It must be noted that *IEE Regulations* are not generally applied retrospectively and that voltage-operated ELCBs may be encountered on older installations. In addition they are still in common usage in parts of the world where the electrical supply authorities do not provide good earth conductors.

The second earth leakage protection principle, of current balance (Figure 6.3), is that of the RCD commonly installed today. Here the phase and neutral conductors both pass through the breaker and are wound a few times around a toroidal transformer core inside. Many turns of a secondary sense winding are also wound round the core, and this winding is connected to a solenoid trip mechanism. In a healthy circuit the current in the line conductor is equal to that flowing in the neutral. Thus magnetic flux induced in the toroid by the current in the line is exactly cancelled by the flux induced by the neutral. The winding direction ensures that the induced fluxes cancel rather than add. With no flux flowing, no voltage is

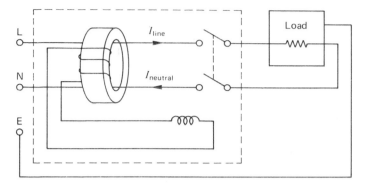

Figure 6.3   *Current balance principle, healthy circuit:*
$I_{line} = -I_{neutral}$ *(courtesy of Strand Lighting Ltd)*

induced in the sense winding and the breaker does not trip. This principle holds regardless of the magnitude of load current flowing in the circuit and demonstrates the first common misconception of RCDs – that they do not provide overload protection! There are, however, combination units of RCDs and overload protection miniature circuit breakers (MCBs) available: these are generally known as residual current breakers with overload protection (RCBOs), and serve to add another dimension to the initials puzzle.

It is extremely important to remember that whilst an RCD will trip if fault current is flowing to earth, clearly it will not if the victim is insulated from earth, and no protection from shock will be provided if both phase and neutral wires are being held. An experienced electrician never holds the two wires at the same time, even if he is 'sure' that the circuit is isolated.

As with most safety equipment, RCDs require regular testing to confirm that they are still functional. BS 4293 requires all RCDs to have an integral test push and to include instructions on its use. Also, *IEE Regulation* 514-12-02 requires a notice to be fixed near the origin of the electrical installation stating that the RCD should be tested quarterly.

If a fault is introduced, causing some current from the line to flow to earth (Figure 6.4), more current will pass through the phase conductor than the neutral. A net flux will be set up in the toroid which will induce a voltage in the sense coil and actuate the solenoid, tripping the breaker and isolating the circuit.

Many touring companies and musicians have built RCDs into their mobile electrical distribution systems for use at venues which do not have a protected installation. However, most RCD manufacturers advise that their products are only suitable for permanent installation as the trip mechanisms are particularly delicate. If RCDs are incorporated into portable equipment it is essential that they are mounted in a manner which will absorb transit shock and that the equipment is adequately packed for transport. All such RCDs should be tested on arrival at their

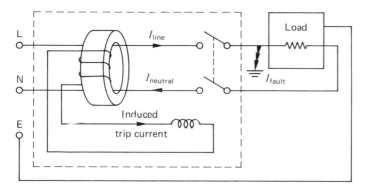

Figure 6.4   *Current balance principle, fault condition:*
$I_{line} = I_{fault} - I_{neutral}$ *(courtesy of Strand Lighting Ltd)*

destination. It is folly to wire RCDs to the ends of extension leads or to store them in cable bins.

RCDs are available in a number of forms for different purposes. The version which plugs into a domestic socket and has a built-in socket into which an appliance can be plugged is familiar to most people. This device has the unfortunate disadvantage of being too portable for use in a place of entertainment and by the frailty of human nature will disappear with the first performance, leaving future performers with no protection. A further disadvantage is that it is too easily bypassed by removing it and plugging the appliance directly into the wall socket when some faulty item of equipment causes it to trip, thus removing the 'safety net' at the time it is most needed.

A number of manufacturers produce domestic-type mains outlets with integral RCDs. These are suitable for protecting feeds to musical instruments in small clubs and pubs provided the following criteria are met:

1 The trip current should not be greater than 30 mA.
2 The device should be of a type specified for use with switch-mode power supplies.
3 All appliance sockets in the vicinity of the stage area must have RCD sockets fitted.
4 Sufficient sockets should be installed.

The third format of RCDs comprises those permanently installed as part of the switchgear. These come in many shapes and sizes and it is important to realize that although an RCD does not provide overload protection, it does have a maximum current rating. A device must be selected with a capacity which is not less than the maximum current which could be drawn through it.

Another factor to be considered when selecting RCDs for part of a fixed installation is the trip current. This is the current flowing to earth which will cause the breaker to trip. It is commonly acknowledged that personnel protection will be reduced significantly if the trip current is greater than 30 mA; in some cases, for example where water is present, even this figure may be too high to afford adequate protection. Large RCDs may have trip currents of several amperes, and are sometimes installed to protect accidental short circuits to earth from overheating and starting a fire: they will, however, provide no protection against electric shock to a person.

RCD protection of a stage lighting installation

The question of whether stage lighting installations should or should not be protected with RCDs cannot be answered with a simple yes or no, as consideration of each venue and its usage may lead to a different conclusion. For example, a well-managed professional theatre with qualified electrical staff and an inventory of maintained equipment may decide that RCD protection of its lighting rig is unnecessary. Conversely a village hall with no permanent maintenance staff which is an occasional venue for the Cub Scout play may chose RCD protection.

In the UK, three guidance publications were produced in 1991 which included recommendations on the use of RCDs.[68] All advise RCD protection of sockets in a performance area into which temporary equipment may be plugged. However, the two publications specific to licensed venues categorically state that RCD protection is not normally required on permanently installed stage lighting circuits.

Regardless of the size of the lighting installation, there are a number of technical factors which must be considered when RCD protection is planned.

The first problem is invariably one of cost. By far the cheapest approach is a single three-phase and neutral RCD connected in series with the incoming feed cable. A typical device capable of passing 600 amps per phase (A/Ph) costs less than £1000, and there is an almost irresistible temptation for planners to specify such an RCD. This is a mistake. If a single earth occurs at any point in the lighting installation downstream of the RCD it will trip, blacking out everything. In addition to the immediate danger to the cast and the obvious disruption to the performance, it will not be possible to restore power until the fault has been found and cleared. Earth faults on line conductors are usually simple to isolate as individual dimmer circuits have fuses or MCBs to protect against short circuits or overload, which will trip and automatically clear a direct short circuit to earth, allowing the RCD to be reset. Leakage faults from line to earth are harder to trace as the MCB (or fuse) will often not blow; however, by switching off MCBs the fault can usually be disconnected and the RCD then reset. However a short circuit or leakage fault between the neutral conductor and earth may also cause the RCD to trip. It may then take several days to locate such a fault, as luminaires may have to be unplugged and wiring from dimmers disconnected.

At the other extreme it is possible to protect each lighting circuit with an individual RCD, but this results in a very high cost. Usually a compromise is adopted, whereby a maximum of 10% of circuits will be isolated should any RCD trip.

A further problem can arise with a single large RCD: that of nuisance tripping caused by cable capacitance. If an RCD is to provide personnel protection its trip current should be less than 30 mA but, in a sizeable lighting rig, currents in excess of this can flow to earth simply via the distributed capacitance of the load cables. The more cable, the higher the total capacitance value and the higher the earth leakage current. For example, consider a typical installation with 200 dimmers, 50 metre cable runs from dimmers to luminaires, and a capacitance of as little as 50 pF per metre:

$$\text{total connected cable length} = 200 \times 50 = 10 \text{ km}$$
$$\text{capacitance (line to earth)} \approx 50 \times 10^{-12} \times 10^4 = 0.5 \ \mu F$$
$$\text{current at } 50 \text{ Hz} = 2\pi f C V = 2\pi \times 50 \times 0.5 \times 10^{-6} \times 240 = 37.7 \text{ mA}$$

An RCD on this system would therefore be impractical. The situation is made even worse by the presence of harmonics. The current waveform through a phase-controlled dimmer set at half conduction can be considered to comprise a fundamental 50 Hz current plus a significant current flowing at each of the harmonic frequencies (100 Hz, 150 Hz, 200 Hz, 250 Hz etc.). The third equation shows that the current flowing from the line conductor to earth via capacitance increases with frequency: it follows that a greater proportion of the harmonics will be coupled to ground. In practice this means that an installation where the capacitive current to earth is below the RCD trip threshold when all dimmers are at full may nuisance trip as lights are dimmed, leaving everyone not only in the dark but also perplexed as to the cause. It should be noted that many older dimmers incorporate large suppression capacitors between phase and earth which will also cause an RCD in the dimmer feeder to trip.

Three-phase RCDs for protection against electrocution have a single toroidal core through which all four conductors (three phases and neutral) pass. However, the diameter of toroids manufactured for this purpose is not large, hence limiting the maximum feeder size which can be protected with an RCD of this type. Devices are available with four separate toroids (one per conductor): the secondary windings are interconnected to cancel out induced voltages in a healthy circuit or trip the breaker under fault conditions. These devices are intended to protect against high currents flowing to earth which may possibly cause a fire, and are not suitable for personnel protection as the 30 mA protection threshold is lower than the imbalance current caused by the tolerances of the four sense transformers. Any attempt to set the device to 30 mA trip level causes constant tripping; unauthorized adjustment of the trip level to a setting well above that affording any personnel protection then follows.

All the above problems are relevant to installations where one RCD is used to protect the feed to a large number of dimmers. There are, however, several factors which must be considered both in this case or when small RCDs are fitted to individual or small groups of dimmers. For example, although the principle of current balance applies to all RCDs there are numerous variations, and it is imperative to select manufacturers' versions which are appropriate for use with phase control.

Most RCDs are designed to operate in circuits carrying continuous 50 Hz sinusoidal AC mains currents. Phase-controlled dimmers, by definition, chop each half of the mains cycle and therefore present a current which is neither sinusoidal nor continuous (Figure 6.5). Because of this, a significant proportion of the total current consists of harmonics; therefore the waveform cannot be considered to be simply 50 Hz. Also, it is possible for a dimmer to become faulty and conduct only in alternate half-cycles of the mains, which results in a direct rather than an alternating current in the load circuit. The effect of all of these factors must be considered in the selection of an appropriate RCD, as shown in the following paragraphs.

Some suppliers offer RCDs with 'electronic trip': these are also known as voltage-dependent RCDs (this term being easily confused with voltage-operated ELCBs). These usually incorporate a semiconductor electronic stage interposed between the sense coil winding and the release solenoid. The electronic circuitry is powered from the line conductor to the RCD (Figure 6.6). Clearly, if these devices are fitted in the load circuit after a dimmer, the voltage available to energize the internal circuitry will be reduced as the dimmer is faded down. Dependent on the exact circuit configuration, the efficacy of the trip function may degrade as the load is dimmed, until eventually the RCD will not trip when a fault is applied. This may occur even though the rms output voltage from the dimmer is still high enough to allow a lethal current to flow through a human body. This type of RCD should not be used between the dimmer and the lamp. Reliability analysis shows these

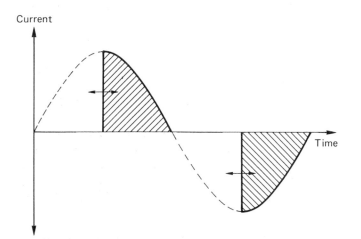

Figure 6.5   *Phase-controlled waveform (courtesy of Strand Lighting Ltd)*

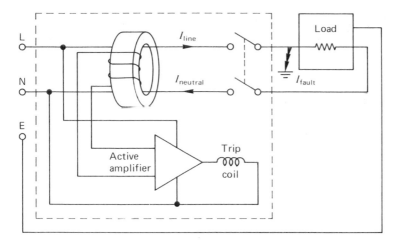

Figure 6.6   *Voltage-dependent (or electronic trip) RCD, fault condition:*
$I_{\text{line}} = I_{\text{fault}} - I_{\text{neutral}}$ *(courtesy of Strand Lighting Ltd)*

versions to be more prone to failure than their voltage-independent counterparts. Furthermore, they will not trip if the neutral conductor becomes disconnected from the feed to the RCD, although the line remains connected.

The standard RCD construction is also unsuitable for use with dimmers, partly because a slight increase in the trip current occurs as the dimmer conduction angle reduces. However, a much greater performance degradation occurs if the dimmer output becomes asymmetrical. Under these circumstances a conventional RCD may not trip even when fault currents of several amperes are flowing. Consequently manufacturers do not endorse this type of RCD for phase-control applications.

All RCDs are fitted with a test button which connects a resistor between the line conductor (before the current transformer) to the neutral conductor (after the transformer), thus causing a current imbalance when pressed. The resistor value is chosen to cause the trip threshold current to flow at full mains voltage. Here also, when the voltage is reduced by a dimmer, the test button will fail to trip the breaker.

Several manufacturers produce a special version of RCD known as a pulsating DC RCD. These respond in the normal manner to symmetrical waveforms, but in addition should trip on phase-controlled or asymmetric pulsing waveforms. They will also trip should a fault occur on electronic equipment with a switching power supply. The principle of operation is similar to the conventional RCD with the following exceptions:

1 The toroidal core material is changed to give better coupling at higher frequencies.

2 The turns ratio is increased to give higher voltage on the sense coil.
3 A differentiating capacitor is connected in series with the sense coil to produce a pulse on the trip solenoid each time the fault current rises or falls.

Needless to say there is a cost penalty associated with these variants, partly due to higher component and manufacturing costs and partly due to lower production volume.

Summary

Installation of a single RCD on the supply feeder should be avoided at all costs, and there is little point in installing one for personnel protection if the trip threshold has to be set above 30 mA to avoid nuisance tripping. Indeed, a false sense of security would be induced in personnel working on the system.

Voltage-operated ELCBs are totally inappropriate for entertainment lighting applications. Although it is unlikely that they would be considered for new installations in this country, there are undoubtedly some already installed and they are still regularly used in some countries.

RCDs which use the line voltage to power an electronic trip mechanism require very close scrutiny before use to ensure that the trip circuit remains functional if the line voltage is phase controlled. Incorporating RCDs into portable equipment requires great care in both construction and use if the devices are to remain effective.

Conventional RCDs designed for 50 Hz sinusoidal currents will not trip should an earth fault occur whilst the dimmer is conducting in alternate half-cycles. Their performance regarding harmonic and non-continuous currents is such that manufacturers will not endorse their use in dimming applications.

Pulsating DC RCDs from *some* manufacturers which are installed on the output of each dimmer appear to offer an approach whereby fault currents of 30 mA will trip the RCD at all dimmer settings above 50 V. However, it should be noted that the variation of tripping time as a result of dimming has not been examined. The declaration of fitness for purpose in this application needs to be provided by the maker of the RCD, who is the design authority for the product.

Finally there is a risk that increased use of RCDs may lead to complacency regarding electrical safety. The use of RCDs is an additional safeguard and in no way forms a substitute for good electrical practice, whether in the field of installation, operation or equipment maintenance.

References

1 International Electrotechnical Commission. *Effects of Current Passing Through the Human Body*, report 479, IEC, Geneva, 1984.

2　Institution of Electrical Engineers. *Regulations for Electrical Installations*, 16th edn, IEE, 1991.

3　Health and Safety Executive. *Memorandum of Guidance on the Electricity at Work Regulations 1989*, HMSO, 1990.

4　BS 842: 1965. Specification for AC voltage-operated earth leakage circuit breakers.

5　BS 4293: 1983. Specification for residual-current-operated circuit breakers.

6　Home Office and Scottish Home and Health Department. *Guide to Fire Precautions in Existing Places of Entertainment and Like Premises*, HMSO, 1990.

7　Health and Safety Executive. *Electrical Safety for Entertainers*, 1991.

8　London District Surveyors Association. *Model Technical Regulations for Places of Public Entertainment*, 1991.

7

Recent developments in luminaire safety

David Bertenshaw

Background

When Captain E. M. Shaw, Head of the London Metropolitan Fire Brigade, made his 1882 inspection of the first theatre to use electric light, the Savoy, he wrote: 'The lighting is principally by electricity, which does not perceptibly raise the temperature and with good arrangements, as in this house, appears to be absolutely safe.' Whilst we know better now of the real risks still being run, the dawn of this new technology finally heralded a practical alternative to the intensive and frequently tragic use of gas lighting during the nineteenth century.

Development of electric lighting

As early as 1808 Humphry Davy had shown that electricity could be used to generate light by means of drawing an arc between two sticks of carbon connected to a battery. Carbon arc lamps were first used in a theatre in 1848, but the noise, constant need for maintenance and inability to be dimmed severely limited their acceptance.

However, in 1879, at a meeting of the Newcastle Philosophical Society, Joseph Swan demonstrated his electric incandescent vacuum lamp. At about the same time in America, Thomas Edison also succeeded in devising the same simple and effective means of converting electricity into light with his carbon filament lamp. By 1881 the incandescent lamp was in manufacture and public use, and rapidly became the universal means of providing stage illumination as public supplies of electricity were developed.

That this new lamp represented such a dramatic safety improvement was evidenced at a public demonstration by their first theatrical user, Richard D'Oyly Carte, at the Savoy in 1881. This involved wrapping a flammable gauze round a lighted lamp and smashing it with a hammer, whereupon the incredulous audience witnessed that the 'flame' (filament) extinguished immediately without even singeing the fabric.

As time went on, the new hazards present with electric lighting became better appreciated and recognized: electric shock, fire from self-heating of the lamp and from poor contacts or wiring, and impact due to mechanical failure. The development of a practical mercury discharge lamp in 1901 and subsequent other discharge lamps brought another real hazard in the form of UV radiation, whilst in 1956 the debut of the tungsten halogen lamp introduced the danger of explosion caused by the high internal operating pressures. Clearly, various standards and regulations were needed to deal with this dangerous but now irreplaceable technique for showing entertainments at their best.

Standards development

As early as 1902 the first electrical inspector of factories was appointed, and the prototypical Electricity Regulations 1908 (replaced only in 1990) recognized the need to regulate the safety of electricity supply. However, on the whole the attitude of UK public administration through most of the twentieth century seems to have had some similarity to the nineteenth century's use of gas: preparedness to regulate the safe use of electricity only in areas of particular public danger. Apart from regulations on a few particular items, UK electrical apparatus in general and entertainment luminaires in particular had no legal need to comply with any safety standards, whereas even theatrical gas lighting was ultimately regulated under the Lord Chamberlain's licences by 1864 (Figure 7.1). There was, though, a steady development of UK voluntary standards and practices, with the *IEE Wiring Regulations* providing evidence of a generally successful self-regulation of electrical installations.

Regarding luminaire safety, UK standards (but not enforceable regulations) were drawn up for the safety of lamps and lamp holders (e.g. BS 5971[1] and BS 5042[2]), and from 1971 BS 4533[3] was introduced (replacing the earlier BS 3820: 1964[3]) covering the safety of construction and use of luminaires. It is interesting to note that this standard provided the model for the International Electrotechnical Commission in the development of IEC 598,[5] now an accepted worldwide safety standard for luminaires.

EEC developments

The UK situation began to change as a result of joining the European Economic Community in 1972. In 1973 the EEC issued the Low Voltage Directive,[6] requiring all low-voltage (under 1000 V) electrical equipment sold in the EEC to be safe as measured by common safety standards. This had the prime purpose of eliminating barriers to trade, by ensuring all states recognized common standards of safety and

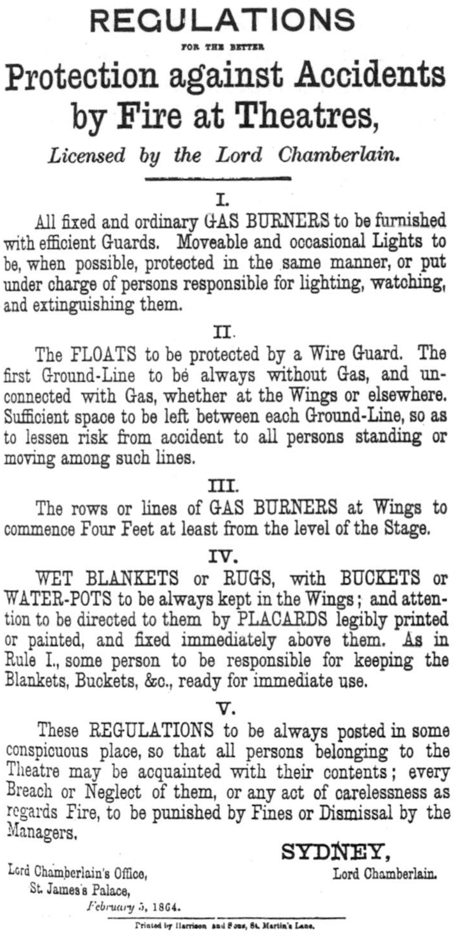

REGULATIONS

FOR THE BETTER

Protection against Accidents by Fire at Theatres,

Licensed by the Lord Chamberlain.

I.

All fixed and ordinary GAS BURNERS to be furnished with efficient Guards. Moveable and occasional Lights to be, when possible, protected in the same manner, or put under charge of persons responsible for lighting, watching, and extinguishing them.

II.

The FLOATS to be protected by a Wire Guard. The first Ground-Line to be always without Gas, and unconnected with Gas, whether at the Wings or elsewhere. Sufficient space to be left between each Ground-Line, so as to lessen risk from accident to all persons standing or moving among such lines.

III.

The rows or lines of GAS BURNERS at Wings to commence Four Feet at least from the level of the Stage.

IV.

WET BLANKETS or RUGS, with BUCKETS or WATER-POTS to be always kept in the Wings; and attention to be directed to them by PLACARDS legibly printed or painted, and fixed immediately above them. As in Rule I., some person to be responsible for keeping the Blankets, Buckets, &c., ready for immediate use.

V.

These REGULATIONS to be always posted in some conspicuous place, so that all persons belonging to the Theatre may be acquainted with their contents; every Breach or Neglect of them, or any act of carelessness as regards Fire, to be punished by Fines or Dismissal by the Managers.

SYDNEY,

Lord Chamberlain's Office,   Lord Chamberlain.
St. James's Palace,
February 5, 1864.

Printed by Harrison and Sons, St. Martin's Lane.

Figure 7.1 *Safety Regulations issued by the Lord Chamberlain (copy in the Public Record Office, LC1/142)*

accepted products for free sale if certified to these standards by a third party or the manufacturer. It also had the intention to ensure that all electrical equipment sold was safe, and it was this, in fact, which required the UK government to enact general legislation for the first time to require all electrical equipment sold to be safe.

This was achieved by the issuing of the Electrical Equipment (Safety) Regulations 1975 and the Electrical Equipment (Safety) (Amendment) Regulations 1976 under the Consumer Protection Act 1961. These were followed in 1977 by a Department of Trade and Industry *Administrative Guidance* publication on the regulations,[7] and in this was contained an explicit reference to BS 4533 as being considered a sufficient safety standard for luminaires. Thus, 94 years after the first theatrical use of electric lighting, there was a legal duty to provide luminaires to a particular safety standard. This, though, was only the harbinger of changes to come, since there was no common agreed EEC safety standard for luminaires and the UK's implementation of the Low Voltage Directive was imperfect.

There are two bodies making European Standards: Comité Européen de Normalisation (CEN) concerned with general engineering and other standards, and Comité Européen de Normalisation Electrotechnique (CENELEC) concerned with electrical standards. Though they are not in fact part of the European Commission, they have an EC mandate to put into place accepted European Standards, preferably by a process of adoption and modification of existing IEC, ISO or member state standards. These are then issued as complete European Standards or Euro-Norms (ENs), or as Harmonization Documents (HDs) where other member states' standards are referred to. Thus, when CENELEC came to consider luminaire safety, IEC 598 was a readily available standard for initial reference. However, being first issued in 1979, this standard was not felt to meet fully the Community's needs. Considerable review of the standard was undertaken until the IEC 598 second edition was adopted, with an agreed set of common modifications, as EN 60 598 'Luminaires'.

The UK government had been quite prompt in implementing the EEC Low Voltage Directive compared with other member states, but the interpretation into legislation was inexact. It failed to acknowledge the primacy of harmonized European Standards and contained many exceptions to suit particular UK practice, thus potentially still allowing UK standards to be used as a barrier to trade. Consequently, replacement regulations acceptable to the EC – the Low Voltage Electrical Equipment (Safety) Regulations 1989 – were issued under the new Consumer Protection Act 1987, and came into force on 1 June 1989. These regulations require compliance with harmonized European Standards as the overriding means of achieving safety. Thus when the new European Standard EN 60 598 on luminaires was completely published in October 1989 (Part 2 Section 17 was published early in January 1989 but the main requirements in Part 1 were not published until October 1989) it became effective and compliance was legally required immediately in the UK and in principle throughout the EC (Figures 7.2 and 7.3).

Euro-Norm EN 60 598-2-17

Since EN 60 598-2-17 is now the particular required standard for live entertainment (stage, film and television) luminaires, it will be of some interest to look at its general structure and content. As is required by CENELEC regulations, EN 60 598 has been published by BSI in the UK as a new version of standard BS 4533: 1990 (reference should be made to the latest issue if any implementation is intended). The structure of the standard is a set of general requirements and tests contained in

STATUTORY INSTRUMENTS

1989 No. 728

CONSUMER PROTECTION

The Low Voltage Electrical Equipment (Safety) Regulations 1989

Made - - - -	*26th April 1989*
Laid before Parliament	*10th May 1989*
Coming into force	*1st June 1989*

Whereas the Secretary of State has, in accordance with section 11(5) of the Consumer Protection Act 1987(**a**), consulted such organisations as appear to him to be representative of interests substantially affected by these Regulations, such other persons as he considers appropriate and the Health and Safety Commission:

And whereas the Secretary of State is a Minister designated (**b**) for the purposes of section 2 of the European Communities Act 1972(**c**) in relation to measures for safety and consumer protection as respects electrical equipment and any provisions concerning the composition, labelling, marketing, classification or description of electrical equipment:

Now, therefore, the Secretary of State in exercise of powers conferred on him by section 11 of the said Act of 1987, by section 2 of the said Act of 1972 and by the Consumer Protection Act 1987 (Commencement No. 1) Order 1987(**d**) and of all other powers enabling him in that behalf hereby makes the following Regulations:–

Citation and commencement

1.   These Regulations may be cited as the Low Voltage Electrical Equipment (Safety) Regulations 1989 and shall come into force on 1st June 1989.

Revocations, disapplications and defence

2.—(1) The Electric Blankets (Safety) Regulations 1971(**e**), the Electric Blankets (Safety) Regulations (Northern Ireland) 1972(**f**), the Electrical Equipment (Safety) Regulations 1975(**g**), the Electrical Equipment (Safety) (Amendment) Regulations 1976(**h**) and the Electrical Equipment (Safety) Regulations (Northern Ireland) 1977(**i**) are hereby revoked.

(**a**) 1987 c.43.
(**b**) S.I. 1972/1811.
(**c**) 1972 c.68.
(**d**) S.I. 1987/1680.
(**e**) S.I. 1971/1961.
(**f**) S.R. & O. (N.I.) 1972 No. 69.
(**g**) S.I. 1975/1366.
(**h**) S.I. 1976/1208.
(**i**) S.R. (N.I.) 1977 No. 137.

EUROPEAN STANDARD
NORME EUROPÉENNE
EUROPÄISCHE NORM

EN 60 598-2-17

January 1989

UDC : 628,977,7 : 654 191

Key words: Lighting fitting; luminaire; film; television; studio; stage; indoor lighting; outdoor; tungsten filament lamp; particular requirements

English version

Luminaires
Part 2 : Particular requirements
Section seventeen – Luminaires for
stage lighting, television, film and photographic studios
(outdoor and indoor)
(IEC 598-2-17 (1984) ed 1 + Amdt 1 (1987))

Luminaires
Deuxième partie: Règles particulières
Section dix-sept — Luminaires pour l'eclairage des
scènes de théâtre, pour prises du vues de télévision
et de cinéma (à l'extérieur et à l'intérieur)
(CEI 598-2-17 (1984) ed 1 + Amdt 1 (1987))

Leuchten
Teil 2: Besondere Anforderungen
Hauptabschnitt siebzehn: Leuchten für Bühnen.
Fernseh-, Film und Fotostudios (Außen und Innen)
(IEC 598-2-17 (1984) Ausg. 1 + Amdt 1 (1987))

This European Standard was ratified by CENELEC on 13 September 1988.
CENELEC members are bound to comply with the requirements of the CENELEC
Internal Regulations which stipulate the conditions for giving this European Standard the
status of a national standard without any alteration.

Up-to-date lists and bibliographical references concerning such national standards may be
obtained on application to the CENELEC Central Secretariat or to any CENELEC
member.

This European Standard exists in three official versions (English, French and German). A
version in any other language made by translation under the responsibility of a CENELEC
member into its own language and notified to CENELEC Central Secretariat has the same
status as the official versions.

CENELEC members are the national electrotechnical committees of Austria, Belgium,
Denmark, Finland, France, Germany, Greece, Iceland, Ireland, Italy, Luxemburg,
Netherlands, Norway, Portugal, Spain, Sweden, Switzerland and United Kingdom.

CENELEC

European Committee for Electrotechnical Standardization
Comité Européen de Normalisation Electrotechnique
Europäisches Komitee für Elektrotechnische Normung

Central Secretariat: Rue Bréderode 2, B-1000 Brussels

Ref. No. EN 60 598-2-17 : 1989 E

EN 60 598-1 (known as Part 1), followed by a schedule of particular requirements for various kinds of luminaires in each section of EN 60 598-2 (Part 2). The controlling standard is in fact the relevant Part 2 section which calls up the required elements of Part 1.

Part 2 currently has 15 sections. Clearly Part 2 Section 17 'Luminaires for stage lighting, television, film and photographic studios (outdoor and indoor)' is of chief interest, though Section 5 on floodlights, Section 20 on lighting chains and Section 22 on luminaires for emergency lighting may prove useful.

Examination of Part 1 shows that safety has to be maintained by attention to mechanical, electrical and thermal properties and use, which in turn depend on the particular electrical classification of the luminaire, i.e. whether Class 1 (earthed) or Class II (double insulated). These requirements may be summarized as follows:

Electrical (if above safety extra low voltage of 50 V a.c.)

- Adequate insulation of live parts and proper earthing of exposed metalwork, or double or reinforced insulation.
- Adequate insulation resistance, creepage and clearances taking account of any HV ignitors.
- Adequate and reliable fastening of wires and contact systems etc.
- Adequate provision, connection and protection for external wiring.
- Protection against electric shock during use (including relamping).
- Adequate system of safe and reliable lamp holders, switches etc.

Thermal

- Adequate endurance with the intended lamp in operation.
- No risk of fire to objects near to the luminaire or on which the luminaire is mounted.
- Safe operating temperatures of parts intended to be frequently manually operated.
- Safe operation during reasonable abnormal conditions.
- Insulating parts to be resistant to heat and ignition.

Mechanical

- Adequate protection against dust and water as required for declared use.
- Adequate retention of electrical components.
- Construction and mechanical components designed to maintain safety in the structure, assembly and electrical protection.
- Suspension system to have an adequate factor of safety.
- Limitation on weight suspended on electrical cables.
- Suspension or adjusting devices to not damage connecting wires.
- Safety shields to protect against tungsten halogen lamp explosion and broken glass risk.

Use

- Durable marking on luminaire to show origin, ratings and any information vital for safe use.
- Instructions to enable and maintain safe use to accompany luminaire.

The extent of the detail requirements in Part 1, extending from the acceptable creepage and clearance distances of insulation to particular requirements on screw terminals, prevents a detailed review here. However, Part 2 Section 17 is particularly relevant to the entertainments industry.

As indicated earlier, EN 60 598-2-17 'Luminaires for stage lighting, television, film and photographic studios (outdoor and indoor)' has many particular extra requirements over Part 1, some of which are indicated below. The general use of high-power halogen or discharge lamps leads to a particular need to protect against broken lamp fragments escaping. This is achieved by limiting the size of any apertures to 8 mm where a shattered lamp's fragments could exit by a direct path and 3 mm where fragments could fall out under gravity. In addition, since an exploding lamp could shatter other glass components in the luminaire, a single lens acting as a shield that may be fractured by an exploding lamp should have a 25 mm mesh guard in front of it, and a safety glass shield should have a 12 mm mesh guard. Precautions must be taken against any UV hazard from discharge lamps.

The generally temporary use and high weight of these luminaires requires a ten times safety factor before permanent deformation in the suspension, together with a proven secondary suspension capable of surviving and arresting 30 free drops of 30 mm, and no risk of accessories falling in any orientation. It must not be possible to insert a lamp into a live lamp holder except in luminaires intended for professional use, and such insertion must always be prevented for luminaires containing high-voltage ignitors generating over 4600 V peak. Luminaires containing high-pressure discharge lamps having an explosion risk must either be prevented from opening until cooled down or clearly marked to be allowed to cool before opening.

Certain extra information must be provided on the luminaire, that is to indicate the top of the luminaire, to state any limits to angles of use, and to warn of the need to isolate electrically before relamping and of the danger of a hot lamp. Also needed is the rated maximum ambient temperature, the maximum luminaire exterior surface temperature and the minimum distances from flammable surfaces to all exterior surfaces of the luminaire and the beam (the test limit is that distance which results in 90 °C in matt black painted wood).

Compliance example

An illustration of how a luminaire's requirements can be met is given by a study of a small theatrical Fresnel luminaire (Figure 7.4). This uses a 650 W tungsten halogen lamp and is intended for use in small civic and professional stages. The

Figure 7.4   *Fresnel luminaire Prelude F (Strand Lighting Ltd): see text for A–G*

mains inlet is via an approved CEE22 plug (A), thus reducing the maximum cable temperature and allowing easy and reliable disconnection for relamping. Only after the plug is removed can the base (B) be opened for relamping. Internal wiring is restrained and has basic insulation, the external metalwork being earthed to class I either by direct connection to earth or via thread-forming screws and paint-cutting lockwashers (C). The hazards from lamp explosion are controlled by the ventilation slots in the base (D) where exit of fragments which could occur under gravity have a 3 mm restriction; all other apertures where fragments could escape have a maximum size of 8 mm. The lens has a 25 mm mesh guard (E) in case of lens breakage. The suspension system (F) exceeds a ten times safety factor and there is provision for a secondary suspension (G).

It should be noted that compliance with EN 60 598-2-17 may be either through certification by an independent test house, or by self-certification by the manufacturer or importer into the EEC.

Further legislation and duties

If the earlier part of the century could be accused of regulatory laxity, that charge can certainly not be levelled now, as three pieces of modern UK legislation put an onus on the manufacturer and supplier to provide safe products.

The Low Voltage Electrical Equipment (Safety) Regulations 1989 were made under the Consumer Protection Act 1987, in turn derived from the EEC Product Liability Directive.[8] In this Act, Part I establishes a civil liability to supply safe products and Part II establishes that new products 'ordinarily intended for private use and consumption' must be safe, with contravention a criminal offence.

Similarly, the Health and Safety at Work Act 1974, Section 6, amended in 1987, places a responsibility on all those who manufacture and supply articles for use at a place of work. They have to ensure that the articles are safe as far as is reasonably practicable, through design, construction and instruction for use, and take into account any reasonably foreseeable use. The last requirement is quite important, since whilst reckless misuse is clearly not intended to be covered, the consequences of reasonable operator mistakes need to be considered. Luminaires are clearly included and, for those intended for use (i.e. handled or operated in some way) at a place of work such as a theatre or concert hall, the responsibility for safety is thus extended to include reasonable and foreseeable misuse.

Yet another UK responsibility for the safe use of electricity was occasioned by the Electricity at Work Regulations 1989, which were also made under the Health and Safety at Work Act 1974 and which came into force on 1 April 1990. These regulations finally replaced the original 1908 Electricity Regulations, and a plethora of subsequent special orders, with a new set of clear and deceptively simple duties requiring the safe installation and use of electrical equipment. Thus, by merely requiring that 'systems (including all electrical equipment from the point of supply to the equipment of use) shall be both constructed and maintained to prevent, so far as is reasonably practicable, danger', a further duty was automatically generated for employers to maintain all electrical appliances (including luminaires) to a reasonable safety level.

This duty is better explained in a *Memorandum of Guidance*[8] as an obligation to perform inspection and maintenance 'of such quantity and frequency that should be sufficient to prevent danger as far as is reasonably practicable'.[9] Since EN 60 598-2-17 is the accepted standard that should now be met for the supply of new luminaires, it must essentially be to this level of safety that existing luminaires should be maintained to comply with the Electricity at Work Regulations. However, much equipment in use was made to older, lower standards (if any) and even modern luminaires can quite rapidly deteriorate in the use and abuse of live entertainment. Thus employers and owners should implement an upgrade and regular maintenance programme on their inventory, reviewed by a competent person to ensure its adequacy, and keep proper records of the maintenance performed and test results. EN 60 598-2-17 sets standards and limits for the main safety risks, principally electrocution, lamp explosion, fire and mechanical failure: hence these must be the areas to check against.

Portable appliance testers provide a ready means of testing insulation resistance (greater than $2\,M\Omega$ at 500 V d.c.), insulation strength (1500 V a.c. for class I) and earthing integrity (less than $0.5\,\Omega$ at 10 A), in conjunction with a full inspection and any required rectification. All exposed metalwork that may become live in case of a failure of insulation must be reliably earthed, and insulation and shields checked or added to protect against the risk of contact with live parts. All wiring, connectors and terminations should be inspected and retightened, or if sufficiently deteriorated (or inadequate as supplied) replaced with new components of appropriate mechanical, electrical and thermal rating and correctly secured. Any signs of thermal overstress should be investigated and rectified, particularly the wiring and electrical components inside the luminaire exposed to high temperatures. The mechanical structure should be checked for security, and alterations may be required to ensure assemblies, accessories and suspensions are adequately robust and secured. Shields may need to be added to protect against the hazard of tungsten halogen or discharge lamp explosion and any subsequent lens/glass breakage if this could constitute a danger in actual use.

Safety in use

Even though a luminaire may be manufactured and maintained to a satisfactory safety standard, if this is not followed by equal care in installation and use, safety may still be seriously jeopardized. This is particularly true of many live entertainment installations where the working conditions are often inadequate, with cramped or difficult access, and ironically, despite the many kilowatts of lighting equipment rigged, are often poorly lit for working.

Consequently there are a number of particular safety practices that warrant attention to maintain safety in use, in addition to the normal personal safety practices appropriate to rigging, focusing and operating:

1 Ensure the support or suspension bar to which the luminaire is clamped is reliably secure through redundancy of support or robustness of design. Lighting stands pose special risks and should be locked out stably and if possible the top tied to an immovable object.

2 Ensure the luminaire is mounted the correct way up if markings show this to be necessary. Whilst this sounds obvious, this simple mistake can cause severe overheating of components that were at the bottom but are now at the 'top'.

3 Always fit a safety chain or bond between the luminaire and the bar or suspension point.

4 Ensure that accessories such as barndoor and colour frames are secure and cannot fall. This may mean fitting a separate safety chain or wire bond to the individual items if their fall could cause injury and they are not otherwise positively restrained.

5 Ensure all electrical cables and connectors are undamaged and their cable clamps are secure and not under strain.

6 Ensure that heavily loaded extension cables are not kept coiled or otherwise unventilated (risk of overheating) and are fully rated for the load. Also ensure that the weight of long drops of extension cable is not taken on normal plug or socket cable clamps, and that extension cables do not obstruct or cause a trip hazard on walkways, entrances and exits.

7 Always disconnect a luminaire from its supply either at the luminaire or (visually) close by before changing a lamp, and do not replace with a lamp higher than the luminaire's rated power.

8 A circuit fuse may fail when a lamp fails and should never be replaced by a larger rating than specified. Any fuse failures or circuit breaker trips not caused by lamp failure should be investigated and rectified before replacement.

9 Always with a discharge lamp and normally with a halogen lamp, allow the lamp to cool before opening a luminaire to eliminate the risk of lamp explosion.

10 Always allow adequate ventilation for the luminaire and ensure the luminaire is at least 0.5 m from any flammable object, further if the object is in the beam. The exact distance will depend on the safe distance marking on the luminaire.

11 Circuits protected by residual current devices (RCDs) should be treated with as much care as those not. The RCD is intended to provide an additional level of safety against an electric shock to earth in areas of high risk, and not to replace good practice. In addition, an RCD may still allow a sufficiently strong shock to be received before automatic disconnection to cause a secondary accident (e.g. a fall from a ladder). Never bypass any RCD protection if equipment causes it to trip, no matter what the urgency of the situation. A serious fault is present and the equipment must be repaired before further use.

12 Any 120 V equipment that is connected in series on 240 V should be fully rated for 240 V, and any series connectors must be designed so that live contacts cannot become exposed if any plug is removed.

Several booklets and guides have now been produced by the Health and Safety Executive,[10, 11] and useful advice is given by Francis Reid and Strand Lighting.[12, 13] Further study of these is recommended.

References

1 BS 5971: 1988. Specification for safety of tungsten filament lamps for domestic and similar general lighting purposes.

2 BS 5042: 1987. Specification for bayonet lampholders.

3 BS 4533: Part 1: 1971 Specification for electric luminaires (lighting fittings); General requirements and tests.

4 BS 3820: 1964. Specification for electric lighting fittings.

5 International Electrotechnical Commission. *Luminaires*, IEC 598.

6 European Communities. *Council Directive of 19 February 1973 on the Harmonization of the*

Laws of Member States Relating to Electrical Equipment Designed for Use within Certain Voltage Limits (73/23/EEC), Official Journal of the EC, L77/29–33, 26 March 1973.

7 *Administrative Guidance on the Electrical Equipment (Safety) Regulations 1975 and the Electrical Equipment (Safety) (Amendment) Regulations 1976*, HMSO, 1977.

8 European Communities. *Council Directive of 25 July 1985 on the Approximation of the Laws, Regulations and Administrative Provisions of the Member States Concerning Liability for Defective Products (85/374/EEC), Official Journal of the EC*, L210/29–33, 7 August 1985.

9 Health and Safety Executive. *Memorandum of Guidance on the Electricity at Work Regulations 1989*, HS(R) 25, HMSO, 1990.

10 Health and Safety Executive. *Electrical Safety at Places of Entertainment*, GS 50, HMSO, 1991.

11 Health and Safety Executive. *Electrical Safety for Entertainers*, IND(G) 1022, 1991.

12 Francis Reid. *The Stage Lighting Handbook*, 4th edn., A&C Black, London 1992.

13 Strand Lighting. *Drama Resource Pack*, 89 300 06, pp. 13–14 and poster 12, Strand Lighting Ltd, 1991.

8
Maintenance of luminaires

John Landamore

Introduction

There is a growing amount of legislation covering working practices for the employee in the workplace and working conditions that must be satisfied by the employer. Because of the nature of some performance work – touring, one night and particularly amateur shows, and the use of casual, enthusiastic but possibly untrained staff – there used to be the risk of developing the attitude of 'that's good enough, it's only a temporary job'. This is no longer acceptable in a world where legislation tries to cover all situations and litigation is becoming more common in the event of an accident. An area where performance environments differ markedly from the usual work environment is that there is public access, not a situation that one would expect to find in a factory or other place of work. Safety in the performance environment therefore affects both staff and, possibly more importantly because they are not aware of the risks, the public. This chapter tries to explain the application of current legislation and good working practice to the maintenance of luminaires in the performance environment. The term 'performance environment' has been used because the equipment discussed is used at concerts, dances and other events, not just in theatres. A lot of what follows is common sense and plain good working practice; however, it has to be applied correctly to be effective.

Maintenance and BS 4533

The safe maintenance of luminaires is a subject that can be handled by any competent people provided that they are made aware of what they have to do, and why, and that they are conversant with the relevant safety standards and have access to test equipment with which to ensure conformance to those standards.

Modern luminaires are designed and built to conform to the relevant sections of BS 4533 'Luminaires',[1] and maintenance of these luminaires must ensure that the requirements of that standard are met and maintained. It is recommended that the full standard is read and understood if luminaire maintenance is going to be undertaken on a full time basis. It is a large document, and the parts relevant here are Part 101 (136 pages) and Section 102.17 (12 pages). Technicians who are regularly involved in luminaire maintenance should have attended a course to make them aware of the implications of the new standards and ideally have obtained a nationally recognized qualification.

Older luminaires were obviously built to less stringent regulations and there are problems maintaining them to conform with BS 4533, particularly with regard to the construction requirements. These requirements govern the size of particle that can fall out of a luminaire in the event of a lamp shattering, the size of mesh required in front of the lens, hanging arrangements, security of accessories, e.g. colour frames and barndoors, and use of a backup suspension system. The standard also specifies the wiring, earthing and labelling requirements, and the tests for insulation resistance, earth continuity, electric strength and leakage currents.

All equipment should be tested according to the standards specified in BS 4533 at least annually. Care must be taken when choosing test equipment to ensure that the test performed are relevant to BS 4533. Some portable appliance testers which may appear to fulfil the requirements do not satisfy the standard with respect to the electric strength test.

Electrical maintenance of luminaires

The maintenance of luminaires cannot be considered in isolation. The electrical installation that supplies them and the mechanical installation that supports them must also be considered in ensuring a safe environment. The safety of the mechanical and electrical installations is beyond the scope of this chapter but they must not be ignored in ensuring a safe working environment.

The luminaire must be wired using 15 A rubber plugs or, in exceptional circumstances, 5 A rubber plugs. The use of any form of hard plug must be avoided to remove the risk of shattering in case of mistreatment. Also by not using 13 A plugs the possibility of connecting luminaires into the domestic supply (with the associated overload problems) is avoided. The 15 A plugs are preferred over the 5 A plugs for several reasons, mainly that the 15 A plug is easier to wire and the installation will then have a greater overload resistance. If 5 A plugs are used then there will be a tendency to use appropriately rated installation cable, and this itself will be overloaded if the luminaire presents a load of more than 1 kW either deliberately or by accident. The 15 A plug and associated wiring will only overload if more than 3 kW is connected to each outlet. The cable grip in the plug, and any trailing socket, must be tight enough to grip the cable firmly without deforming the insulation and cores, causing subsequent damage. Obviously the plug must be correctly wired!

In the context of the plug and socket, both experience and documentation have shown that any screwed electrical connection loosens with time. Further information on this subject may be found in the letters pages of *Electronics and Power*.[2] The loosening of the terminal screws means that both the socket and the plug need to be opened when they are subjected to the regular maintenance tests. (This loosening of threaded electrical connections also has implication within control racks for both terminal blocks and connections to thyristors if they are of the bolt and eye type.)

Over the years, electrical cables of various construction have been used for application in areas of high temperatures. Some of the more common constructions of these older types of cable are separate cores and fibre insulated, asbestos insulated and butyl rubber insulated cables. It must be noted that all these types of cable represented the best of technology at the time that they were used in luminaire manufacture. These older cables all have problems and should be replaced with the present recommendation, i.e. high-tear-strength silicone rubber insulated cable of an appropriate rating. The butyl rubber cable is still sold as heat resisting cable, but its temperature tolerance is not sufficient to allow its use in rewiring luminaires. The cable should be of 15 A rating for all luminaires using lamps of a power between 500 W and 3 kW inclusive. The cable must be suitably uprated for luminaires of a greater power. The use of silicone cable does not prevent cable faults occurring, as even silicone cable dries out and exhibits cracking after prolonged use at high temperatures. A regular check therefore needs to be kept on cables and damaged or suspect cable replaced. Cables insulated with PTFE are available with a higher temperature rating than silicone insulation, but these cables tend not to be as flexible and therefore their use is not recommended except in unusual circumstances.

The cable tends to fail in one or more of four regions, namely the areas around the strain relief gland into the lamp body, the strain relief gland on the lamp tray, around the lamp base which is the region of highest temperature, and at any point along the interior cable length where abrasion occurs between the cable and luminaire body when the lamp tray is moved. Because of the tendency of silicone cable to dry out with prolonged use, it is recommended that when the cable is renewed the single cores leading to the lamp base should have an extra sleeve of glass fibre insulation covering them. Also where the cable goes through the cable gland either in the body of the luminaire or on the lamp tray, the cable should either have a glass fibre sleeve put along it for a short length or have glass fibre tape wound around it to provide some protection. The protection of any internal length of cable that flexes during focusing, and could abrade, is a problem. The internal cabling is subject to prolonged high temperatures during operation of a luminaire. Any protective covering obviously needs to retain the same flexibility as the cable after exposure to continuous high temperature. A tendency to harden may either result in cracking of the protection when flexed or hinder the smooth operation of the focusing arrangements. The materials investigated to date have all been glass fibre based and harden when exposed to high temperatures. In the absence of any suitable material, present practice is not to sleeve the silicone cable where it flexes inside the luminaire.

At the lamp tray, any connector block is subject to the previous comment about the loosening of screws with age and the lamp base itself must be inspected. The electrical connections, usually hidden within the base, again need checking for tightness, correct connection of cable and quality of insulation of cable. Corrosion within the base, which occurs primarily on the live contact, both causes and is caused by sparking which often occurs with prolonged use. The sparking can result in the lamps being welded into the base and it may also generate radio frequency interference, possibly affecting sound equipment and contravening the forthcoming electromagnetic compatibility (EMC) regulations. Mild corrosion can be removed by gentle cleaning with fine emery cloth, but if the contacts are heavily pitted then the lamp base must be replaced. The older centre-pin-style lamp bases use a spring to ensure that there is a good connection to the lamp: the play in this spring must be checked to maintain the quality of connection. These springs are not usually replaceable: if prolonged use has resulted in spring deformation, then the lamp base must be replaced.

The existence of the older type of lamp base means that a change of lamp type is also often considered when luminaire maintenance is being undertaken. The older tungsten filament lamp has been replaced with the tungsten halogen lamp which has a longer life and a better quality light output. There are conversion kits available which allow the use of these newer lamps in old luminaires, but in fitting these kits several points must be remembered. The old ceramic lamp bases had an insulating disk underneath them to prevent arcing between the connectors on the underneath of the lamp bases and the lamp tray. The conversion kits usually have the connectors mounted on the side of the lamp base, and if this is the case the insulating disk should be removed to ensure that there is a good earth contact between the lamp tray and the conversion kit. If the connectors are under the conversion, and it has a metal base, then the insulating disk should be used and arrangements made to earth the conversion kit unless the installation instructions state otherwise. The tungsten halogen lamps are also smaller than the tungsten filament type and available in a wider range of powers. There is a temptation to put larger-power lamps in luminaires to increase the light output. Whilst this is usually all right for a power increase of about 25%, e.g. 500 W to 650 W, doubling of the power should not be attempted. This increased power will result in the luminaire running hotter, and this must be remembered for both handling considerations and thermal stresses. Use of a larger lamp may yield better light output but it may also result in the more rapid deterioration of internal components.

Of equal importance to the electrical safety of the luminaire are the earthing arrangements, and here the earlier comments apply about the quality of cable insulation and connection tightness. On older luminaires the earth connection is not usually bonded between the lamp tray and the body of the luminaire. Therefore when the luminaire is rewired the possibility of fixing such a bond wire should be investigated, provided that the fixing of such a wire does not compromise the usability or safety of the luminaire. To ensure the quality of the earth continuity it must therefore be checked between the earth pin on the plug and various parts of the external luminaire body, including the suspension stirrup, which is also known as the trunnion arm or hoop.

It is now necessary for the electrical tests specified within BS 4533: Part 101 to be elaborated upon. The standard specifies that compliance with the earthing requirements shall be checked by inspection and by the following test:

A current of at least 10 A, derived from a source with a no-load voltage not exceeding 12 V, shall be passed between the earthing terminal or earth contact and each of the accessible metal parts in turn.
The voltage drop between the earthing terminal or earthing contact and the accessible metal part shall be measured and the resistance calculated from the current and the voltage drop. In no case shall the resistance exceed 0.5 Ω.
Note: In the case of a luminaire with a non-detachable flexible cable for the supply connection, the earthing contact is at the plug or supply end of the flexible cable or cord (Section 7.2.3)

For a luminaire provided with a connector socket for a mains supply, the earth contact shall be an integral part of the socket (Section 7.2.5)

The following tests of insulation resistance and electric strength apply to Class 0 and Class I luminaires, the classes that the vast majority of luminaires fall into. The only luminaires that are not covered in these classes are those that rely on double or reinforced insulation for protection against electric shock (Class II).

The standard specifies that the test of insulation resistance is conducted as follows:

The insulation resistance shall be measured with a d.c. voltage of approximately 500 V, 1 minute after the application of the voltage.
The insulation resistance shall be not less than the values specified in Table VII. (Section 10.2.1.)

Table 8.1 is part of Table VII in BS 4533, and refers only to Class 0 and Class I luminaires.

The standard specifies that the test of electric strength is conducted as follows:

A voltage of substantially sine-wave form, having a frequency of 50 Hz or 60 Hz and the value specified in Table VIII, shall be applied for 1 min across the insulation shown in that table.
Initially, no more than half the prescribed voltage shall be applied, then it is raised gradually to the full value.
For the high-voltage transformer used for the test, when the output terminals are short-circuited after the output voltage has been adjusted to the appropriate test voltage, the output current shall be at least 200 mA (Section 10.2.2.)

Table 8.1   *Minimum insulation resistance*

Insulation	Minimum insulation resistance (MΩ)
Between live parts of different polarity	2
Between live parts which can become of different polarity through the action of a switch	2
Between live parts and the body*	2
Between accessible metal parts and metal foil on the inside of insulating linings and barriers	˙2

*The term 'body' includes accessible metal parts, accessible fixing screws and metal foil in contact with accessible parts of insulating material.
Source: BS 4533 Table VII.

Table 8.2 is part of Table VIII in BS 4533, and refers only to Class 0 and Class I luminaires.

The luminaire is deemed to have passed the electric strength test if no flashover or breakdown occurs.

The requirements of the leakage current test may be summarized as follows: the leakage current from each pole of the supply to the body may not exceed 1 mA/kVA in a Class I luminaire under normal operation.

The use of specialist test equipment, even when used as specified in BS 4533, will not guarantee the detection of insulation failure on the internal wiring. If the insulation failure occurs where the cores are separated or beneath supplementary insulation then only visual inspection will find the fault before a failure to earth occurs. This highlights the point that maintenance must rely on a combination of close visual inspection and the proper application of the correct test equipment.

Mechnical maintenance of luminaires

Unlike electrical faults, mechanical faults can usually be uncovered by a close visual inspection of the luminaires. The first visual inspection should always be of the rigging arrangements. There should be a safety factor of ten in all equipment associated with the rigging of luminaires, including both the structure it is suspended from and the suspension equipment on the luminaire. Hardware is available, or can be designed, to allow the safe rigging of a luminaire in any orientation. The misuse of rigging equipment, e.g. standing hook clamps up from lighting bars, should never be allowed. There must also be a secondary suspension system implemented such that if the primary system fails the secondary system prevents the luminaires falling. In the professional theatre this secondary system

Table 8.2   *Electric strength*

Insulation	Test voltage (V)
Between live parts of different polarity	$2U + 1000$
Between live parts which can become of different polarity through the action of a switch	$2U + 1000$
Between live parts and the body*	$2U + 1000$
Between accessible metal parts and metal foil on the inside of insulating linings and barriers	$2U + 1000$

U = working voltage.
*The term 'body' includes accessible metal parts, accessible fixing screws and metal foil in contact with accessible parts of insulating material.
Source: BS 4533 Table VIII.

usually takes the form of a chain or wire rope around the luminaire suspension stirrup and also around the supporting lighting barrel.

All bolts associated with luminaire suspension should either have locking nuts or use locking washers under flat nuts to prevent the nuts unscrewing in use. When the bolts are used without nuts, e.g. threaded directly into a metal casing, then some means must be provided to prevent the bolt unscrewing with use. Any other bolts or screws used in the construction of the luminaire should be checked regularly, as both the focusing action and thermal stress can loosen them. Tables of recommended tightening torques are available for various sizes of bolts and it is recommended that a torque screwdriver and torque spanner are used in tightening screws and bolts to avoid the problem of overtightening the thread and stripping it.

There is an increasing use of thread-forming screws in the construction of modern luminaires. Whilst these ease the problems of manufacture, the thread produced by the screw is not as good as that produced by machine tapping: care must be taken when inserting these screws into already threaded holes not to form a new thread, or, when tightening, not to strip the thread in the body of the luminaire. These screws are often relied upon to provide the earth path in the luminaire body and therefore both they and the mating holes should have clean metal surfaces.

The focusing of the luminaire moves the lamp tray and lens(es) relative to each other, either by moving the lamp tray and having fixed lenses, or vice versa. There are a few examples where both lens and lamp tray move. There are three basic forms of focus adjustments: those relying on friction, those using gears and those relying on a screw thread to alter the relative positions of the lens and reflector. The focusing arrangements should be in good repair, and obviously the less force that is needed to focus the luminaire the better. The friction type of adjustment is easy to maintain: just ensure that the threads on the locking system are in good condition and that the moving parts travel freely. The gear system just needs to be kept clean and any rotating parts lightly lubricated with a dry agent like graphite powder. The screw-type adjuster needs more attention to keep it in good condition. The thread and any other guide rods must be clean and dry to ensure easy travel for the moving carriage. The use of oil, grease or any other easing agent, whilst possibly easing the travel of the carriage in the short term, will cause problems as such agents will eventually carbonize, become sticky and attract dirt over time and will severely inhibit the carriage travel. If the guides are already in this condition they must be cleaned back to bright metal using a degreaser and possibly fine emergy cloth to remove baked-on deposits. Similarly, the guideways in the carriage must be cleaned to remove any deposits restricting travel.

The profile type of luminaire is usually equipped with one or two sets of beam-forming shutters. These shutters corrode because when used they absorb a proportion of the heat generated by the lamp. The use of lubricant to ease the operation of these shutters may provide short-term relief but, like the threaded focus mechanism, this may carbonize with the heat and actually worsen any sticking. Corrosion on shutter blades is removed by extracting the blades from the shutter gate and polishing with varying grades of emery cloth. Any corrosion inside the shutter gate should be removed by wire brushing. If the shutter gates are riveted together then it is not advisable to drill out the rivets to split the gates owing to the difficulty in obtaining some of the special rivets used. When reassembling the shutters a small spray of silicone release agent may be used on the blades. The same comments apply regarding corrosion on the irises used for reducing the beam diameter.

Rough handling either in transit or from luminaires being dropped can cause deformation of the body of the luminaire and cracking of the lenses. The deformation of the body stresses bolts as well as causing misalignment of the optics and reducing the quality of light output. Depending on the extent of deformation, either the body casing can be rebuilt back to the true shape or it will have to be replaced. The internals are usually undamaged, the casing having protected them, and they can be salvaged as spares or for use with a new casing. Any damage to the lens may not be obvious at the time of the incident. Obvious damage is usually spotted when the luminaire is picked up and can then be repaired, but more dangerously the incident can seed a crack which the thermal stresses of use can cause to propagate. If the lens then cracks whilst in use it can fall out of the luminaire. It is therefore strongly recommended that any lens that is badly chipped or shows signs of cracking or abuse is replaced. The fixings for the lens must not be so loose that the lens can fall out; however, if the lens is clamped too tightly then the expansion of the lens housing with use can crack the lens. The use of some form of spring leaf clip is recommended if possible, to allow for expansion whilst holding the lens firmly in place. The use of wire grilles in front of the lens is recommended for old luminaires and is mandatory for luminaires conforming to BS 4533 unless they have multiple lenses. The standard governs the size of mesh required for these grilles, which differs depending on the construction of the luminaire. Unfortunately these lens-retaining grilles are often difficult to obtain, particularly for older luminaires.

Any accessories used with the luminaire, e.g. barndoors, colour frames and lens grilles, must be attached to the luminaire so that they cannot fall from the luminaire regardless of its orientation.

Acknowledgements

Extracts from BS 4533: Part 101: 1990 are reproduced with permission of the British Standards Institution. Complete copies of the standard can be obtained by post from BSI Sales, Linford Wood, Milton Keynes, MK14 6LE.

References

1 BS 4533: 1990. Luminaires.
2 Institution of Electrical Engineers. *Electronics and Power: Journal of the Institution of Electrical Engineers*, pp. 304, 431, 491, 1987 (now *IEE Review*).

9
Smoke and fog machines

George Thompson

Introduction

It is perhaps a strange situation that whereas most employers and government agencies are striving to reduce the levels of airborne pollution, and weather forecasts frequently give indications of 'air quality', theatres and discos deliberately introduce pollution into the atmosphere by means of smoke and fog effects!

Smoke and fog machines usually have two purposes: to produce a heavy fog or mist which adds an air of mystery to the performance or to produce a thin, almost invisible, haze which serves to scatter light and so reveal the path of beams from spotlights and other lighting effects. The two requirements are to some extent conflicting, and various types of machine have evolved in the last ten years to meet them.

The heavy fog is widely used in the theatre, and in fact it is almost impossible to go to a major show without eventually seeing a mist of some description swirling about the stage. A thinner fog is also used to a large extent in discos to add atmosphere, but it is not so dense as to obscure the action, as is sometimes necessary in theatrical productions. On the other hand, the fine light-scattering haze is used predominantly in discos and rock and pop performances to reveal and enhance the lighting effects, which are often a very important feature of the show.

Many different devices, systems and materials have been used in the past to produce such effects and there is no doubt that some of them have presented a hazard to human health and are still in use around the world. Some of the devices have involved the burning of various substances, the chemical products of which have been largely unknown. In other cases all kinds of unsuitable substances have been blown into the atmosphere with wild abandon just because they looked good, without any thought being given to their toxic properties, i.e. how dangerous they are. It will not be possible to cover all these methods in this chapter, and so attention will be concentrated on the commonest to be found on the British entertainments scene.

Although the devices used to produce these effects are often called smoke machines, this is something of a misnomer and may have led to some of the bad publicity which has surrounded them in recent years. They do not produce the fairly large solid particles associated with bonfires and other forms of burning, nor does the chemical composition of the fog even remotely resemble that of cigarette smoke. Certain special pyrotechnical effects do produce airborne particles, but these are dealt with in the chapter on pyrotechnics (Chapter 10). Unfortunately, the term 'smoke machine' is now so widely used that it is virtually impossible to change it.

The machines to be described here produce their effect by means of airborne dispersions of mainly liquid droplets, accompanied by a small amount of vapour. The size of the droplets depends on the type of machine and the chemicals used. From the point of view of health hazards, the greatest unknowns lie in the chemicals and their effects on the human body. These aspects, together with some research findings, will be dealt with in detail later in the chapter.

Types of machine

There are three main types of machine: dry ice, cracked oil, and fog fluid.

Dry ice

The dry ice machine uses solid carbon dioxide which is heated to produce carbon dioxide gas at a temperature considerably lower than ambient, which in turn condenses the water vapour in the atmosphere to produce a dense white mist. As carbon dioxide is heavier than air and only the water vapour in its path is made visible, the resultant mist tends to roll along the ground and create an atmosphere of mystery and yet does not rise up to obscure the artistes. These machines are generally only used where a particularly low-lying fog is required and nothing else will do, as the raw material is more expensive than fog fluid for the same amount of mist and it requires special arrangements if it is to be stored for any length of time. It is also one of the 'greenhouse gases' and thus contributes to global warming, but this is not really a factor in deciding whether or not to use it, as the amount generated by all the entertainments venues worldwide is a minute fraction of that produced by other sources.

Cracked oil

The term 'cracked oil' used to describe this type of machine is much misunderstood. In the petroleum industry, 'cracking' refers to the process of reducing crude oil to numerous smaller components using catalysts and heat: such 'cracked' oils are likely to be carcinogenic. Most people in the entertainments industry, however, seem to think that 'cracking' is the process of atomizing the oil which takes place in the machine. Also, the term 'cracked oil machine' is sometimes loosely used for any type of machine which uses oil as the medium.

On no account should catalytically cracked oils be used in fog machines as they could cause a serious health hazard. To avoid the risk of confusion, a better term for all such machines would be simply 'oil-mist machines'.

There are two subtypes of oil-mist machine, one in which the oil is heated and one in which it is not. In the first type the oil is heated to boiling point and then cooled to produce a dense white mist which is pumped out of the machine. In some cases a compressed gas such as carbon dioxide is used as a propellant. A variant of the arrangement is known in which the oil is allowed to fall on heated wires or plates, but this must raise doubts about the chemical composition of the resulting mist.

In the other type of machine no heat is used, the light mineral or vegetable oil being atomized into an almost invisible mist by being forced through a very fine nozzle by a compressor. This method is much used for enhancing lighting effects, and has the advantage that the mist can be pumped up above the stage well before a performance and will remain there for hours.

A drawback of both these systems is that the oil in the mist must eventually fall to the ground. Since it is an oil, its rate of evaporation is low, with the result that everything and everyone in its path may become coated with a thin sticky film.

Fog fluid

The third type of fog generator, the fog fluid machine, uses a liquid which is heated to form a white cloud of a mixture of droplets and vapour which can be very dense, depending on the fluid used and the operator's requirement. Some machines use an inert gas such as nitrogen to propel the cloud over the desired area.

The liquid is generally one of the family of polyfunctional alcohols from the glycol group. The chemical family of alcohols is a large one and only a few of them give rise to the euphoric feeling associated with wines and spirits, which is caused by ethyl alcohol. The glycols do not have this effect. This machine is one of the most common types and considerable experience has built up in its use and operation. It has become very popular as it is easy to use and relatively cheap, and the fluid requires no special storage arrangements. Like the oil mist machine, however, the mist must fall to the ground eventually and can give rise to some staining and stickiness of surfaces.

General safety considerations

All of the types of machine usually have an electrical input and most of them require heating elements, so that care must be taken in their use. All manufacturers issue comprehensive instructions with their machines and these should of course be followed to the letter. As far as the safety of the mechanical and electrical parts of the machines are concerned, these will already have been incorporated into the design of units purchased from reputable manufacturers, so it is only a matter of following the instructions and using common sense to avoid trouble.

However, it should be noted that under the terms of the Electricity at Work Regulations 1989, regular maintenance must be carried out on all portable electrical appliances and records must be kept.

All machines using heaters are provided with thermostats (often electronic in nature) to keep the fog medium at its working temperature, and cut-out thermostats or thermal fuses are also fitted to switch the machine off in the event of failure of the heating thermostat. Despite these precautions, machines have been known to overheat and burn out but the fluids used do not ignite and a serious conflagration due to a flaming liquid is not possible. A health hazard may still occur as overheating could raise the chemicals above their decomposition point to form other undesirable substances. Obviously, a machine should never be operated under such conditions. Care should always be taken to site the machines away from materials which are ignitable, and they should be in view of the operator at all times when fog is being produced.

The safety hazard due to the fine film of oil or fluid causing surfaces to become slippery has resulted in this class of machine being withdrawn from some venues, although a well-designed machine should be able to produce a large volume of mist lasting for several hours using only a tablespoonful of liquid. Eventually, however, even this small amount will fall to the ground over a wide area, and users must take particular care to see that stairways and emergency exits do not become so slippery that after many performances the persons using them can fall over and cause a further hazard to others.

All three types of machine use a chemical substance or combination of substances as the medium, and clearly attention must be paid to any possible hazard to life. As mentioned above, the chemical hazards of the dry ice machine are easy to comprehend and easy to deal with, but until fairly recently it was often difficult to find out what chemicals were used in proprietary liquids as the exact formulation was a closely guarded trade secret. However, following the Health and Safety at Work (H&SW) Act 1974, Section 6, and the Control of Substances Hazardous to Health (COSHH) Regulations 1988, manufacturers must provide adequate information about any risks to health or safety of their product. This is generally in the form of data sheets, and full account must be taken of the conditions of use if known.

The major manufacturers of fog fluid machines in this country have taken their responsibilities for the welfare of the general public seriously, and all of them have had extensive research carried out on the toxicity of their products by independent laboratories. In many cases the machines have been submitted to various public bodies all over the world for approval.

However, manufacturers need not disclose the exact composition of a substance unless there are any hazardous components in the product, in which case the user must be told so that he can independently assess the risks in the specific circumstances of his use.[1] Consequently, any attempt at secrecy would tend to indicate the presence of a dangerous chemical, and manufacturers are now more willing to give the composition of their fluids, although it must be borne in mind that this can change overnight if the manufacturer so decides.

Chemistry and toxicity of the media

Dry ice machines

Chemically these machines are the simplest as their medium is a single chemical, carbon dioxide (CO_2), whose properties are well known and can be found in every elementary chemical textbook. In use, the dry ice becomes mainly water droplets condensed by the cold carbon dioxide from the vapour which is always present in the atmosphere. The carbon dioxide gas also has the twin hazards that it does not support life and is heavier than air. These two properties in combination make it a system which must be handled with forethought. It must be remembered that, as the fog disperses, the gas becomes invisible and will sink to the lowest part of any building or site and may remain there for a long time if there is little or no ventilation. Orchestra pits are of course particularly vulnerable and there are apocryphal stories of whole orchestras passing out, but the hazard is not that great as in most performances the absence of sound from the orchestra would not go unnoticed for long! Far more dangerous are off-stage basements or rooms which may be lower than the source of the fog, and if these are occupied when dry ice is used, particularly during long rehearsals when other trades may be using them, a dangerous situation could arise where there is little or no ventilation. In such rooms or areas a CO_2 alarm should be fitted with the sensor in a position just below normal head height.

Oil-mist machines

Since the mist is airborne and is very slowly falling, some of it will be inhaled and/or ingested by the artistes and possibly members of the audience (or the dancers in a disco). In recent years considerable interest has arisen over possible deleterious effects to the body, such as whether the oils used are carcinogenic or mutagenic (i.e. liable to induce cancer or to cause subsequent birth defects). The amount taken into the body may be small at any one performance, but if there are daily performances an appreciable quantity could be built up in the lungs of the artistes over a period.

To decide if any hazard exists it is necessary to know what kind of oils are used and what is known about them. The manufacturers generally describe them as light mineral oils or white oils, whilst in some cases it is claimed that vegetable oils are used. As the latter are used extensively in cooking, the small amount used in oil mist generation should be harmless in the long term, although even here, since the oil is mostly inhaled rather than ingested, there could be short-term effects on lung capacity. It is also possible that problems could be caused in a very small number of cases owing to an allergic reaction to vegetable oils.

Considering the most serious possibility first, namely carcinogenicity, the Health and Safety Executive (HSE) has published a guidance note (EH 58) on this very subject, and what follows is largely taken from that note.[2]

One factor which becomes immediately clear is that in no circumstances should an operator use just any kind of oil that happens to be around, either as a desperate measure when just before a show it is discovered that the oil has run out, or as a means of saving money. It cannot be too strongly emphasized that only oil supplied by the machine manufacturer specifically for the purpose of producing theatrical fog or smoke should be used, and even then, on first purchase the manufacturer should be asked to state in writing that the oil is safe for that use. This is important, as the oil may have been purchased from a chemical or petroleum company which may simply claim that it is not toxic in normal use, without having any idea that it will be used in the form of a very fine aerosol, possibly heated as well. Such an assurance from the manufacturer is essential, as the H&SW Act lays the responsibility for employees' health fairly and squarely on the employer, who must ensure that no dangerous substances are used without the proper precautions. Failure to comply with the Act is a criminal offence.

Some mineral oils are undoubtedly carcinogenic, these being:

- unrefined or mildly refined vacuum distillates
- catalytically cracked oils with boiling points above 320 °C
- used engine oils.

It thus becomes further apparent that the term 'cracked oil machine' should not be used, as this can cause confusion with 'catalytically cracked oils' which, unless they have low boiling points, should never be used in such machines.

The kind of mineral oil which is not a carcinogen and would therefore be reasonable to use in a fog machine is that defined by the HSE as 'highly refined lubricant base oil', sometimes known as light oil or white oil, the latter being of medicinal quality. It should be noted that the word 'oil' does not specify a standard product, as any one oil will be made up of possibly hundreds of different compounds and even when highly refined, such oils still contain some sulphur, nitrogen and oxygen compounds, together with traces of metal.

The problem of oil mist as a health hazard occurs in many other places beside the entertainments industry, and the oil industry has looked into this in some detail, culminating in a report in which some 80 international studies on human reaction to oil mist were surveyed. The following comments are based on extracts from that report.[3]

The cancer-causing properties of crude oil are due to the presence of substances known as polycyclic aromatic hydrocarbons, which fortunately are removed if the product is 'highly refined'. This is a relative term, and once again emphasizes that the oil should only be obtained from a source where there is sufficient knowledge to distinguish the various oil products.

Once the oil mist has been generated it is important to know how it enters the body, and this naturally depends on the size of the droplets. Although measurements for the size of the particles in theatrical mists vary, the fact that they can persist for hours in the air indicates that the size must be of the order of 1–5 μm. Particles in the 5 μm region will be deposited mainly in the throat and nose, eventually finding their way into the stomach. Smaller droplets will be drawn into the alveoli of the lungs where, if in considerable quantity, they are likely to affect lung function, at least in the short term.

Obviously the effects of oil mists on humans cannot be safely studied by direct experiment, so it is usual to extrapolate from the results of animal studies. However, care must be taken in doing this as of course the relative sizes of the lungs of small mammals and those of humans are considerably different, and this may have a marked effect on the rate of absorption of oil mist and the distance it penetrates into the lungs.

Short-term effects will be fairly obvious to see, but other effects may be more insidious and may not become apparent for some years. In the short term it has been found that mineral oil droplets remained in the lungs of mice for up to 90 hours, but edible (vegetable) oils progressively decreased during the period, probably due to metabolic processes. Other work found that below a concentration of $200 \, mg/m^3$ there was no effect on respiratory function, but at concentrations above that level lung compliance was reduced. This is a high level, and is only likely to occur where machines are used for fire training purposes, in which cases the trainees would be wearing some form of breathing apparatus. This level is far above the $5 \, mg/m^3$ recommended by the HSE, and well beyond most practical situations for theatres or discos. Singers have often reported having difficulties when working with smoke machines, but it is doubtful whether a build-up in the lungs equivalent to $200 \, mg/m^3$ could be reached even after many long rehearsals.

A curiosity found in one experiment was that several days after exposure to high concentrations of certain oils there was evidence of a protection from the effect of sulphur dioxide, ozone and nitrogen dioxide in the lungs of small mammals. This could be a useful side-effect in industrial areas with high atmospheric pollution!

In long-term studies, rats and rabbits were exposed to high concentrations of lubricating oils for up to a year without any significant adverse effects being seen. Animals have also been exposed for up to two years to a white mineral oil mist at a concentration of $5 \, mg/m^3$ without any toxic hazard being reported. In other studies, no carcinogenic effects have been found for concentrations of light mineral oils within the HSE guideline.

Although as mentioned earlier it is not ethical to initiate experiments directly on human beings using a substance which may be carcinogenic, a large number of post-exposure studies have been carried out on workers, mainly in engineering plants, who have been exposed to oil mists of various kinds. It is, however, difficult to apply the results to the disco/theatre situation as in many of the cases the type of oil and its concentration were not given. It is known that high concentrations will affect the lungs, causing inflammation and fibrosis, but the levels appear to be far beyond the HSE recommendations. To add to the difficulty, some of the reports have been conflicting. The CONCAWE report[3] concludes that although no definitive study has demonstrated that exposure to oil mist alone has caused any adverse human health effects except at levels greatly above 5 mg/m^3, it cannot be concluded that this is an acceptable exposure limit for all types of product. This is all the more reason to use an oil which is known to have no carcinogenic properties.

Fog fluids

The medium used here is a water-based fluid which has one or more glycol compounds mixed with it and may also contain additives in the form of scents and colours. The fluid is heated to form a dense white cloud of droplets and some vapour. A propellant such as nitrogen is used in some cases.

The glycol family of chemicals has 11 members and 20 derivatives, but not all are suitable for use in fog generation as some have undesirable side-effects. This is a reason again for purchasing supplies of fluid only from reputable manufacturers, and on no account should a glycol compound produced for any other purpose be used for theatrical effects.

All fog fluids are not identical in composition, as the various manufacturers have their individual preferences, with the consequence that the appearance (and perhaps the side-effects) will differ. In this country all of the fluids are based on demineralized water with a low bacteriological count, whilst the glycols are selected from the following list:

- triethylene glycol (TEG)
- monopropylene glycol (MPG), or 1,2-propanediol
- dipropylene glycol (DPG), or propanol
- butylene glycol (BG), or butanediol
- glycerin, or glycerol, or 1,2,3-propanetriol.

Unlike the oils, all of these are fairly simple compounds and consequently there are no polycyclic aromatics and hence no risk of cancer from that source. The entire glycol family is used extensively in industry, so that fortunately there is a considerable body of literature regarding their effects when in contact with humans.

As with most chemicals, if taken in sufficient quantity in a short period the glycols are capable of causing death, but the quantities required far exceed those which it would be possible to obtain at a theatre or disco, apart from actually drinking an entire bottle of the fluid! For example, a disco lasting for 6 hours would use about 150 ml of fluid, most of which would be carried away by the ventilation system or fall to the ground.

As with the oil mist, much of the data on the lethal dose for glycols have been obtained from tests on animals, but it should be pointed out that nearly all these tests were carried out by the chemical and food industries over the last half-century, and no smoke machine manufacturers in this country are known to be carrying out tests on animals at present. Also, although it does not necessarily follow that the amount of glycol which proved fatal to a mouse can be scaled up to give the lethal dose for a human, at least some idea of the amount can be obtained.

As most of the glycols have been in use for a number of years, a considerable body of literature about their chemical properties exists which it would be impossible to even summarize here. A good reference source is *Patty's Handbook of Industrial Hygiene and Toxicology*,[4] from which most of the following material is taken. In general, all of the glycols listed above have low toxicity when used in the bulk form, although not so much is known about the effects when used as an aerosol. We now look at each constituent in detail.

Triethylene glycol is used industrially as a plasticizer and solvent, and has been used in skin preparations as an absorbent. It is said to be flammable in the mist form, but since fog fluids are made up with a large proportion of water this hazard is extremely low and there have been no reported cases of fires due to its use in entertainments venues. Rats and monkeys have been exposed to the saturated vapour for over 18 months without any apparent ill effect, and its toxicity is so low that it has been claimed that the inhalation of atmospheres containing it does not pose any health hazard. It is not irritating to the eyes or skin and has been found to be far less toxic than ethylene glycol (anti-freeze) or diethylene glycol. It is for these reasons that triethylene glycol is widely used by reputable manufacturers. Since at least 1943, triethylene glycol has been used in air conditioning systems as a sterilizer without any adverse effects being reported. It could be argued therefore that the use of fog machines with this chemical could have a beneficial effect on the atmosphere in crowded theatres and discos!

Monopropylene glycol has also been used in air conditioning systems, pharmaceuticals and foods for over half a century, so there is considerable experience of its use with human beings, and there have been no reported incidents when it is used at low levels. It has even been fed to farm animals as a source of carbohydrate to increase the weight of lambs and chickens and the milk yield of cows! It is not injurious to the eyes and, although it may cause slight stinging and bring tears, there is no permanent effect. It is possible that this is the ingredient of some fog fluids which causes audiences to complain of watering eyes.

Dipropylene glycol is not used as extensively in industry as the previous glycols but its toxicity is also known to be very low. Rats have been exposed to the smoke without any adverse effects being found 14 days later, and there were no abnormalities at the subsequent post-mortems. This chemical does not cause significant eye irritation.

Butylene glycol is different from the other glycols in that it exists in various forms known as isomers: these are compounds having the same chemical composition but different internal molecular linkages and therefore different chemical properties. These arrangements are coded to indicate the structure, and for this compound there are the 1,2,- the 1,3,- the 1,4- and the 2,3- isomers. Commercial fog fluids use the 1,3- isomer as being the least toxic and it has also been used in cosmetics and pharmaceutical products. Once again, rats have been subjected to the vapour without apparent harm. Unusually, 1,3-butylene glycol has been directly tested on human volunteers, both internally by mouth and externally on the skin. At quantities of up to 10% of diet for a week there were no adverse effects as seen by blood tests, although the level of blood glucose fell slightly. No signs of skin irritation were found in 200 volunteers in the age range 6–65 years. In undiluted form 1,3-butylene glycol causes painful stinging in the eyes, but there is no permanent damage. A 10% solution has no effect but it is possible that anyone actually in the fog could experience a slight stinging.

Glycerin is of course very well known and is used in a wide variety of foodstuffs, pharmaceuticals and cosmetics. It also has a very low toxicity but is capable of a violent reaction when mixed with oxidizing agents such as peroxides or permanganates. This is unlikely to happen when it is used as a fog fluid, but is yet another reason for purchasing fluid only from the original manufacturer and not attempting to mix an in-house formula. Taken in quantity, glycerin can have some unpleasant side-effects, as a single dose of around 100 ml will cause headache, dizziness, nausea and vomiting. However, this is quite a large amount and far in excess of that which could be ingested at an entertainments venue.

Concentration levels in the atmosphere

Concentration levels of all substances known to be harmful to man are set in the UK by the Health and Safety Executive in the guide EH 40 *Occupational Exposure Limits*.[5] There are two parts to the guide: maximum exposure limits (MELs) and occupational exposure limits (OELs). MELs are set for the most dangerous substances, and workers must never be exposed to greater concentrations: in fact, every endeavour should be made to reduce the levels where possible. On the other hand, OELs are levels where, as far as is known, there is no evidence that anyone will be harmed by being exposed to those levels day after day. Not all of the materials used in the machines described in this chapter are included in the guide, but of those that are, all fall into the latter category. However, one must take note of the caveat 'as far as is known'.

Two different concentrations for each chemical are generally given in the guide: the long-term 8 hour average ('time-weighted average' or TWA) and the short-term 10 minute average. It is all very well to set an exposure level, but problems arise when it comes to measuring that level in the theatre/disco environment. To be absolutely safe, the concentration level should be continuously monitored in all parts of the venue where staff and the general public are to be found. However, this is a good deal easier said than done, as owing to air currents and the movements of the audience/dancers, the concentration will vary from moment to moment and place to place. Also, apparatus for making a direct measurement is not easily portable and the results are not immediately available: the alternative is a light transmittance meter or densitometer which is calibrated in terms of the substance being monitored.

Carbon dioxide

Because this gas cannot support life there is a concentration level above which it becomes dangerous. The HSE guide EH 40 sets this at $9000\,mg/m^3$ for an 8 hour period and $27,000\,mg/m^3$ for the 10 minute exposure. Gas monitors are available commercially to check the level.

Oil mist

Occupational exposure standards for mineral oil mists are given in HSE guide EH 40 as $5\,mg/m^3$ (8 hours) and $10\,mg/m^3$ (10 minutes). Reference is made to the guidance note EH 58 mentioned earlier, where warning is given of the possible carcinogenic properties of some oils. These levels also have a certain degree of international status, being used in both the United States and the former USSR.

One company has had measurements carried out under controlled conditions in a demonstration studio.[6] In the first test the machine was run for about 30 minutes to give a relatively high density of mist, whilst in the second test it was run for about 5 minutes to give the density which would normally be used in a theatre or disco to enable the light beams to be seen. The results, given in Table 9.1, show that at a high density of smoke the concentration level at a fairly short distance from the machine is just within the HSE guideline, whilst under normal operating conditions the concentration can be at least an order of magnitude below the recommended level.

Fog fluids

Only two of the substances listed earlier have concentration levels set in the HSE publication EH 40, these being monopropylene glycol (listed as propane-1,2-diol)

Table 9.1 *Oil mist machine test results*

Observed smoke density	Location	Concentration (mg/m^3)
30 minute run		
High	Next to smoke generator	12.55
High	2 m from smoke generator	4.56
Medium	Under stage light	2.25
5 minute run		
Low	Next to smoke generator	0.34
Low	2 m from smoke generator	0.09
Low	Under stage lights	0.40

Source: reproduced courtesy of Samuelson Concert Productions Ltd.

and glycerin (listed as glycerol mist). This does not necessarily mean that the other ingredients can be used without restriction, as the HSE attitude is that the absence of a listing merely indicates that no serious problems with the substance have been brought to their attention, which in view of the fact that some of them have been in industrial use for over 50 years, is very reassuring.

Of the two substances that are listed, the limit for monopropylene glycol is 470 mg/m^3 as total particulate and vapour, and 10 mg/m^3 as solely particulate. The boundary between the two states is difficult to define, but HSE advice is that the output of fog machines should be treated as a particulate and its concentration limited to 10 mg/m^3.

As with the oil mist machines, actual measurements of concentration levels produced by fog fluid machines at two nightclubs have been made by an independent laboratory on behalf of a manufacturer.[7] The results are shown in Table 9.2. It will be seen that, except for the DJ station in nightclub A, these figures are well within the HSE guidelines. Taking into consideration the errors arising from the limitations of the experiment, even the DJ station figure is reasonable. It should also be borne in mind that the recommended limits are averaged over an 8 hour period, whereas the average disco only lasts for 5 hours and the average theatrical performance for 3 hours. If the above results are multiplied by 5/8 and 3/8 then the concentrations do not pose any hazard.

Checklist for operators

Safe operation of smoke and fog machines depends mainly on common sense, but attention to the following points will prevent any hazards arising:

1 Machines should only be used in well-ventilated spaces, never in tightly closed rooms, and any ventilating grilles on machines must be kept clear.

Table 9.2 *Fog fluid machine test results*

Location	Total glycol concentration (mg/m^3)
Nightclub A	
1 m from generator	> 0.80
DJ station	5.19
Above bar	2.03
Nightclub B	
DJ station	1.50
Open area	2.14
Behind bar	1.08

Source: reproduced courtesy of JEM Smoke Machines Ltd.

2 Machines should be frequently cleaned internally, with particular attention being paid to heat exchangers where fitted.

3 Most machines have a 'machine ready' lamp or indicator and no attempt should be made to use them until they are ready.

4 The amount of medium in a machine should be kept at a reasonable level and not allowed to run out.

5 If a machine has a heater, the smoke at the outlet will be very hot and there should be a clear area in front of the machine for at least 2 metres. If the machine is standing on a floor or mounted near a ceiling, make sure that neither of these is composed of easily flammable material. Where the machine uses a petroleum-based fluid, the clear area should extend for 5 metres and it is essential that open flames are not within this area.

6 If there is any smell of burning or other unusual odour, the machine should be instantly switched off, as the smell may indicate the machine is overheating, with possible decomposition of the oil or other fluid.

7 If the machine is operated by remote control, the outlet must be visible to the operator at all times.

8 Only trained personnel should be allowed to use the machines, and training must include a study of the manufacturers' operating instructions.

9 Regular maintenance should be carried out by qualified staff, and it is advisable to return a machine to the manufacturer or the appointed agent for a complete overhaul after extensive use.

10 For fog fluid and oil mist machines, only fluids supplied or recommended by the manufacturer should be used.

11 Dry ice can be purchased from a variety of sources but it must be handled with care. It can easily give severe 'cold burns' and must never be handled without protective clothing, especially gloves and goggles. No parts of the body should be left exposed when handling dry ice, as small pieces can break away from the main bulk of the material and cause deep burns before being discovered and removed.

12 The electrical supply to all machines should be switched off before filling, and those with heaters should be allowed to cool for a reasonable period.

13 Smoke or mist must never be blown directly into the face of any person.

14 A machine must never be left unattended for long periods with the heating elements operative.

Acknowledgements

The assistance of the directors and staff of the following companies in the preparation of this chapter and in granting permission to publish previously confidential information is gratefully acknowledged:

Concept Engineering Ltd
JEM Smoke Machine Co Ltd
LeMaitre Ltd
Roscolab Ltd
Samuelson Concert Productions Ltd.

References

1 Health and Safety Executive. *Substances for Use at Work: The Provision of Information*, HS(G) 27, HMSO, 1989.
2 Health and Safety Executive. *The Carcinogenicity of Mineral Oils*, EH 58, HMSO, 1990.
3 CONCAWE Health Management Group. *Health Aspects of Worker Exposure to Oil Mists*, report 86/69, CONCAWE, Den Haag, 1986.
4 *Patty's Handbook of Industrial Hygiene and Toxicology*, Wiley, Chichester.
5 Health and Safety Executive. *Occupational Exposure Limits*, EH 40, HMSO, 1992.
6 Neville, S. *Measurement of Oil Mist Concentrations from the Cirrus Smoke Machines*, Rendel Science and Environment, London, 1991.
7 Holehouse, M. D. *Airborne Glycol Concentrations during in situ use of JEM Smoke Machines*, National Occupational Hygiene Service Ltd, Manchester, 1989.

10
Pyrotechnics

Rodney Clark

Introduction

Pyrotechnics are now used increasingly in film, television, rock and pop concerts and of course theatrical applications. Indeed the use of pyrotechnics in these situations is now commonplace, whereas only a few years ago it was much rarer.

One of the *Oxford Dictionary* definitions of pyrotechnics is the art of making and displaying fireworks. However, it is important to understand the difference between what most people understand by the term 'fireworks' and the devices used by the entertainments industries (Figure 10.1). Furthermore, as fireworks are explosive, the dangers inherent in the types used for entertainment purposes should also be understood.

Explosives for non-entertainment use are generally designed and manufactured to have a considerable destructive force, e.g. for the military. Sadly, one of the most well-known examples of this is Semtex, an extremely efficient destructive explosive. Explosives for entertainment purposes are designed and manufactured chiefly for their artistic visual effects, e.g. gerbes or fountains which produce a constant spray of particles, usually silver.

A simple definition of the difference between outdoor firework displays and stage pyrotechnics is that firework displays are generally intended as entertainment in their own right. An example known to all of us is the annual 5 November shows which take place across the whole of the UK. Pyrotechnics in the theatre or at rock and pop concerts are used to enhance a particular scene or song, or to draw the audience's attention to or from a part of the stage set, an example being the genie appearing in a pantomime following a puff of smoke.

It must be understood that all pyrotechnic effects produce light, colour, heat, sound and smoke or a combination of two or more of these elements. With one or two exceptions such as slow burning smoke powder, pyrotechnics rely on the ignition of a continuous chemical combustion. This can be either spontaneous as in flash effects, or over a longer period as with smoke effects. Once ignited, pyrotechnic devices are virtually impossible to extinguish. Indeed, certain devices

Figure 10.1   *A selection of stage pyrotechnic effects*

will continue to burn even when immersed in water; in fact water can cause some devices to burn more intensely and possibly explode. It should be apparent therefore that effects must be chosen carefully and only fired via a purpose-built pyrotechnics control system which is operated by an experienced and responsible person. Obviously, the overriding and deciding factor when considering the use of pyrotechnics in any show must be safety. This applies to all shows, be it a pantomime with one or two flash effects, or a rock show with 100 or more effects during the performance.

There are three main ways of ensuring safety. Firstly, the effects themselves should be obtained from a recognized manufacturer. Home-made effects are illegal – you need a licensed factory to produce explosives of any type – and dangerous. The effects must be designed and manufactured so that no risk is taken if they are used correctly and the manufacturer's instructions are followed. Consequently, they will function as intended, produce the desired effect, and produce that same desired effect time after time. Secondly, the effects themselves should only be fired via a control system that has been designed and manufactured with adequate safety features built in, both electrical and mechanical. Lastly, the user, i.e. the operator, should have enough experience and knowledge to ensure not only that the effects are used correctly and safely to produce the desired result, but also that he or she can cope with any unforeseen circumstances. Remember, even the smallest effect is an explosive, so handle and treat it with respect at all times and never become complacent. Injuries caused by maroons and flash effects can be very severe and painful.

All aspects of pyrotechnics are subject to considerable legislation regarding manufacture, transportation, storage and use. These include the Explosives Acts of 1875 and 1923 and the Health and Safety at Work Act 1974, and an employer's obligation under these Acts should be borne in mind at all times. There are also various guides published by national authorities which interpret and clarify the laws. Indeed it is these guides that various officials generally refer to when inspecting a show or event. The most recent of these is the Home Office *Guide to Fire Precautions in Existing Places of Entertainment and Like Premises*. There will shortly be available the revised edition of the guide known to most people in the industry as the 'Pop code', but its official title is *Guide to Health, Safety and Welfare at Pop Concerts and Other Similar Events*. However, the draft version of this covers pyrotechnics mainly as an outside event and does not concentrate on stage effects, although most of the precautions are relevant to any kind of performance.

One of the major problems with using pyrotechnics is the lack of pre-planning. The person responsible for the show is often aware that such effects are to be used, but leaves the decision very late and then tries to incorporate them into the show: instead, with careful planning and positioning, the effects can provide an even more spectacular visual enhancement. Those involved with show planning should think about the effects at an early stage, i.e. in which scene they are to be used, where they are to be sited, where the operator will be sited etc. To leave this to the last minute introduces an unnecessary element of risk, not to mention annoying the cast considerably when green flashes are suddenly introduced into their carefully rehearsed scene!

Purchase and storage

The purchase and storage of standard or normal stage pyrotechnics in Great Britain is relatively straightforward, but users in Northern Ireland should check with the RUC as different laws apply there. Generally, pyrotechnics come under the HSE classification of 'Shop Goods, Fireworks' Class 7 Division 2, and, providing the purchaser is over 16, no purchase licence is necessary. The exceptions to this can be where items such as fuzeheads, certain types of safety fuse and certain powders need to be purchased. For these, police authorization in the form of a licence or certificate may be required. For more details on these it is always best to check with the manufacturer for classification and any documentation needed for purchase.

Storage methods are known as either mode A or mode B. Details of these modes are given in the *Summary of Acts Concerning Premises Registered for Gunpowder or Mixed Explosives* available from the Health and Safety Executive. Briefly, mode A is for large amounts up to 1 tonne, and mode B is for amounts up to 250 kg. However, these amounts may be reduced by the relevant authorities. As mode A is for amounts not usually required by most users, mode B is the one generally used. This mode of storage means a substantial receptacle inside a building, the receptacle being constructed and lined so that any exposed iron, steel etc. is covered, for example with wood. Any screws or nails should be of copper, brass or zinc. The point of this arrangement is to prevent any form of ignition via sparks.

Naturally, the receptacle should be locked with an appropriate warning sign on the lid. It should also be kept in a room designated for that purpose, and 'No smoking' and 'No naked flame' signs should be fixed to access doors. The room should be cool and dry, and other flammable items and liquids such as paint must not be stored in the same room. Where fuzeheads, powders or safety fuses are purchased and therefore stored, they must be stored in their own separate receptacles and not stored together. The appropriate fire extinguishers should be easily accessible, placed by the exit door of the room.

Registration of premises with storage mode B is compulsory with the local authority. The department responsible for this is usually the trading standards department: an annual fee is payable. There are no powers of refusal for this registration, provided the conditions are met, but the authority should always be notified as soon as it is planned to provide a store. It is also wise to inform the police, as they can advise on security. The fire service should also be informed, as in the event of a fire they should be aware that explosives are stored in the building. Many users overlook advising their insurers, but it is as well to do this to ensure adequate cover is available.

Transport

It is extremely unlikely that users or operators will transport quantities of explosives by road, but some brief details may be useful.

The carriage of explosives by road is governed by the Road Traffic (Carriage of Explosives by Road) Regulations 1989. Briefly, it is permissible to carry up to 50 kg net explosive content in a private car or van in Great Britain, but this should be avoided if at all possible! Amounts over 50 kg may require trained drivers, specialist vehicles (known as powder wagons in the trade) and documentation which varies according to the classification of the product carried. For example, unlimited amounts of class 1.4S (usually signal smokes etc.) can be carried, but there are stricter load limits on other classifications up to class 1.1 (usually products with a mass explosion risk).

It is illegal to use the mail to send any explosive product. Nor can any form of public transport be used, e.g. railways or coaches. However, 2 kg can be sent by taxi, providing the driver is aware of what he is carrying.

If a freight company is used to transport show effects, for example on a tour, then the packaging must comply with the Dangerous Goods Packaging Regulations. The cartons must be of an approved type and the appropriate hazard warning stickers must be affixed to the carton. Of course, the agreement of the carrier must be obtained before any goods are sent by this method.

At this point the European situation should be mentioned, as more and more shows and productions now visit the Continent. All European countries (both EC and non-EC) have varying regulations covering explosives in relation to purchase, use, transport and storage. These are complex and vary from country to country. Unfortunately, terrorism has played a part in much of this legislation, and the authorities in some countries can regard a simple flash effect as being as undesirable as any other explosive.

There are very few ports in the UK licensed to have explosives within their boundaries, and there are even fewer international freight forwarders willing to transport these items. In some countries only a licensed pyrotechnician can use stage pyrotechnic effects, no matter what they are. It is also worth pointing out that if one is caught with illegally imported pyrotechnics the penalties can be severe, even to the point of vehicle confiscation! Therefore, when one is taking a show abroad with pyrotechnics featured in it, the manufacturer's advice should be sought first. Most UK manufactured stage pyrotechnics are available abroad, or the manufacturer can advise on how to get them there.

Notification of use

Once it has been decided to include pyrotechnics in a show, the relevant authorities must be notified in writing of their intended use with seven days being the minimum period of notice required. A licence issued by the inspecting authority must be obtained for the use of pyrotechnics, and do not forget to inform the venue as well.

The inspecting authority responsible for the use of pyrotechnics varies from region to region in the UK. It is more often than not the officer responsible for entertainment from the local fire service, or the Environmental Health Officer, or the Building Inspector. Bear in mind that their decision is final, so ensure all precautions are in place and that the operator will be available for a demonstration at the agreed time.

At present in the UK there is no course which leads to a licensed pyrotechnician qualification. The person who is made responsible for the pyrotechnics on a show – and there must be one person only – should be a competent adult operator who is aware of all safety requirements, knows how the control system works, what effect the chosen pyrotechnic produces, and has sufficient strength of character to resist pressures from actors, musicians or production to fire the effects regardless. The operator's decision must be final, no matter how strong the pressures are on him or her to fire the effects.

Firing/control systems

The firing or control system must be specifically designed for pyrotechnics. A recognized manufactured system should always be used (Figure 10.2). Home-made

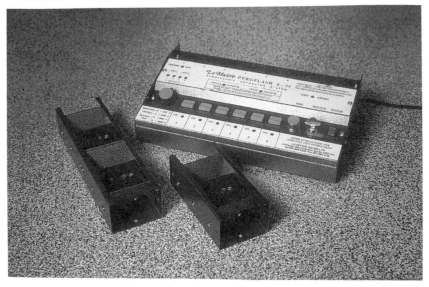

Figure 10.2   *A typical pyrotechnic firing system*

devices can and do lead to accidents and will not have been tried and tested for this use.

Whilst mains voltage will fire pyrotechnic effects it is unnecessarily hazardous: indeed, the results of certain effects fired in this way could be more spectacular and dangerous than planned. All normal manufactured systems employ a transformer which reduces the voltage from 240 V to between 24 V and 50 V, depending on the make. There are very few battery powered units available, such units being notoriously unreliable. When transformer systems are used, the drop in voltage and hence power that will occur with long cable runs, owing to possible high resistance, should be borne in mind.

There are commercially available systems which work on a discharge principle. They are capable of working away from a mains supply for a considerable number of ignitions or firings and will safely fire up to 100 effects some quarter of a mile away. Whatever system is used, it should have a minimum of three safety features incorporated before detonation of a device is possible. The whole system should be capable of being isolated via a key-operated power isolation switch, so that without the key being inserted, nothing can be fired. The key must be kept with the operator at all times and *never* left in the system, except when effects are to be fired. The second safety feature is channel switches: these control which devices are selected. The third feature is the fire button itself, which must be of the shrouded type, as an unprotected fire button is easily pressed or knocked.

The positioning of the controller is critical, and the operator must have a clear line of sight to see all effects clearly. It is for this reason that the pyrotechnic operator is sited on or near the stage and not front of house, with for example the lighting director, or backstage where effects are not visible. We are all too well aware that no matter how well rehearsed a show is, or how many times the same show has been performed, once the adrenaline is flowing – people forget. It has been suggested that control and firing of pyrotechnics be carried out 'automatically', for example by the lighting designer or audio engineer, but this is totally unacceptable, as another element of risk is introduced. Whilst the main reason for this suggestion is to have the effects fired on cue, it is extremely dangerous unless the person having control of the firing can see the position of the pyrotechnic devices relative to the performers.

The operator must also be able to warn absent-minded personnel that effects are to be fired and be readily available to deal with any unforeseen incidents. Most modern controllers do have test facilities built in which enable fault conditions to be recognized, including faulty pyrotechnic effects. Where test facilities are not a feature of a controller then, by using a continuity meter (a device that will pass a very small current of not more than 10 mA), checks can be made. The control system should be kept in good serviceable condition at all times, being serviced by the manufacturer at regular intervals to ensure safe operation.

Most stage pyrotechnic devices are now of the pre-packaged type. The use of loose powders is widely discouraged and indeed is not allowed by an increasing number of licensing authorities, which from the safety aspect is a step in the right direction. Effects produced by the use of loose powders can be unreliable, owing to the ignition methods used, and dangerous, as loose powder is easily displaced from its firing tray. For example, an actor walking past a firing tray with a flowing costume can easily displace the powder, and end up with some of it on the costume itself, thus presenting an additional hazard.

The actual effects are pre-loaded into cartridges, and therefore they cannot be accidentally knocked over or spilt. Where reloading during a performance is necessary, this is very easily achieved by simply unplugging a used effect and plugging in the next.

The traditional method of achieving a flash effect was to use a flash box with fuse wire or a detonator as the source of ignition. Ideally it was necessary to apply enough power to make the fuse wire atomize into small white-hot droplets rather than to glow red-hot, sag and break. The powder was placed on top, in an amount according to the effect required. A detonator could also be used, although this could be unreliable owing to the detonator blowing away from the powder immediately following ignition. There are various ways of overcoming these problems, but all involve a considerable amount of unreliability. There are though one or two powder effects which are still in use and do not provide the significant hazards associated with flash powders.

Slow burning smoke powder, which is a fine white powder in appearance, can only be ignited by placing it on a slow burning smoke box. This box usually consists of a small box with a 750/1000 watt heater element. The element is in close contact at the top with an aluminium or mica plate. A small amount of powder is placed on to the tray, and when power to the box is turned on and the plate has heated up, a wispy smoke is produced.

Reasonably accurate control can be achieved by connecting the circuit to a dimmer, thus enabling temperature control and hence the amount of smoke output. Slow burning smoke powder is really the only pyrotechnic smoke that is controllable. It is ideal for effects such as witches' cauldrons and artificial log fires. It is a useful effect when smoke is required over a prolonged period. *Lycopodium* powder is a fine yellowish powder derived from a clubmoss, but it is not an explosive powder by itself. The main use of this powder is to produce or simulate a flame where the use of flammable liquids would be hazardous. It is used by blowing or throwing the powder through a small flame, resulting in a billowing flame effect with little heat. Professional pyrotechnic companies use this with *Lycopodium* guns and compressed air. However, there are now available other pyrotechnic effects which produce flame more easily and safely.

Before any pyrotechnic effect is used in a show, the operator must be satisfied as to its suitability. If the operator has any doubts then advice should be sought from the manufacturer. In the unlikely event of this not being available, a trial run should be made outdoors well away from everyone and everything. An old but very apt saying is, 'if in doubt – leave it out.'

Code of practice

A code of practice should be drawn up by all users and followed both by themselves and by other visiting acts or shows. A suggested code of practice for the use of stage pyrotechnics is as follows:

1 Pyrotechnic special effects can be extremely dangerous if misused and should only be used by competent adult persons following the manufacturer's instructions fully and with care.
2 Always remove the key and put it in your pocket before plugging in the controller. Keep it in your pocket during set-up and loading. Only put it in the controller when you are to fire the devices.
3 Ensure that suitable fire fighting equipment is to hand and that personnel are trained in its correct use.
4 Ensure that a suitable first-aid kit is available and that personnel are trained in its use.
5 There must be no smoking, naked flames or any source of ignition in the vicinity of pyrotechnic materials at any time.
6 All pyrotechnic devices must be sited so that they are clear of obstructions and cannot set fire to adjacent materials, fabrics, costumes or scenery.
7 All pyrotechnic devices must be sited so that there is no possibility of injury to persons.
8 Only approved controllers and firing boxes/pods from a reputable manufacturer are to be used. Home-made or adapted firing systems are not permitted.

9 Ensure that the pyrotechnic operator sites the control box so that he/she has a direct view of all devices at all times.

10 Only take sufficient pyrotechnic devices for each performance from the main store. Do not store excess material on stage.

11 One person should be made responsible for the setting up and firing of pyrotechnics.

12 Only pre-packaged pyrotechnic devices from a reputable manufacturer will be permitted. The use of loose powders is not permissible.

13 Use only the smallest device available to achieve the desired effect. If there are any doubts about the effect produced, contact the manufacturer for advice before use.

This code of practice is intended as a guide only and is by no means exhaustive.

Choosing effects

The choice of effects should be given careful thought, as there are many available. Always use only the smallest effect available to achieve the desired result.

Never attempt to create effects by mixing manufactured effects powders, as many of these are not compatible. Mixing is a very dangerous practice and is illegal under the Explosives Acts. Manufactured effects should not be changed, tampered with, reloaded or refused; this is illegal and dangerous. If a specific effect that is not readily available is required, then always consult a licensed manufacturer.

Of the vast choice of effects available, the most commonly used are as follows. These are all standard products and readily available.

Flash effects

These produce a brilliant flash which is usually white but can be coloured, e.g. red or green. The initial flash is followed by a cloud of white smoke rising upwards. The effect is used in theatres to announce the arrival or departure of the witch. Flash effects can also have the addition of silver or gold stars which are thrown into the air with the flash. It should be noted, however, that lower lighting levels should be in operation when gold is used, because gold is less intense than silver.

Smoke puffs

These produce a cloud of smoke but without the brilliant flash associated with flash effects. They are especially useful where TV cameras are used because smoke puffs will not 'blind' the camera.

Coloured fire

Coloured fire, or transformation as it is traditionally known, creates a coloured flare effect. The duration of this varies, but approximately 6 seconds is common. The effect burns very bright and produces intense heat, together with white smoke. Although the smoke can appear to be coloured, this is in fact only a reflection from the flare, which can be of various colours: the effect should not be confused with coloured smoke. This effect is best used where the actual flare is hidden and only the reflected colour is seen or viewed from a distance.

Coloured smoke

This should be used with care as it contains dyes. The effect is available in various durations and colours which are usually very pure and dense. Obviously, care must be taken when using these near personnel, scenery and equipment as they may cause staining.

Gerbes

Gerbes are effects which produce a spray of sparks, usually gold or silver, over a timed period. Types with varying heights and durations are commonly available. Some newer versions can have other effects incorporated, for instance a red flare. Care should be taken when using these effects as the sparks are hot, and with larger versions the sparks can remain hot for some time. A cousin of the gerbe is the jet effect. This is an instantaneous, very bright effect with no fallout from the sparks, i.e. the effect disappears before it falls to the floor. Various heights are available.

Whistler effects units

These produce a high-pitched screaming and whistling noise.

Streamer/glitter/confetti units

These produce visual effects which are the only type that can be directed towards the audience, although not pointed straight at them. Following a medium report, a shower of glitter, confetti or streamers is propelled upwards and then floats down. These are very spectacular effects which can be used in musicals and wedding scenes.

Fault simulators or robotics

These are used to re-create, for example, electrical faults, possibly a sparking fuse box or wall socket. They are small units, far less powerful than, for example, the silver star flash effect.

Flame effects

Flame effects are generally used by experienced or professional operators only, owing to the nature of the effect. They can be usefully employed to simulate the aftermath of explosives or of gas main explosions. They are not for casual use and licensing officers are, quite rightly, very strict over their use. They are generally gold or yellow in colour, but it is possible to colour the flame otherwise.

Cannons

These employ a maroon to propel confetti or glitter a considerable distance into the air, which then flutters down in a snowstorm effect. These units are for use in large venues only, and should be used with great care. Under no circumstances must they be pointed at people or other equipment. The contents are propelled at great speed for some 10 m before starting to lose velocity.

Maroons

Although widely used, maroons are possibly the most misused and potentially the most dangerous effect. Theatrical maroons explode and fragment with great force and produce a loud report. They must only be used in a properly constructed bomb tank. Do not use dustbins, waste paper bins, old water tanks etc.

A bomb tank is constructed of heavy-gauge steel with an open top (Figure 10.3).

Figure 10.3   *Purpose built bomb tank for maroons*

This top must be covered with a strong wire mesh lid which must be capable of being fixed shut when in use. The maroon is suspended inside the tank away from the sides and bottom. Because of the dangerous nature of maroons, the wires must never be allowed to come into contact with even the smallest electrical source during transportation, storage and loading, and the electrical circuit must be physically isolated before and during loading. As a final precaution, the operator's back should be turned to the bomb tank when connecting the maroon wires to the firing circuit.

Bomb tanks should be sited off the stage area and clear of all personnel and flammable materials such as curtains. Careful positioning is essential, especially with regard to light fittings or other items immediately above the tank. When the bomb tanks are in use, warning notices which read 'Danger, explosives, keep clear, bomb tank in operation' should be sited at all access points (Figure 10.4). The operator must be extra vigilant and keep all personnel away from the area in which the tank is situated. The bomb tank must always be emptied of debris before attempting to reload. An often disregarded aspect of maroons is that if they are fired near speaker systems, damage to the systems can occur: the sound engineer should be warned.

Miniature maroons known as microdets are also available to simulate gunshots. Again, these should be used in bomb tanks. Non-fragmental versions are also available, but professional advice should be sought before they are used. It is sometimes thought possible to simulate body or bullet hits on personnel with microdets. In theory it is, with the use of the appropriate body armour and protection, but again professional advice must be sought first. Do not try this effect out with or on inexperienced persons.

Figure 10.4   *Warning sign for use with bomb tanks*

Fuzeheads will also produce a small crack if fired on their own. These small devices look like a match head with two extending wires. As mentioned earlier, a police licence may be required for the purchase of these.

Disposal

In the unlikely event of an effect not firing during a show, the circuit to which it is connected must be isolated and left alone until the end. Once the public have left, all connections should be checked and the circuit reconnected to the firing system. If the effect should still fail to fire, it should be left alone for 15 minutes and then removed to a safe place. It must not be thrown away with other refuse or given to others, but should be returned to the manufacturer for safe disposal. From experience, the great majority of failures of pyrotechnics are the result of poor electrical connections and badly maintained systems.

Conclusion

There are numerous other pyrotechnic effects available. However, they are less commonplace, or are only used by professional pyrotechnicians.

As shows, concerts and productions in general are becoming more ambitious and spectacular, pyrotechnics play an ever increasing role. The duty of everyone involved with pyrotechnics is to ensure their safe use, both legally and morally.

References

1 *Explosives Act 1875*, HMSO, 1923.
2 *Explosives Act (Repeals and Modifications) Regulations* 1974, HMSO.
3 *Explosive Substances Act 1883*, HMSO.
4 Home Office and Scottish Home and Health Department. *Guide to Fire Precautions in Existing Places of Entertainment and Like Premises*, HMSO, 1990.
5 Health and Safety Commission and Home Office. *Draft Guide to Health, Safety and Welfare at Pop Concerts and other Similar Events*, HMSO, 1991.
6 Health and Safety Executive. *Summary of Acts concerning Sale of Explosives*, HSE, Current edition.
7 Health and Safety Executive. *Summary of Acts concerning Premises registered for Gunpowder or Mixed Explosives*, HSE, Current edition.
8 *Control of Explosives Regulations* HMSO, 1991.
9 *Road Traffic (Carriage of Explosives) Regulations*, HMSO, 1989.
10 *Packaging of Explosives for Carriage Regulations*, HMSO, 1991.
11 *Classification and Labelling of Explosives Regulations*, HMSO, 1983.
12 *Consumer Protection Act*, HMSO, 1987.
13 *Air Navigation (Dangerous Goods) Regulations*, HMSO, 1987.
14 *Dangerous Substances in Harbour Areas Regulations*, HMSO, 1987.
15 *Merchant Shipping (Dangerous Goods and Marine Pollutants) Regulations*, HMSO, 1990.

11

Lasers, light and the eye

Stephen Day

Introduction

Special effects based on the use of lasers have become increasingly popular during the last twenty years. Lasers are able to create lighting effects which are spectacular and unattainable by practically any other means. Whether it be a low-powered unit to simulate Tinkerbell at the local provincial theatre's production of *Peter Pan*, or several high-powered units in a stadium to provide various effects at a major open air concert, their use is continually growing. The beams most generally used are however hazardous, with the eye being particularly at risk. Nevertheless, by following the guidelines given in this chapter, it is possible to create laser lighting effects which are both visually pleasing and safe to all concerned.

This chapter will discuss what a laser is, what it is capable of doing, why it is potentially hazardous and what measures can be taken to make it less so. It will also look at the relevant UK legislation and how to comply with it, and suggest a code of good practice.

What is light?

Before understanding a laser it is essential to know something of the nature of ordinary light and its properties. Put simply, light is a form of energy. It may be quantified by measuring its energy in joules or its power (i.e. rate of energy production) in watts.

When physicists look at the propagation of light they normally describe it in terms of a stream of particles called photons. Light is created by internal energy changes within atoms. An atom can be thought of as being made up of a central nucleus surrounded by a number of orbiting electrons in discrete energy levels. If energy is given to an atom it can have the effect of promoting the electrons from one energy level to a higher level. When this happens the atom is said to be in an excited state. Some time after being excited the electron will fall back to its original or ground state and a photon of energy equivalent to the difference between the two states will be emitted.

The photon also exhibits properties which cause it to behave partly as a small particle and partly as wave motion. The colour of the light seen by an observer is determined by the wavelength of this wave motion, and may vary from blue (400 nm) through to red (700 nm). Wavelengths shorter than 400 nm are referred to as ultraviolet (UV) and wavelengths above 700 nm are referred to as infrared (IR).

White light, such as that from a hot body like the sun or the filament of an electric light bulb, is a continuous spectrum of many different wavelengths or colours. That this is so may be demonstrated by passing a beam of white light through a prism or a diffraction grating which will split the light into its component colours. Such light does not exhibit any polarization, i.e. the vibrations occur in all directions about the axis of propagation. Each photon of light energy is emitted independently of every other, and the waveform of each is out of phase with every other. Light from the sun or a lamp is produced in all directions and not as a beam. Thus, ordinary light has a continuous range of frequencies, and is unpolarized, out of phase and not directed: such light is called incoherent.

When light falls upon any object it will be either absorbed, transmitted or reflected or often a mixture of all three.

What is a laser?

The word 'laser' is an acronym for Light Amplification by the Stimulated Emission of Radiation. A laser, therefore, is a light amplifier, and the amplification is achieved by stimulated emission which produces a stream of photons having identical frequency, phase, direction and polarization. Because of these attributes, it is called a coherent beam of light.

How does a laser work?

For stimulated emission of radiation to occur it is necessary for some atoms to exist in an excited energy state. In an excited atom an electron may decay to a lower energy level by emitting a photon. This is known as spontaneous emission or luminescence and is the process which occurs in, for example, a light emitting diode. If the emitted photon passes close to another atom in a similar excited state, it may induce an identical transition. In this case the emitted and stimulating photons are identical in every respect and, since they will have the same frequency, phase, direction, momentum and polarization, they will be coherent. This is the stimulated emission of radiation.

A laser consists of three basic components: an optical cavity, a lasing medium and a pump or energy source (Figure 11.1). The optical cavity is, in essence, a tube

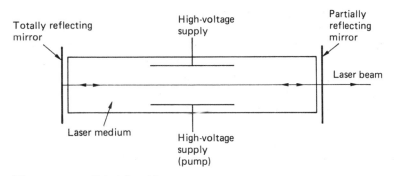

Figure 11.1   *Principles of laser operation*

with a mirror at each end. Any rays of light travelling along the axis of the tube will be continually reflected between the mirrors, while rays travelling at any other angle will escape through the side walls.

The lasing medium may be a solid, a liquid or a gas. It is simply a material in which it is possible to induce a situation where more atoms exist in an excited state than in their ground state, which is known as population inversion. In a solid-state laser the lasing medium is normally in the form of a cylindrical single crystal whose end faces have been highly polished and mirrored so as to form the optical cavity. In a gas or liquid laser the lasing medium fills the transparent tube which forms the optical cavity.

The pump is an energy supply which causes and maintains the population inversion within the lasing medium. The pump is usually a high-powered flash lamp or an electrical discharge. In display lasers, the lasing medium is usually argon or krypton gas and the pump is an electrical discharge (sometimes called the exciter).

In a gas laser, an inert gas, or sometimes a mixture of gases, is contained in a tube. An electrical discharge ionizes the gas inside the tube: the plasma so formed contains many atoms in excited energy states, and population inversion is achieved. Some of the radiation emitted will be in a direction parallel to the tube bore. The rest will be lost through the walls of the tube and does not contribute to the laser operation. For a photon travelling along the bore, there is a chance of passage close to a second excited atom and the stimulation of emission of another identical photon. The probability of this occurrence depends on the gas density and the length of the bore. For a single pass along the bore the probability is of the order of 10%.

If mirrors are placed at either end of the tube, photons are reflected many times along the length of the bore and in this way the likelihood of stimulated emission is further increased. Each stimulated photon is capable of stimulating another and each is in perfect coherence with those already present, so achieving light amplification.

Laser tube mirrors have a very high reflectance at the wavelengths of interest, but transmit unwanted laser frequencies. By retaining only the desired wavelength photons in the bore, amplification is restricted to this wavelength only. Similarly, misdirected radiation of the desired wavelength escapes from the bore and is not amplified. Thus the highly directional nature of laser output is achieved. In order to make use of the desired laser radiation, some of it must be allowed to escape from the cavity as a beam. In practice one of the mirrors is coated to permit about 1% transmission of the laser wavelength. It is this 1% of light which escapes that forms the usable output of the laser.

Why is a laser dangerous?

The previous section showed that the laser output is bright, monochromatic, coherent and unidirectional. The emitted beam is extremely narrow and intense and will not undergo any significant divergence over quite considerable distances. As a result, a lot of energy is concentrated into a small area and the power density of a beam is extremely high. To put this into perspective, the power density of sunlight on a bright day is about 10 mW per square centimetre, equivalent to the irradiance of a very modest, low-powered laser.

Such high-energy density of laser radiation striking human tissue either directly or by reflection is capable of inflicting varying degrees of damage. The principal concern is with eye damage, since that organ is capable of increasing the power density by many thousands of times through its focusing effect. While the hazard to the skin is of a secondary nature, these effects can be considerable too and should not be underestimated, particularly when dealing with the higher-powered lasers encountered sometimes today.

In order to understand how a laser beam can damage the eye, it is necessary to examine its structure. The eyeball is approximately spherical in shape; its interior volume is filled with a clear viscous liquid called the vitreous humour. Surrounding the vitreous humour are three basic layers: the outermost layer, which is known as the sclera or the white; the middle, which comprises the choroid, the ciliary muscles and the iris; and the inner layer or retina, which contains the light sensitive surface.

At the front of the eye, the choroid becomes the ciliary muscle which is attached to the lens, and this muscle changes the shape of the lens to provide focusing (Figure 11.2). Also at the front, the sclera becomes the cornea. Sandwiched between the lens and the cornea is the aqueous humour. The lens is in turn covered by the pigmented iris and in the centre of the iris is the pupil, an opening through which light can be admitted. The muscles in the iris alter the quantity of light entering the eye by changing the size of the pupil.

The retina is the inner layer of the eyeball and contains the photoreceptor cells. Two types of receptor cells exist: rods, which exhibit strong sensitivity to low light levels but are incapable of discerning colour; and cones, which are capable of discerning colour but which are not so light sensitive as rods. Both types are

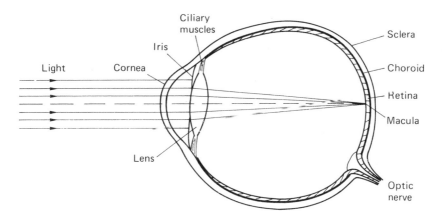

Figure 11.2   *Structure and function of the human eye*

attached to nerve endings which join together from all parts of the retina to form the optic nerve, which passes through the rear of the eyeball and goes to the brain.

The macula or fovea is a tiny part of the retina which lies opposite the lens and is the area of greatest visual acuity. Focusing of light on to the fovea by the lens can increase the power density of any incident light by a factor of up to 100,000. Since laser radiation is so much greater in intensity than normal light, the focusing effect can readily cause an eye hazard.

Tissue damage mechanisms

Thermal effects

These are responsible for the major type of damage. As energy is delivered into a small area of tissue, the tissue will heat up. This is especially dangerous in the eye as it has no cooling blood supply like other parts of the body. If the rate of energy deposition is greater than the rate of dissipation it will become very hot very quickly. Damage may vary from nothing at all, to erythema (a reddening of the skin), steam generation, charring or explosive disruption. The retina is most at risk from the effects of heating.

Photochemical effects

Photochemical changes are most likely to be caused by ultraviolet radiation and wavelengths towards the blue end of the spectrum. The cornea is the part most at risk from UV since it is absorbed here and cannot penetrate through to the retina. The skin could also be affected, and erythema is caused by chronic exposure.

Chronic exposures

There are very few data available on this topic, though it is known that long-term exposure to UV causes premature tissue ageing, and similar exposure to IR causes the formation of cataracts on the cornea. It is conceivable that a person who is occupationally exposed to low levels of laser radiation over a long period could develop a previously unrecognized chronic disability, since this is still a young technology.

Factors which contribute to tissue injury

Wavelength

Some wavelengths are more readily absorbed than others by certain tissues.

Tissue absorption

The cornea, lens and humour all transmit wavelengths between 400 and 1400 nm and are therefore not at risk from exposure to visible and near infrared radiation. The choroid and retina do however absorb quite strongly within the range and are thus very susceptible to thermal effects. Below 400 nm the cornea absorbs very strongly.

Beam power

The strength of the beam is obviously a very important factor, since the higher the beam power, the greater is its potential for damage.

Beam size

The diameter of the beam is critical, since the greater its diameter for a given power output, the lower the power density and hence the potential for causing damage.

Exposure duration

If a direct exposure to the beam is likely to be limited to a short pulse, for example because the beam is being scanned, then the amount of energy being received is always going to be fairly low.

Pupil size

The amount of energy which is received by a tissue is proportional to the area over which the exposure occurs. The pupil of the eye can vary in size from about 1.5 mm diameter in bright direct sunlight to about 7 mm diameter in a dark room after full dark adaptation. The pupil will transmit about 20 times more energy in the latter case than in the former.

Location of the retinal injury

A burn on the fovea would cause the most dramatic reduction in vision, but a similar-sized burn on the peripheral retina would probably go unnoticed after the initial trauma.

Distance

The hazard from a beam decreases with distance from the source. This is due to absorption by moisture and contaminants in the air and the fact that the beam does have a slight divergence. This may not be noticeable over short distances, but over extended distances the beam diameter can grow sufficiently for the power density to be reduced to a safe level. This leads to the concept of the nominal ocular hazard distance (NOHD), which is the minimum distance from a source at which it is safe for direct viewing of the beam, i.e. allowing the beam to terminate on the surface of the eye.

Lasers used in places of public entertainment

All the foregoing has been general information pertaining to laser light, optics and their associated hazards. The specific case of laser systems used in display applications will now be considered.

Nearly all laser systems consist of three basic components:

- a laser
- an effects head and/or an optical table
- a computer-based controller.

The laser itself has already been described, and its function is simply to provide a bright, parallel source of light. Lasers are bought as a component from a manufacturing company, the two most favoured types being argon ion and krypton ion.

An ingenious feature about a laser display is its optical system and its computer control. The output beam from the laser is usually engineered to be directed on to a section called the optical table. Here, through a complex system of shutters, fully reflecting and semi-reflecting mirrors, it can be split into several less powerful beams which may in turn be directed to pass through various optical components from which the beams will ultimately be projected out into the theatre, hall or open air.

The most commonly used effects are as follows.

Beam chases

In this effect the primary laser beam is directed on to one or more mirrors on the optical table which direct it to a remote site around the venue. Very often a beam will be projected from the table to a mirror mounted on a wall or in the lighting truss above the stage, and from there to another mirror mounted say on the foot of the stage; from there further reflections may be generated. In practice it is not usually feasible to have more than about three successive reflections after leaving the optical table since the quality of the beam starts to deteriorate owing to the imperfect nature of the remote mirrors usually used. The effect is usually terminated by projection over the heads of the audience and into a dead area of the theatre. Usually a number of differing beam paths are constructed which may be projected either simultaneously or in rapid succession, but these sequences are generally pre-programmed and stored in a computer memory, with the computer activating the various devices on the optical table at the appropriate cue.

Diffraction gratings

In this effect a beam is shone either directly on to a diffraction grating on the optical table or effects head, or else on to a mirror on the table from where it is reflected to a remotely mounted diffraction grating or more usually a diffractive mirror. The effect from any of these is the same. When the raw beam from the laser is diffracted, it is broken up into its component wavelengths, with the result that a series of fingers of different coloured light are projected from the grating in a fan-like pattern. Several successive sets of this diffraction pattern are generated, each identical to the next but with decreasing power as the angle between the pattern and the incident beam becomes greater. These repeating patterns are known as the orders of diffraction and, by convention, are numbered from zero, with the zero order being the most powerful and the first, second, third, fourth etc. orders becoming less and less powerful with each generation. Various refinements of the basic effect are often used, such as mounting two gratings perpendicular to one another to achieve a three-dimensional effect, or mounting a grating on the spindle of a small motor to achieve a more dynamic effect.

Line scanning

In this case, the primary beam from the laser is deflected on to a mirror mounted on a galvanometer. The galvanometer then has a rapidly oscillating voltage applied to it, and this has the effect of moving the reflected beam back and forth at a high velocity, which is usually arranged to be sufficiently fast to make the resultant reflected beam appear as a solid sheet of light. The image projected on to a screen will appear as a straight line.

X–Y scanning

If a second galvanometer is now introduced which oscillates at right angles to the first scanner and at the same frequency, the resultant emitted light will appear to be in the image of a cone and will be three-dimensional. This image projected on to a screen would be a circle.

Graphics and writing

This is a special case of X–Y scanning. If the voltage applied to both the scanners is now varied, it is possible to see how the pattern traced out by the beam may be controlled, and a variety of shapes, patterns and characters may be projected on to a screen. This is where the third component of a display laser is important – the computer. A computer or microprocessor can be programmed to alter the voltage applied to the scanners and thus to control the shape traced out by the beam. In this way it is possible to write messages or draw patterns of quite intricate complexity. Because of the speed of the scanners the image will appear to be continuous, provided that the scan pattern is continually recycled.

Mirrorballs

In this effect a beam is projected from a previously aligned mirror on the optical bench to a remotely mounted mirrorball (usually suspended from the ceiling). The mirrorball, with its multifaceted surface, will redirect the incident laser beam to form many smaller moving point sources which will scan across a stage, a dance floor, an audience etc.

Cone spinner

This is a device which consists of a plane mirror mounted on the spindle of an electric motor, the plane of the mirror being a few degrees offset from the axis of the motor. When the motor is switched on and a laser beam is projected on to such a device, the reflection appears as a hollow cone. Very often, this effect is enhanced by projecting a small scan pattern on to the cone spinner rather than a single beam.

Video projection

This is not a common effect at the time of writing. Nevertheless, a system has been developed which will project a raster-type video scan similar to that which forms the image on a television set. This uses dye-tuned lasers to generate the primary red, blue and green colours of a video signal. These are modulated and then combined by an optical system to provide a beam which is projected on to a vertical scanning galvanometer and from there on to a rotating drum with a precision aligned, multifaceted mirror surface. This is then able to generate the 625 line raster scan which conforms to the television standard and which may be projected over any distance subject to power. It has the unusual and very valuable property that the image is always in focus no matter at what distance the beam strikes an object.

Fibre optics

A fibre optic cable may be used to transmit a beam from the laser to a remote effect, and it may be used to feed an effect which would be otherwise inaccessible. The losses along the cable are likely to be fairly high, although the emergent beam may still be high powered. It is sometimes used simply to form an outline or a shape on stage, e.g. a piano or a violin bow.

These nine effects are the basis of all lighting effects likely to be encountered with lasers, and any not specifically described here will be a derivative of one of them.

Standards and legislation

In the UK, the primary piece of safety legislation is the Health and Safety at Work Act 1974. The requirements of this Act should already be familiar but briefly, it is an enabling Act which places a duty on manufacturers, designers, suppliers, installers, operators etc. to ensure the health and safety of anybody who might be adversely affected by their operations. This is achieved through the implementation of a written safety policy which details the arrangements for instigating a safe system of work, training of staff etc.

To assist employers in carrying out their duties, the Health and Safety Executive publishes a series of guidance notes for specific industries. As far as display lasers are concerned, guidance note PM 19,[1] in the plant and machinery series, is the recommended guide to safe practice. This note does not have legal status as it is purely for guidance. However, if a prosecution were brought under the Act and the recommendations of the note had not been followed, it would be up to the defendant to prove to the court that he or she had been acting in a safe manner, and to explain why it was not considered necessary to follow the recommendations. Most local authorities, who are responsible for licensing places of public entertainment, make it a condition of granting a licence that the requirements of PM 19 are met.

Guidance note PM 19 refers to the recommended control procedures as set out in British Standard BS 7192: Parts 1, 2 and 3.[2] Part 1 gives the basic definitions and outlines the biological effects of different types of exposure. Part 2 gives a detailed specification for the manufacture of laser products. It gives a classification scheme which enables the devices to be separated according to their hazard potential by assessing the maximum level of hazard to which access is possible (accessible emission limit or AEL). Part 3 gives general guidance to users of lasers on how to establish safe working practices. It also sets out recommended maximum permissible exposure (MPE) levels to which AELs can be related.

Once a manufacturer has classified his laser product, the standard then goes on to specify a range of engineering control features such as protective housings, key switches and beam stops, and outlines the range of information to be supplied to the user. All lasers are grouped into the following classes:

Class 1   Inherently safe. Either the MPE cannot be exceeded under any conditions, or the product is totally enclosed in an interlocked system.

Class 2   These are low-power devices emitting radiation in the visible part of the spectrum, i.e. 400 to 700 nm. They are not inherently safe but protection may be afforded by the body's aversion reflexes, i.e. closing the eyes to avoid a bright light.

Class 3A   The output power does not exceed 5 mW emission in the visible range. The irradiance at any pont in the beam must not exceed 2.5 mW per square centimetre. Protection to the eyes is usually afforded by the aversion responses. Viewing the beam directly with optical aids may be hazardous and any such optical equipment should have suitable filters built in.

Class 3B   Emission may be either visible or invisible at a power of less than 500 mW. Direct viewing of the beam and specular reflections is hazardous, but they may safely be viewed via a diffuse reflector under the following conditions: (i) a minimum viewing distance of 50 mm, (ii) a maximum viewing time of 10 seconds and (iii) a minimum diffuse image diameter of 5.5 mm.

Class 4   High-power devices with outputs exceeding those specified for class 3B and capable of producing hazardous diffuse reflections. They may also present a fire hazard and their use requires extreme caution. Most lasers used for entertainment fall into this category.

Considerations of safety

How is it possible to define which effects are safe and which are not?

The primary laser hazard is excessive exposure to the eyes, and it is important to emphasize that the crucial factor is the exposure and not just the power. Common sense dictates that a high-powered beam is inherently more dangerous than a low-powered one, but the duration of any potential exposure to the radiation is equally important. It is the product of the power and the exposure time which ultimately determines the safety or otherwise of an effect.

There is a basic conflict in the application of lasers in the area of public entertainment which does not exist in any other application because, in most other laser applications, it is neither necessary nor desirable to look directly at the beam. In a public display, however, the whole purpose is to see the beams – and, by and large, the closer one approaches a beam, the more spectacular is the effect. This contrasts sharply with safety considerations, which would dictate that the viewer and the beam are kept as far apart as possible.

The majority of lasers used in public entertainment have a power output of somewhere in the region of 0.5 W to 20 W and are therefore capable of causing permanent eye damage within 1 to 0.1 μs exposure time! Great care is needed: taking the nine basic effects referred to earlier, the following is a guide for safe operation.

Single (primary) beams

For single beams forming a beam chase from the optical table to one or more remote mirrors, it is likely that the beams are going to be very powerful and will need to be kept away from the audience, the performers on stage, and the crew or technicians working in the area. Direct beam viewing should be absolutely prevented, and it is suggested that a minimum separation of 2.5 m between a beam and any personnel be created. Such effects projected into the auditorium would naturally need to terminate well away from any members of the public. If beams are reflected around the stage, say from the lighting truss to the floor, it is recommended that performers be given a cueing mark on the stage floor where they should stand and that the effect is not operated if the performer(s) are not in their correct places. When this effect is being used, it is safer if everybody on stage is prevented from moving around.

Diffraction effects

If the primary beam from the laser is directed straight at the diffraction grating then the low-order beams will be almost as powerful as those in the previous effect, and the same considerations must apply. With higher-order beams, however, it may be possible that they are sufficiently low in power to permit them to be projected into an occupied area. In order to judge whether this is so, it is essential that the power density of any beams entering an occupied area is measured with a calibrated laser power meter. For the purposes of deciding the maximum permitted power, it is probably safe to assume that nobody would be able to stare directly into a beam for more than 10 seconds and the power should be set accordingly, i.e. approximately 0.1 mW.

Primary scanning

Effects achieved solely through the use of scanning galvanometers, i.e. line scanning, cone scanning, graphic projections and laser writing, often cause the most controversy when directed at a populated area.

The repetition rate of the scans is normally high enough to ensure that the duration of exposure to the eye would be sufficiently short to permit a relatively high-powered incident beam to be used. All the time the beam is being scanned at this rate, the maximum exposure to a direct viewing observer would be within a safe limit. However, a problem arises in that this effect relies upon the fast movement of the beam to ensure an observer does not receive an excessive exposure. If the scanners were to fail, being low-inertia devices they would quite possibly stop dead and allow a single powerful beam to be emitted which would undoubtedly cause instant and permanent eye damage. Even if the scanners were not to fail but to slow down, exposure to an observer may become unacceptably high.

When a system such as this fails it is said to fail to danger, and this is bad design practice as far as health and safety is concerned. It is usual for scanners to be interlocked to a shutter at the laser, so that in the event of a scanning malfunction the shutter will drop and the beam will be terminated. The drawback with this type of interlock is however twofold. Firstly, it only monitors the feedback voltage from the galvanometer and not the motion of the mirror. It is quite possible that a mirror could become detached from its driver whilst the galvanometer spring is still oscillating and hence giving a feedback signal to the shutter. In this event the laser would continue to operate even though a beam had become stationary. Secondly, and perhaps more importantly, if a situation arose where the beam became static and the interlock did operate, it would probably take somewhere in the region of a quarter of a second for the shutter to operate. As most scanned effects need at least a 1 W input beam to make them visually acceptable, this reaction time would be approximately 1,000,000 times too slow. The only type of interlocking device which would be acceptable in this situation is one which could react this quickly, but at the time of writing there is nothing readily available which could meet this criterion, although the situation could conceivably change in the future.

It is therefore essential that primary beams are not scanned on to an audience, a performer or a technician.

Secondary scanning

This is the term given to the effect achieved when the scanned output from a pair of galvanometer scanners is projected on to a remote moving reflector such as a mirrorball or a cone spinner, i.e. the scanned image is itself scanned by a second device.

Providing that the device is fitted with a motion-sensing interlock it would be safe to allow a beam of up to 2.5 mW per square centimetre to reach an audience, i.e. the class 3A exposure condition. Thus the greatest irradiance of an observer would be the class 3A limit, and this would be only momentary until the interlock operated the shutter. Whilst the beam was being scanned normally, the actual exposure would be considerably less. Class 3A exposure of audience or performer would be permissible only in an emergency during the short period it took for an interlock to operate.

Video projector

This is similar in principle to the secondary scanned effect. The multifaceted cylindrical mirror is mounted on an air bearing and revolves continuously at very high velocity. If it were to slow down, a motion-sensing interlock would operate the shutter and the inherent high inertia of the mirror would ensure that it would not be able to come to a sudden halt.

Fibre optics

Fibre optics are not often used as an effect in themselves but are used to transmit the laser light to some remote effects head. Wherever they are used, the ends of the cable should be capped if not plugged into some optical device, since the emergent beam could still be very powerful. Any scattered light emerging through the side walls of the fibres would be safe to view.

General points relating to the installation

1. The laser should be securely and rigidly mounted, as should the optical table and the effects head. Any small movements or vibrations at the source could lead to quite considerable movements of the beam at some distance away.
2. The system should only be used by competent, trained personnel. There must be some form of control against unauthorized use, e.g. a keyswitch or a password entry system into the controller.
3. There should be a clearly marked emergency cut-off switch to enable the system to be closed down quickly by anyone in the event of an emergency.
4. The display area should be clearly defined before setting up a show, and no beams should be permitted outside this area.
5. The laser controls should be sited in a position where the operator is able to see all the beam paths.
6. During the setting up and beam alignment, the power output should be reduced to the minimum required to see the beams. The designated area should be clear of all personnel during the alignment process.
7. As far as possible, keep all beams out of any areas accessible to the public. The only class of beam which is inherently safe and which may therefore be projected into an audience is a class 1 beam. As has been mentioned earlier, the exposure is determined by the power density and the duration, and in order to remain within this class the typical combinations of power and exposure time shown in Table 11.1 are required. Clearly, only very low-powered beams are safe to be viewed for any length of time, and therefore any higher-power output must be kept out of the audience, since there is no way of ensuring a sufficiently short exposure to the beams. Any beams which are designed to be projected into a public area must be measured with a properly calibrated laser power meter.

Table 11.1 *Class 1 laser: typical power and exposure combinations*

Power (mW)	Exposure (s)
0.1	100
0.4	10
1	0.2
5	0.001
10	0.00001
100	0.000001
1000	0.0000001

8 Any beams which could give rise to an exposure greater than class 1 should be at least 3 m above any floor surface where anybody is likely to stand and be at 2.5 m away laterally.

9 In the case of a scanned effect which is directed near to an audience, but not deliberately at them, an aperture mask should be fitted to the front of the scanner housing which will only permit the effect to be emitted provided it follows the predetermined path. Should a fault develop in a scanner which would result in a beam being projected into the audience or any other unwanted area, the beam will be stopped by the mask and not be able to cause any unplanned exposure.

10 Any remote reflectors should be securely mounted and rigidly locked. It is generally acceptable to use adjustable mountings when the installation is a temporary one, but in a permanent situation the mirror should have a secondary fixing to prevent any movement over a period.

11 Interlocks should be fitted to all secondary scanning devices, i.e. mirrorballs and cone spinners. These should be able to detect the actual motion of the device and should be connected to a shutter.

12 The laser should be equipped with a gravity-operated shutter held open by a solenoid. This may then be linked in to any interlocking device and to an emergency switch so that in the event of a malfunction or emergency the beam can be terminated.

13 All the above relate to optical hazards. Lasers normally require high-voltage three-phase electrical supplies, and all the usual safety considerations when handling these need to be adopted.

References

1 Health and Safety Executive. *Use of Lasers for Display Purposes*, PM 19, 1980.

2 BS 7192: 1989. Radiation safety of laser products.

12

Stage equipment safety considerations

Richard Brett

Introduction

No equipment installation can be made totally safe. However, a very high level of safety can be achieved on theatre stages by:

- the use of common sense
- proper supervision
- compliance with codes and regulations
- application of engineering and technology

This chapter reviews a number of questions regarding equipment safety which can arise in the stage and over-stage areas of opera houses, theatres, community halls and similar venues, in which musicals, drama, dance and other productions are presented.

A theatre stage is a *potentially* dangerous place, and it is important that everyone working there is conscious of this. However, good working practices have been established for most activities and, when these are followed, the likelihood of serious injury or a fatality is minimized. This requires those with experience or who have been fortunate to have received proper training to be constantly alert to malpractice, whether or not they are in a supervisory role.

The risks to people on stages and in associated areas may appear to be a consequence of moving equipment and scenery, but two deaths which occurred in the UK in recent years have been due in one case to the failure of a floor surface and in the other to poor scenery stacking practices. Without making any implications as to responsibility for any theatre backstage accidents, it is likely that in almost any situation the lack of application of common sense and responsible supervision may have a part to play. It is also a fact that familiarity and repetition of a tiresome routine dulls the senses and can lead to proper working practices being altered to be easier or quicker to carry out. One of the questions which must be asked in respect of all backstage activities is: 'Is this process as *easy and as straightforward* as it can reasonably be?' If not there is a very real chance that people will develop short cuts, which are potentially bad practices, in order to reduce the effort or time they have to spend on their tasks. A similar question must also be applied to equipment: 'Will the equipment be able to do *what is demanded of it*, or will it always be at potential risk of being overloaded or modified to run faster because it is actually inadequate?' Examples of this include strapping counterweight bars together to carry greater loads, or increasing motor powers without due consideration of the increased mechanical loads on transmission systems or of safe stopping distances and similar parameters.

It is not acceptable for venues requiring the facility to suspend heavy loads to have to jury-rig the inadequate equipment provided by the architect or builder because of their failure to obtain professional advice during design of the building. It is preferable to expend a limited budget on the appropriate basic structural or equipment provisions, rather than force future users to attempt to take risks with safety. Present-day requirements for lighting and sound suspensions in multi-purpose halls are considerable, and even the basic structure must be designed to accept multiple point loads of 1000 kg or more.

Familiarity is also dangerous in potentially passive situations. There are many examples of technicians and performers falling and being shocked, if not injured, when a rostrum, a stairway or even a stage elevator platform was not in the position it was expected to be. Senior personnel at both the Royal Opera House in Covent Garden and the Bayerische Staatsoper in Munich have been injured by falls into the hole created by a lowered stage elevator in their own theatres. In production situations it is not always practicable to erect a safety barrier and, whereas technicians and performers rehearse a production and thereby learn where things are, occasional visitors to the stage, even from within the theatre's own technical direction, will be more at risk. These examples serve to stress the importance of barriers or some form of warning at a significant change of level, even if it is not practicable to erect a full handrail. During fit-ups or when the stage or setting is left unattended by responsible crew or stage management, it is essential that the practice of erecting a barrier be enforced.

During the commissioning of the Drum Revolve stage in the Olivier Theatre in the Royal National Theatre building in London, a full set of barrier rails was provided to surround the 11.8 m diameter revolving stage, half of which could drop at any time to form a 12 m deep hole. On occasions when contractors' staff were in attendance on stage and the barrier was not erected, it was interesting but alarming to see the attraction and fascination that this hole had for many of the theatre personnel crossing the stage! However, it was the oblivion with which some unsuspecting people set out to walk straight into it which made one realize that we must all be protected from the unexpected.

Simplicity in operational processes is important. The risk to personnel of any injury or strain in carrying out their duties must be minimized. This does not mean that they should not have to pick up heavy loads, work hard or handle difficult objects: what it does mean is that they must be provided with a safe means of carrying out these duties. On stage this will include sufficient staff and proper handles for lifting heavy objects, mechanical equipment to assist with tiring tasks and proper access to all working areas.

This applies also to the correct design of the theatre technical spaces such as grids, loading and fly galleries, lighting bridges and similar. These are all areas in which a lot of time is spent by the technical crew carrying out repetitive, and sometimes labour-intensive, tasks. Guidance as to the correct design of some of these areas can be obtained from reference works, such as those published by the Association of British Theatre Technicians,[1] but care must be taken to ensure that the principles shown are correctly interpreted for the specific project. Blind application of a general principle can result in an unworkable situation. In designing equipment it is important to eliminate the detail that will catch a finger or toe: examples are rope locks which clamp fingers, or counterweights with no finger recesses to make them easy to handle. In achieving coordination with the structure in a new or refurbishment project, it is important to watch at the drawing stage for low-headroom steels or support members which are just above the gallery or grid flooring level. It is amazing how, under the pressure of the design timetable, the most rational architects and structural engineers will assume that only dwarfs are employed in the higher levels of theatres!

In reviewing some of the safety aspects of specific parts of a typical theatre stage and the more common equipment found there, a start will be made on the grid at the top of the flytower. This book is not a design manual: its intent is to point the way to the application of good safety practices. In this chapter, which relates to the safety of permanently installed stage equipment, some recommendations as to design approaches are included, but these must be verified as applicable in any specific situation before being implemented.

The grid

A theatre grid, consisting as it does of a timber or steel floor with a series of small openings in it, is more dangerous for people on the stage below than for those working on the grid itself. A typical modern British grid will consist of a number of parallel 100 mm × 50 mm steel channels welded 50 mm apart: the 50 mm spacing provides the gap through which hemp and wire ropes and electrical cables can be rigged. Other grid decking includes steel egg-crate, which is used in many forms in the USA, and proprietary steel storage or access walkway decking have been found to be economic. These are mounted with gaps between them so as to provide the necessary openings for spot lines and similar. The fact that the grid must be perforated means that *no loose equipment* should be used on the grid whilst work is going on below, and that all parts in use on or above the grid must be restrained. Small removable parts which can pass through the grid slots or holes, such as clamps for spot-line pulleys or removable sections of the grid itself, must be *made captive* with adequately rated wire rope slings or similar.

In older theatres the grid was used to carry the suspension pulleys for hemp or counterweight flying installations. Modern installations usually attempt to place the counterweight or motorized suspension diverter pulleys above the grid and use the grid as a walking surface on which spot-line diverter pulleys and point hoists may be located. As such, it is essential that the grid decking be adequate to support these additional loads and that all equipment is provided with suitable carrying handles so that it may be moved around the grid.

In order to accommodate hemp rope suspensions, it has been the practice to create a 'hemp slot', which is a wider gap at the edge of the grid over which head pulleys are mounted and through which the hemps pass to the working gallery below. Some form of clearly marked and captive covers should be available for protecting this slot. The slot through which drop the counterweight pipe or power suspension wire ropes will have to be of adequate width so that the wire ropes do not wear on the edge steels when swinging. This slot should be protected by clear marking and will often be apparent by the wire ropes themselves; remember, however, that in all stage areas the work is often carried out in poor and changing lighting conditions, so very clear safety markings are essential. Neither of these slots is wide enough for anyone to fall through, but they could cause injury if someone lost their footing while crossing.

It is good practice to limit those with access to the grid to people who have a need to be there and to allow only responsible persons to take tools and loose equipment into the area. Loose parts left by accident could be vibrated free and fall unexpectedly to the stage below.

Flytower galleries

The galleries in the flytower of a theatre are important working spaces and must be designed to accommodate the personnel and equipment necessary. They are generally unique to each theatre and, while standardization would be a benefit, they are often dependent on the form of construction of the flytower (steel frame, concrete) and on the preferences of the structural engineer. Experience indicates that the best galleries have resulted when the detailed operational requirements have been determined by the theatre consultant who has then collaborated with the structural engineer. Some perfectly workable and safe galleries have been obtained within quite unusual structural forms. A number of very useful general recommendations as to flytower gallery sizes and handrail heights are published by the Association of British Theatre Technicians.[1]

Counterweight installations are to be found in most theatres with flytowers and these, to some extent more than with hemp or powered systems, raise some special safety considerations in respect of the working galleries. The process of loading and unloading the counterweights requires the gallery to be at the correct height so that this labour can be carried out without strain and without climbing on to handrails or other steelwork in order to reach the weights. Additional galleries must be provided between the fly gallery and the loading gallery in professional theatres with heavy-capacity sets and where double-purchase counterweights are used, so that all the weights can be reached without gymnastics.

The detail of the gallery depends to some extent on the counterweight system being installed. The gallery must be provided with a handrail and kickedge on the counterweight (off-stage) side but cannot, for practical reasons, have a lower rail on this side. This would obstruct the loading and unloading of the counterweights. The on-stage edge of the gallery must be designed to carry stacked weights and be so protected that these cannot fall to the stage. Similarly, a weight dropped accidentally while loading must not be free to fall on stage, and the lower part of the counterweight installation should be enclosed with wire mesh panels to prevent this. These have the additional advantage of protecting stacked scenery or personnel from the moving ropes and counterweight cradles, but should be easily removable to allow inspection and maintenance. In double-purchase installations where personnel can move beneath the counterweight cradle zone, adequate structure must be provided to stop a falling weight safely. Standard steel weights are normally around 6 kg or 12 kg, although some heavier weights may be used permanently in the bottom of the cradle to balance the empty pipe.

Counterweight equipment

The details of a counterweight installation will be determined by a consultant or specialist manufacturer, and generally the safety of a correctly designed and installed system will be dependent on the way it is used. It is easy to use a counterweight installation incorrectly and thus to make it a potentially dangerous piece of equipment. Flying systems must be operated by personnel who have been correctly trained or who are supervised by those with training or proper experience. To assist with the dissemination of the correct practices, the Association of British Theatre Technicians has prepared a 'Flying code of practice'[2] which lays down the principles for safe working of all types of flying systems.[2] This should be consulted by all those who design or use such systems.

Some obvious practical design points affecting the safety of suspension systems for scenery, lighting and other equipment include the need to ensure, throughout the life of the equipment, that wire ropes cannot wear on fixed steelwork or come out of pulley grooves under any conditions, that all pulleys are rotated by movement of the wire ropes in their grooves, and that the correct wire rope fixings are made at all tie-off points. While regular inspection of mechanical equipment is essential to ensure reliability, the frequent inspection of wire ropes is vital to safety.

The capacity of the system must be suitable for the venue and type of scenery and shows anticipated. The rope lock must be robust and capable of taking the considerable strain put on it by the operators. Not all manufacturers' standard rope locks are suitable for professional usage. Some locks also distort the rope more than others, although the bad practice of using a rope lock as a braking device by applying it on a moving counterweight set is the worst cause of rope wear. The resultant reduction in rope diameter can cause the lock's effectiveness to be reduced and the sets to be less stable when the lock is applied. This can be particularly dangerous when loading or unloading of counterweights is taking place. The strength of the suspension pipe must be related to the uniformly distributed and point loads that it will be expected to carry (this is not necessarily solely dependent on the counterweight capacity).

Power flying systems

The safety of power flying systems will be dependent upon the mechanical, electrical and control design features as well as upon the operation of the equipment. Depending on the degree of sophistication of the control system, such equipment can be largely protected against mistakes by the stage crew and operator. For example, it is normal for the most basic equipment not to run when overloaded, whether the overload is applied statically or in motion, or when a wire rope goes slack. Both of these are operational snags and can be caused, however careful an operator is, by picking up a misplaced piece of scenery or lowering scenery on to an obstruction. In addition to stopping when *one* of the wire ropes goes slack, the mechanical design of the system must prevent this wire rope coming out of the groove on the winding drum. This is sometimes achieved by a keep mounted just clear of the winding drum, but is best achieved by a moving pulley which takes up the slack whilst the drum comes to a standstill and keeps the tension on the wire rope in the drum groove. Such systems allow freedom for rigging operations and a safe restart, under the operator's control, when the load is again applied.

Most advanced power flying systems will feature software monitoring of motor performance, load, speed and other parameters and constantly compare these with command signals derived from the control panels. In the event of one of these parameters being outside a preset tolerance band, the system will react to the malfunction, whether it is caused within the control system itself or externally. It is good practice to duplicate the essential checks and to include mechanical detectors where appropriate as backups.

It is normal for the control systems on powered flying installations to require a specific action by the operator in order to initiate any motion or to restart after any snag or trip. A snag or trip is defined as an operational error rather than a malfunction. Such systems must not allow any movement to commence unless a specific action is taken by the operator. With the ability to control groups of hoists together to pick up extensive or heavy pieces of scenery, it is necessary that such a group is made inviolate so that any snag or malfunction affecting one hoist brings it and all the others in the group to a stop in synchronization and in a controlled way. In Germany there are regulations restricting the maximum speed at which loads carried by powered flying systems can move, the distance which the hoists can travel before stopping in the event of a snag or malfunction, and the number of pieces of scenery which one operator can control. In the UK there are no such regulations at present, but the Association of British Theatre Technicians has included some useful operational points in its 'Flying code of practice'.[2]

Although there are more power flying installations in mainland Europe, the development of the operational features for such systems has probably been more extensive in the UK. Much of the same operational flexibility has been reflected in recent developments in Scandinavia and Australia. The UK philosophy has been to permit one operator to control all the moving pieces in the flytower, as might be required in a large transformation scene, but to provide additional safety controls so that, in the event of a physical problem, the appropriate group of hoists can be stopped.

Users elsewhere may also find the maximum speed permitted in Germany somewhat restrictive in large theatres. The argument is whether speed is in itself dangerous, and this will depend on the ability of the control system to detect snags or system faults rapidly and of the hoists to decelerate the relevant loads safely. Kinetic energy is proportional to the square of the velocity, and so four times the energy has to be absorbed on stopping if the maximum speed of a system is doubled. The mechanics of the system must be designed in accordance with the forces which such deceleration will create, and in these combined respects a correctly designed powered system may well be safer in some applications than the equivalent manual system. A good operator can run a counterweight at an average speed of about 1.4 m/s but has difficulty in stopping it accurately from this sort of speed. Correctly designed power systems can offer higher speeds, where appropriate, and rapid controlled deceleration.

A safety audit must be done for any equipment installation, particularly where there is the potential danger of items falling or of hazards being created. A safety audit involves verifying that the equipment installation will be safe under all circumstances when used within its design capacities. It requires the safety factors of every component to be checked and related to ensure that none are exceeded under all foreseeable conditions. It will include checking the effect of one or more simultaneous failures on all other components. A basic check on a flying system would be the effect of the failure of one wire rope on the remainder of the suspensions. Checks on apparently peripheral fittings must be made. Hoists and pulleys must remain securely fixed down under all circumstances and not be ripped off their mountings, as happened during an emergency stop test on one power flying installation.

The type of installations more likely to be a safety hazard are those which have been put together for limited expenditure and for which a full safety audit has not been carried out. Such an installation could involve using a winch to overhaul counterweights so that they do not need to be loaded when heavy scenery or lighting equipment is hung. If fitted with some overload and slack wire rope detectors, a basic installation of this type may be safe when used correctly, but without safety features it would be potentially dangerous. It must be incumbent on the designers and suppliers of such installations to ensure that the limitations of the equipment and detailed methods of use are clearly understood and displayed along with other data essential on all powered systems, such as the safe working load. It is always safer to use a proprietary winch or hoist system (standard chain hoists are used extensively throughout the entertainment industry) for the purpose for which they were designed, rather than to attempt to create a system which may have potentially dangerous conditions.

Safety curtains and dividing doors

The equipment which is used in the larger theatres to divide the stage from the auditorium or one part of the stage from another, for example the side stage from the main stage, has a potential to injure. The dividing doors are often, for space reasons, hoisted vertically into the flytower. They are usually heavy sound-attenuating panels which are counterweighted and descend slowly under the control of an air or hydraulic damper. It is necessary to ensure therefore that they do not lower on to scenery or personnel, and this can be achieved by incorporating a contact detector on the bottom surface of the door. Some types of useful contact and vicinity detectors are discussed later in the section on stage elevators. A further safety feature is to allow a large door of this type to be initiated to descend under its own control to about 2.5 mm above the floor and then to stop and await a further constant pressure on the 'down' button to make the door close and seal. This has operational benefits on stage also.

Safety curtains have, over the years, saved a number of theatres from total destruction, but they have also been the cause of some injuries and deaths. The most horrifying was the decapitation of a woman in the audience in a continental theatre where the safety curtain landed on the very front of the stage, just in front of the audience. In her enthusiasm for the performers she had leaned across into the stage and was not aware of the descent of the curtain. This incident led to the authorities requiring the safety curtain to be set upstage where it could not cause such an injury. In the critical downstage zone of a professional theatre, this could distance the audience from the setting line by an additional 0.75 m, which would not be welcomed by set designers or directors.

The elimination of this distance was behind the thinking on the safety curtains in both the Lyttelton and Barbican Theatres in London, where the theatre design requires the safety curtain to be set as far downstage as possible. Because these theatres both have stage elevators which can be set to different levels, including being levelled with the front auditorium floor, it was essential that the curtain was right at the front of the stage. These curtains are split in two unequal pieces horizontally, the lower part being about a third of the total and acting as a partial counterweight to the top section. When open, the lower part actually forms the stage riser. However, when the curtain closes, the lower part rises, thus making its movement clear to anyone in the vicinity, and when the two parts close together the join is arranged to be some 4 m above the auditorium floor and well out of reach. The movement of the two parts simultaneously also minimizes the time taken to seal these large proscenium openings.

Stage elevators

The term 'elevator' is used here to refer to a platform forming part of the stage or auditorium floor surface which can be raised, lowered or tilted to create different levels on the stage, to move scenery or to change the form of the venue. Stage elevators are not lifts, in the conventional English use of the word; they are specifically designed pieces of equipment used in theatres, opera houses, convention halls and community centres for changing the level of all or part of the floor. Elevator equipment can involve large areas of floor (an opera house may have three elevators, each 20 m by 6 m in plan) and these may move both above and below the fixed stage floor level by as much as 12 m. The Opéra de la Bastille has elevators which lower some 21 m. Even units which travel small distances must be used with care, and all elevator equipment must be designed so as to ensure that, whilst in motion or stationary, either they create no hazard or any hazard which is created is guarded.

Considering first the problems that can arise when the elevators are stationary, these will generally relate to the changes of level. Unless these are always going to be anticipated and clearly visible, as at the front of the stage (the stage riser) or in a set of orchestra risers, or are part of a setting which requires no barriers (as in a quayside, built as part of the scenery), such changes in level must be protected by steps or barriers. It is also important to mark the edges of raised elevators wherever possible so that personnel are made aware of the location and start of descending steps or ramps. Where a very deep unprotected hole is required for effect as part of the scenery, the circus technique of using a safety net must be borrowed. It is not possible to define what height might constitute a dangerous fall (people have fallen into orchestra pits and got up and walked way), but the risk in each individual case on stage must be assessed and protected.

There is no situation in which an unprotected drop would be acceptable in an auditorium or in any space accessible by the public. Thus, where elevators are used to reformat an auditorium, automatic or manually fitted handrails must be provided on all elevator edges which are not against walls or otherwise protected. This applies particularly to elevators which are used to lower or raise the part of the auditorium near to the stage to form an orchestra pit. A robust and secure rail, complying with statutory requirements, must be erected along the edge of the auditorium floor as soon as the elevator is lowered. Such an elevator may well also be able to be raised to stage level in order to form a forestage, and in this situation the front edge (the riser) and any other accessible edges should be faced with solid material so as not to create a hazard.

The next major hazard with elevators is that of guillotine edges where two elevators or a fixed and a moving edge pass. Such dangerous situations must be eliminated or provided with a fail-safe form of edge protection. Wherever possible such edges should be located out of reach. In concert halls, conference venues and community centres it is often possible to provide the elevator with fascias, or skirts, on all the vertical surfaces which may be exposed to personnel, thus eliminating the guillotine edges. In practical terms it is often necessary to set the fascia back from the edge of the elevator platform by 10 mm or so and to install a vertically tapered lead-in to the edge of the actual platform. This tapered edge is intended to push any obstruction clear as the gap closes. Allowing 10 mm each side means that some 20 mm clearance is obtained between the moving faces of the elevator and thus these will not rub together or get damaged in normal use.

Such a technique should be used on mechanized orchestra risers, for example, but it has to be said that very few buildings are planned with sufficient depth or spaces to permit such a simple and fail-safe form of guillotine edge protection. Adequate space allowance in the early days of planning and budgeting buildings, including concert and conference halls (which are often to be provided with platform elevators), would often lead to simpler, and less costly, mechanical installations. Safety requirements can represent a large proportion of the complexity necessary.

Where an elevator cannot have fascias because, for example, it is necessary to leave access to the underside, there will be guillotine action when the exposed edge passes a similar fixed edge on the structure or on an adjacent elevator. When the exposed edge of an elevator lowers past a stationary floor we have the typical toe trap.

Although stage and auditorium elevators are not normally expected to be moved with personnel on them, there are times when it is very cost-effective to allow the crew, who have loaded the scenery on to the elevator, to travel on the elevator in order to move the scenery off. There are also situations in which performers may be required to travel on elevators for effect. Where the personnel involved are responsible, have had the movement and dangers explained to them by the person responsible for the installation, and have a means of stopping the elevator in an emergency, it is hard to argue against permitting such a controlled usage. Under these circumstances, it is good practice for a responsible person to be designated to be in charge of all entry and exit movements to and from the elevator and to have an emergency stop control to hand. Thus personnel on an elevator in motion, although having been instructed to keep away from the edges, are potentially at risk of any exposed guillotine action.

Where it is necessary to have passing edges within reach of personnel for the reasons explained above or others, there are methods by which injuries can be effectively eliminated. These require the application of similar detection and machine stopping devices to those used throughout manufacturing industry. The methods of detecting a limb or obstruction do, however, have to be selected with the theatre application in mind. This means that use of many photo-electric devices cannot be recommended, as the light source could affect a blackout on stage and the signal from them might even be falsified by unintended stage lighting angles. Whilst often used in off-stage applications, many of the pressure mat devices are also impracticable on stages, but the air pressure or vaccum tube contact detectors have been used successfully on theatre equipment. Satisfactory installations using mechanical bar detectors which lift against springs and operate lever switches or similar devices have also been manufactured. Some of the later developments of optical fibre technology offer interesting features. One available product consists of a tube moulded within a block of aerated neoprene. When this is slightly distorted by pressure on one surface, an internal light path is broken and the detector reacts, stopping the equipment. This sort of product is fairly robust and can be manufactured so as to eliminate any dead ends or non-active joins which otherwise might put someone at risk.

Having identified a satisfactory detector in principle, it then becomes essential to ensure that it can be applied to the elevator or other equipment which has to be stopped. The critical parameter in most theatre applications is the over-travel that the device can accommodate, which is the distance that the detector can be compressed or moved before the equipment can be brought to a halt, i.e. the stopping distance. When an obstruction is detected, the detecting device has to reduce its dimension or its mounting has to move to accommodate the ongoing motion of the equipment as this is brought to a standstill. In this way a hand or foot caught in a guillotine edge will not be harmed as the elevator is designed to stop within the over-travel of the detector and without excess pressure being put on the obstruction. Thus the stopping distance of the elevator must be known *under all conditions of loading and operation* for the right detecting device to be selected.

As was discussed earlier, it is not practicable to have gates or automatic barriers on many of the levels served by stage elevators. However, where the elevator and the access point to it are not on stage or forming part of the setting, then it is important to incorporate interlocked gates to prevent personnel, who may not be seen by the operator, moving on or off or between elevators. Usually under the stage the elevator moving parts can be guarded and normal handrails provided.

The operational position for stage elevators is normally at stage level or on a perch platform with a view down on to the stage. It must not be assumed, however, that the operator will be able to see everything which happens: quite often he will be cued verbally or by lights and may also have a number of performance-related things to do at the time of the movement. Under these circumstances a second person must be delegated to watch for any danger: it is good practice during complicated scenery movements for the operator to have assistants, with either emergency stop buttons or dead man's handles, on stage or on a flytower gallery where they can see all elevator or other scenery movements. These controls can be used to stop the equipment in an emergency, as the dead man's handle has to be kept pressed for the movement to take place, whilst the emergency stop has only to be pressed to stop the movement. However, it must be realized that the danger with a properly designed and engineered elevator installation is not so much in its motion as in the holes and openings that this equipment creates in the stage floor and the potential danger from insecure scenery.

Stage wagons and revolves

The most commonly used items of stage floor equipment are revolving stages and stage wagons. These two items of equipment are similar, although stage wagons will normally travel on the surface of the stage whilst revolves are generally set into the stage floor or are provided with a fixed surround extending the stage floor around them. Revolves are sometimes set into wagons so that they may be stored in a side or rear stage area and brought on to the main stage when required. Where stage elevators are installed, such a revolve wagon will normally be lowered on the elevators until it is flush with the floor.

Many of the principles outlined previously apply to these items of equipment. Controls should be where an operator can see the danger areas. Complex movements should not be attempted without an assistant to watch for potential hazards. The speed of the equipment must be commensurate with its ability to stop in a controlled way. The movement of a stage wagon, which is usually a fairly large area of low-height construction, must be signalled to personnel in the vicinity: if this is not practicable in a production, assistants must ensure the path is clear before allowing the movement to take place. Whilst this appears obvious, it is surprising how the pressure of a rehearsal or production can cause this simple rule to be overlooked. The writer has personal experience of nearly being struck by the surprisingly silent motion of a large stage wagon in a German opera house! Such equipment is unlikely to cause a fatality but can cause foot and leg injuries.

Revolves are normally located in one place or, if mobile, take up fixed positions on stage when used. Stage wagons in major theatres move in straight lines and are generally guided. A number of auditorium installations built in recent years use air castor technology, in which the hovercraft principle – of blowing low-pressure air out of suitable orifices under a heavy item of equipment – lifts the equipment sufficiently to minimize the friction and allow one or two people to push it around on a level smooth floor as they desire. This has been used with particular effect in the Derngate in Northampton, where large units of raked seating and side-wall towers, with two levels of seating on them, are moved about to change the form of the auditorium and stage. This is a basically safe method of handling large items, as the low-friction effect can be eliminated very quickly by cutting off the air supply. The low friction is caused by a very thin film of air under the flexible membrane forming the air castor. The air castor fills with air under pressure, raising the equipment some 20–25 mm above the floor. Provided the edges of the moving equipment are suitably designed and faced, there is a minimal hazard for toes. As with any moving item, however, care must be taken that the movement route is not obstructed and the operator has control of the air supply.

One of the more dangerous items sometimes used on the stage floor is the travolator which, in theatrical form, is a continuous strip of moving floor on which performers act out a moving scene whilst remaining in a more or less static position. A revolve is also sometimes used for such scenes (as in a famous *Mother Courage* at the Old Vic in London) and is probably less dangerous, in that the flooring does not have to turn and disappear under the stage to reappear at the other side. It is this edge effect of a travolator which has been the cause of foot and ankle injuries, in the same way that the major hazards on an escalator are at the edges and where it links to the fixed flooring. Escalator manufacturers go to great lengths to comply with the regulations which apply to moving floor equipment for use by the public, a complexity which is impracticable in most limited stage productions. This type of equipment is seldom, if ever, installed permanently in theatres but may be required in a particular production.

In respect of the design and use of all specialized moving equipment, an independent qualified person, who must not be under any financial or time pressures which might compromise safety, must be appointed to judge the safety of any equipment built for a show *in the context in which it is to be used.* Greater safety precautions must be taken on all moving equipment where the performers are wearing full length costumes, which might get caught in the edges or gaps, or where they are occupied in some way such as playing musical instruments, in a stage fight or even performing a soliloquy. Account must also be taken of the amount of lighting in which the scene will be played, as this can have a direct effect on the hazards.

Emergency stops and safety systems

Where there are a number of powered items such as elevators and scenery flying equipment installed in or above the stage, it is important that methods of stopping this equipment be immediately available to personnel in the main working areas. The placing of emergency stop buttons and the items which they stop requires careful thought. Is a single series of push buttons around the stage, which stop everything, correct in a theatre context? Or should, for example, the elevator or wagons be stopped without affecting the power flying system? Separation of these functions may be appropriate in a heavily mechanized stage, but it is essential that no one is confused by the duplication of push buttons. Where two emergency stop circuits are provided, pairs of pushes, one for stage floor equipment and one for over stage, should be mounted in each location and clearly marked as to their function. Emergency stops normally consist of mushroom head pushes which lock in when pressed and have to be turned or otherwise manipulated to release them. The pushes should have an adjacent indicator light and also be traced through the control system so that the equipment operator knows which push has been activated. After an emergency stop incident, no movement of the equipment should occur or be possible until the push is released, and the operator has reset the system and has selected and restarted a motion.

A safety strategy which has been used successfully for a major stage floor installation combined the emergency stops with a safe access system. Technicians and performers require access from under stage to this equipment, which consists of two elevators mounted within a revolving stage and with a separately revolving half-circle revolve on top. In order that no motion can be started whilst anyone is at risk within the equipment, a set of small traffic lights is combined with each of the emergency stop pushes fitted around the equipment.

Each emergency stop push is always operational and will stop all parts of the equipment which may be moving. When the equipment is stationary, the red light is normally showing, indicating that the equipment is potentially hazardous to enter because it could move at any time. However, pressing an emergency stop push whilst the equipment is stationary puts the system into an unavailable state and the green traffic light shows. The operator can set up his next movement on the control panel but cannot implement any motion whilst the emergency stop remains locked in and people are moving around under stage. This state is indicated to the operator, together with which of the pushes has been pressed.

If the pushes have not been released when the operator has a cue approaching, he can cause the amber lights on each traffic light signal to flash, indicating to the crew that a cue is imminent. The crew finish their work and, with any performers involved, take up safe positions on the elevators or outside the equipment and release the pushes. The lights then indicate the red state and the operator is free to carry out the cue. At any time during the motion the emergency stop pushes will decelerate the moving parts rapidly to standstill. The principles behind combining the safe access and emergency stop pushes were simplicity – to have only one method of dealing with safety on the stage – and familiarity because, as personnel get used to pressing the pushes, such an action does not appear so dramatic in an emergency.

A further important aspect of emergency stopping is that the system must be designed to bring the equipment to a stop safely and as rapidly as possible. It is not, as is often thought, only necessary to take the main power off the system and let the brakes or friction bring the equipment to a halt. In many installations, the opposite is true: the equipment can be brought to rest more rapidly by powering it down a rapid deceleration curve. This is particularly applicable where full electronic closed-loop control is installed and the brakes, whilst fully capable of decelerating and holding the load, would not respond so quickly or smoothly. Application of the brakes may also put a major shock into the mechanical system and cause scenery to be dislodged. In such advanced systems the powered deceleration must be implemented first, followed, where appropriate, by isolation of the power supplies. Suitable protection must be provided to ensure power isolation and the application of the brakes if the rapid powered deceleration was not detected within a few milliseconds of initiation.

Methods used for the construction and fixing of scenery must also be considered where powered systems can be brought to a stop quickly. This is a separate and important discipline where supervision by a senior responsible person is essential as it may cross boundaries between scenery construction, stage crew and equipment operation. A flown piece of scenery which is in itself securely constructed, but which has a door held on with lightweight pin hinges, might lose the door if the flying bar to which it is attached stops rapidly. On a stage wagon system or revolve it is important that the methods used to fix down the scenery will prevent it falling over and causing injury in the event of an emergency stop.

Emergency stops are primarily to halt the motion of potentially damaging loads and items of equipment which could cause physical injury. All the electrical equipment must be enclosed and protected in accordance with relevant codes and regulations: hence the isolation of the power from the system, motors, brakes, racks of electrical equipment and similar, is the function of an isolator, not necessarily of an emergency stop system. It might be felt appropriate to provide separate remote control of the electrical power supply isolator from the control desk or from a position on stage. To enable maintenance of the electrical or electronic equipment to take place, separate and appropriate safety interlock systems must be installed for use by the authorized technicians.

Examination of the limited number of serious accidents which occur on stages or with stage equipment emphasizes the importance of the application of common sense and of proper supervision in safety. Many of these few accidents could have been eliminated, or their effects mitigated by a more sensible approach to the work or by the monitoring of activities by a senior person or, in some circumstances, even by just another person. Work should not be undertaken alone on electrical equipment or where there is a need to get near or inside moving equipment, as for inspection or testing. Pressure to complete a task, to modify something quickly, or tiredness, which at times affects everyone at work in the theatre, must not be allowed to degrade proper working practices. Interlocks and technical safety devices must not be shorted out without taking all the necessary consequent precautions.

Apart from such operational responsibilities, it is essential that the equipment installations be inherently safe. Here cost and competitive tendering are both factors, because unless the equipment is comprehensively specified from the point of view of safety as well as of its theatrical performance, contractors will not give priority to safety features which might lead to their equipment being more expensive than that of their competitors. As there are no relevant standards for much stage equipment in the UK at present, widely varying bids can be received for poorly specified installations. It is noticeable that sketchily specified works, which are the result of accepting the lowest bid, often feature weaknesses and limitations which would not be found where a consultant, or even a single nominated contractor, has been involved. In some of these instances even basic safety features are not provided and, unless all those operating the equipment have the knowledge and experience of the installation contractor, such equipment can put personnel at risk.

Equipment installations must start with the right concepts, be provided with adequate spaces, be given realistic budgets and be properly specified for performance and safety. Tenders for the equipment should only be sought from fully pre-qualified contractors with adequate experience of this type of equipment. The selection should be made on the quality of their submission and their design approach, rather than just on price. When the contractor is appointed, his drawings should be reviewed, the results of his safety audit examined and inspections made of equipment in manufacture and while being installed. Finally, testing should be independently witnessed and the users fully trained in operations, in safety procedures and in first-line maintenance of the equipment. Such a procedure, properly carried out, will lead to stage equipment installations which are operationally satisfactory and safe.

References

1 Association of British Theatre Technicians. *Code of Practice for the Theatre Industry*. Part 2, Chapter 1: Design guide: guard rails, 1987.
2 Association of British Theatre Technicians. *Code of Practice for the Theatre Industry*. Flying code of practice, in press, 1993.

13

Sound levels and noise control

Ken Dibble

Introduction

Some may express surprise at finding sound levels and noise control included in a reference volume concerned with event safety. However, this is an aspect of event management which is taking on increasing importance as more legislation and codes of practice concerning exposure to loud sounds or noise in the community are introduced. Three different areas are of concern to the authorities:

1 the level of sound emanating from the event giving rise to nuisance complaints from nearby residents or other noise-sensitive locations such as hospitals
2 the level of sound to which event staff are exposed over a working day
3 the level of sound to which the audience are exposed during the event.

The first two are subject to actual legislation: Section 80 of the Environmental Protection Act 1990, and the Noise at Work Regulations 1989 arising from the Health and Safety at Work Act 1974. The third is an area of more recent interest and is one of the many aspects of event safety addressed by the Health and Safety Commission in its 1992 *Guide to Health, Safety and Welfare at Pop Concerts and Other Similar Events*. In addition to the legislation itself it is standard practice for the licensing authority to require details of the arrangements and to satisfy itself that these three aspects will be controlled before a licence is granted.

So the control of sound has become an important aspect of event management. Contravention will guarantee that any subsequent licence application will be refused, and may incur substantial fines or even lead to imprisonment!

Some basics

Before becoming embroiled in the numerics of the various regulatory requirements, it is as well to have at least a basic understanding of the units employed in the measurement of sound levels and the nature of the problem that has to be addressed.

Decibels

The decibel is the basic unit of sound level measurement. The physics of its derivation need not concern us here, but Figure 13.1 will serve to give some meaning to the values one so often hears being bandied about. Because the human hearing system has a logarithmic response to changes in amplitude, so the decibel is a logarithmic unit of measurement. Thus a 10-fold increase or decrease in sound pressure level (SPL) gives a measured increase or decrease of 10 dB, a 100-fold change gives plus or minus 20 dB, a 1000-fold change plus or minus 30 dB etc. One or two useful rules of thumb are as follows:

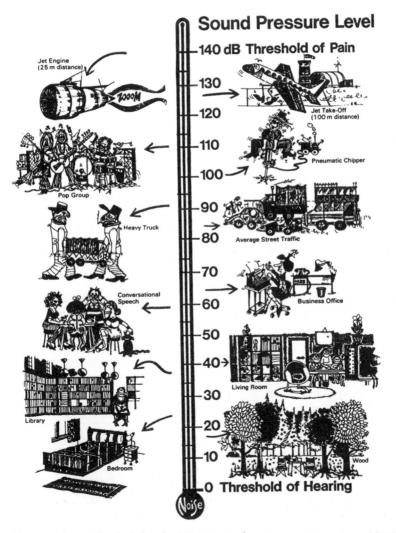

Figure 13.1   *The decibel scale: SPL in typical environments (courtesy of B&K UK Ltd)*

- A 10 dB increase or decrease in SPL produces a perceived doubling or halving in volume.
- Doubling or halving an amplifier output power produces an SPL increase or decrease of 3 dB, i.e. an increase from 1 W to 2 W produces +3 dB, whilst an increase from 1000 W to 2000 W also produces +3 dB!
- In free space (i.e. an outdoor arena), SPL will decrease by 6 dB each time the distance from the loudspeaker system is doubled, e.g. 100 dB at 1 m will reduce to 94 dB at 2 m, 88 dB at 4 m, 82 dB at 8 m, and so on. Figure 13.2 shows the relationship and will serve as a handy ready reckoner.

Frequencies

The other important concept is the relationship between frequency and music. Again we need not be concerned with physics, but we do need to understand the basic principles.

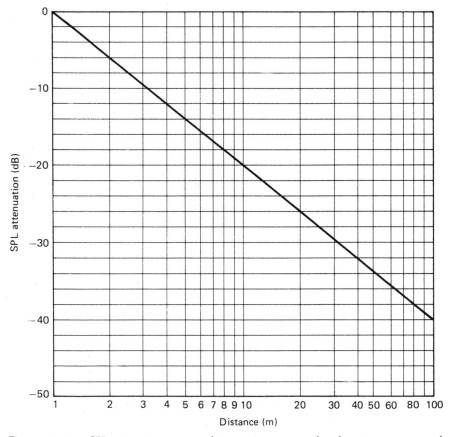

Figure 13.2   *SPL attenuation versus distance from source, based on inverse square law calculation 20 log (distance)*

Essentially, a perfect ear has a nominal sensitivity range from 20 Hz to 20 kHz: this is reduced by ageing, by injury (i.e. exposure to excessively loud sound over long periods) and by disease. Frequencies up to about 200 Hz are considered to be bass or low frequencies, those between about 200 Hz and 800 Hz are considered low midrange, those between 800 Hz and about 3.2 kHz are upper midrange, and those above 3.2 kHz are high frequency or treble. Figure 13.3 shows a useful relationship between the musical scale, frequencies, wavelength, and standard octave (1/1) and one-third octave (1/3) bands such as are to be found on a typical graphic equalizer. Again, one or two useful rules of thumb are as follows:

- Open bottom E string on bass guitar is 41 Hz.
- Concert pitch A is 440 Hz.
- Each doubling (or halving) of the frequency is equivalent to a musical change of one octave.

A-weighting

Now we have a grasp of decibels and frequencies, we can consider frequency weighting. Just as the ear does not have a linear response to sound level, nor does it have a linear frequency response. What is more, its frequency response characteristic is different at different listening levels. Figure 13.4 shows equal loudness contours. It can be seen that at low listening levels the ear is extremely insensitive to low frequencies; it is at its most sensitive at 4 kHz, and its response

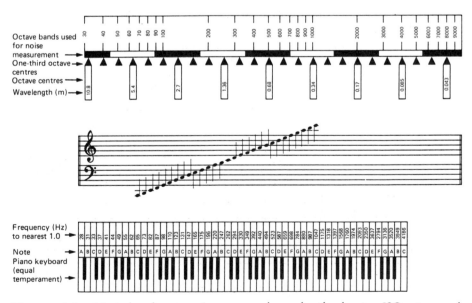

Figure 13.3 *Musical scale versus frequency and wavelength, showing ISO octave and one-third octave centre frequencies*

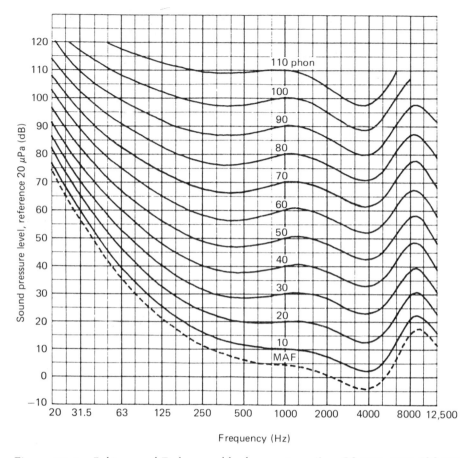

Figure 13.4   *Robinson and Dadson equal loudness contours (from BS 3383: 1988, ISO 226: 1987). The phon is the SPL relative to 20 μPa of a pure 1 kHz signal. The broken line shows the minimum audible field (MAF)*

flattens out as the sound pressure level is increased. Because of this phenomenon, the SPL is invariably measured via a special (equalization) filter intended to compensate for the ear's characteristics. This is known as A-weighted measurement and is expressed as dB(A). Figure 13.5 shows the A-weighted filter slope which, as can be seen, is more or less the inverse of the equal loudness curves at the lower listening levels.

Integrated A-weighted sound pressure level LA$_{eq}$

This is a unit which is widely used in determining noise exposure and in arriving at an average SPL over a given period. It is essentially an integration of dB(A) with time and is usually expressed as such, e.g. 102 dB LA_{eq} 15 minutes.

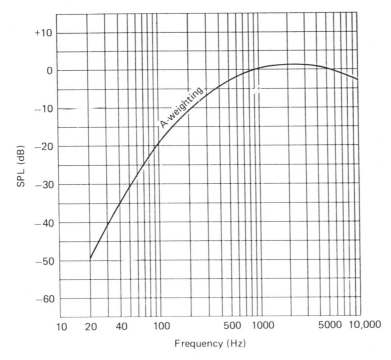

Figure 13.5   *A-weighting characteristics (based on BS 5969: 1981, IEC 651: 1979 Table IV)*

Background noise level LA$_{90}$

This is defined as that SPL which is exceeded for 90% of the time. In practice it relates to the quiet lulls between passing traffic or other transient noise events. Its value is dependent on what the actual background noise level would be in the absence of the transient noise events, on the level of the transient noise events themselves, and on the proportion of time for which those noise events are present during the measurement period. It is almost universally the unit used to determine the background noise level.

Transmission loss (TL) or sound reduction index (SRI)

This is the amount by which sound is attenuated across a particular space or across a particular barrier, e.g. a tract of land that separates the venue from a particular noise-sensitive location, a wall, a roof, a whole building or marquee, a barrier screen etc. In its simplest form it is the difference between the sound level measured at the source and that measured at the receiving location, and is expressed as the simple dB difference.

Typical music levels and spectra

This information has been included in order to provide a basic understanding of the nature of the problem we are trying to address.

Figure 13.6 shows a series of one-third octave level versus frequency analyses of some typical event noise sources: these are known as one-third octave spectra. Figure 13.6(a) shows a typical rock music concert, 13.6(b) a discotheque, 13.6(c) rave music and 13.6(d) an excited crowd at a football match.

Note the emphasis on the bass frequencies in the music spectra. If the value of the bass energy is read off the dB scale it will be found to be considerably higher than the dB(A) broadband SPL figure. To take the rave music plot shown in Figure 13.6(c) as an example, a bass peak of 120 dB is recorded in the 63 Hz one-third octave band whilst the broadband A-weighted SPL is 97–98 dB(A). This is due to the effect of the A-weighted filter shown in Figure 13.5. Thus it is quite common for the sound level in particular one-third octave bands to be considerably higher than the broadband SPL measurement such as might be measured on a conventional sound level meter. Experience suggests that this is an essential prerequisite to a successful rock or rave music event, and without this bass emphasis the broadband SPL would need to be considerably higher to achieve the same degree of audience satisfaction.

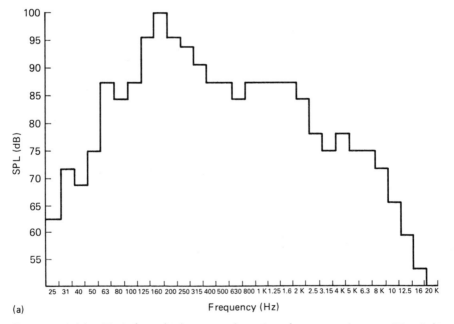

(a)

Figure 13.6(a)   *Typical one-third octave analysis of a rock concert performance (Tom Robinson Band) at circle front, Edinburgh Empire Theatre, 1986: broadband SPL 96 dB(A)*

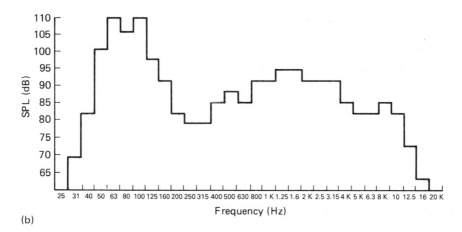

(b)

Figure 13.6(b)   *Typical one-third octave analysis of discotheque dance music, Romford Hollywood, 1988: broadband SPL 96 dB(A)*

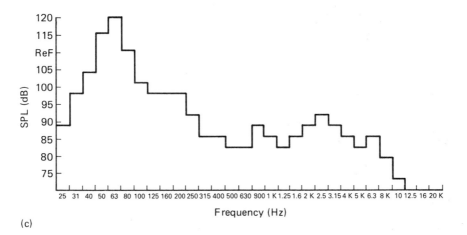

(c)

Figure 13.6(c)   *Typical one-third octave analysis of rave music, Raindance Promotions, Jenkins Lane, Barking, 1991: broadband SPL 98 dB(A)*

Having now established the basic principles we can address the three main issues: noise nuisance, staff exposure and audience exposure.

Noise nuisance

The primary concern of the noise nuisance legislation is to ensure that residents living in the vicinity of the event site are not unduly disturbed by excessive noise

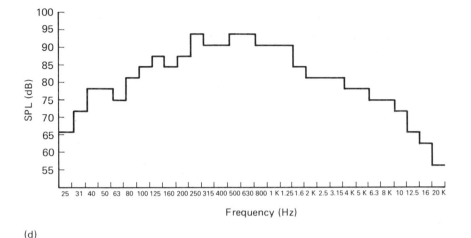

(d)

Figure 13.6(d)   *Typical one-third octave analysis of football crowd, City Stand, Carrow Road, Norwich, 1988: broadband SPL 96 dB(A)*

levels. It is the responsibility of the event promoter to ensure that this requirement is complied with.

The law

The principal instrument in law is the Environmental Protection Act 1990, of which Section 80, Subsection 1 states:

Where a local authority is satisfied that a statutory nuisance exists, or is likely to occur or recur . . . the local authority shall serve . . . an abatement notice imposing all or any of the following . . .

(a) requiring the abatement of the nuisance or prohibiting or restricting its occurrence or recurrence
(b) requiring the execution of such works, and the taking of such other steps as may be necessary for any of those purposes.

Note that it is the local authority, not the police, which is empowered under the Act, and that the authority only has to be satisfied that a nuisance *may* exist before action can be taken. The term 'nuisance', however, is not defined and the criteria used in its determination vary from one authority to another.

Subsection 7, however, provides that:

In any proceedings for an offence . . . it shall be a defence to prove that the best practicable means were used to prevent, or to counteract the effects of, the nuisance.

And in Subsection 9, the term 'best practicable means' is defined:

(a) 'Practicable' means reasonably practicable having regard among other things to local conditions and circumstances, to the current state of technical knowledge and to the financial implications.
(b) The 'means' to be employed include the design, installation, maintenance and manner and periods of operation of plant and machinery, and the design, construction and maintenance of buildings and structures.

All of this is straightforward enough but, because of the onus of proof of nuisance, the lengthy procedures associated with Section 80 enforcement and the existence of the 'best practicable means' defence, many local authorities do not consider the Act an effective regulator when amplified music is the cause of the complaint.

Licensing

Given that such entertainment normally takes place on premises which are licensed for the purpose by the local authority, a more expedient means of control is provided by the inclusion of noise criteria as a condition of licence, and this is usually how the local authority will deal with the problem. Thus, the granting or renewal of the public entertainment licence, any liquor licences and any special hours certificates will be subject to recommendation by the environmental health department, whether or not any Section 80 abatement notice is served.

Nuisance criteria

The need to balance the rights of the individual to the peaceful enjoyment of his or her home against the right of people to be entertained was recognized as long ago as 1963 by the Wilson Report to Parliament (Cmnd 2056) where, under the heading 'Noise which is occasional but predictable', Lord Wilson counsels:

457: This group . . . covers noise produced by events which occur infrequently, but predictably, at particular places . . . Their common features are that their noise is part of, or an inevitable accompaniment to, the amusement and pleasure they provide to the people who attend them. They are relatively infrequent and last for a limited time . . . Many, perhaps most of them, take place out of doors.

458: . . . These activities are not subject to controls under the . . . planning legislation as they involve only the temporary use of land and little or no works. We do not think that further control should be sought in this direction.

459: We do not think that the nuisance provisions of common law . . . are likely to be effective . . . Neither, in our view, is total prohibition the right answer as this would not hold a reasonable balance between the liberty of those people who enjoy the noisy activity and those who are disturbed by the noise.

What absolute common sense!

Considerable research has since been carried out in an attempt to determine what level of disturbance the community may reasonably be expected to accept, mainly by the former GLC Scientific Services Department in connection with pop music events at Wembley Stadium, Crystal Palace, Reading Rock and Knebworth Park. Four primary factors have emerged:

- frequency of events held at a particular venue
- amount by which the level of residual noise from the event exceeds the neighbourhood background noise level
- time of day
- climatic conditions.

The compounded chart of Figure 13.7 shows the numbers of complaints received in relation to these four factors during a busy summer season at Wembley Stadium in 1988. All the events were scheduled to finish at 2230 hours. The upper dotted line shows the audience volume level and the lower bold line the 15 minute LA_{eq} residual noise level at the nearest residential premises, over a series of 11 concerts. The points of note are the increase in residual noise when the wind is unfavourable and the sudden increase in complaints after 8 events, when the public were clearly becoming fed up with the disturbance, even though the SPL on day 9 was less than on days 1, 2 and 3. In general the GLC found that provided the frequency of events was controlled and a 2230 finishing time was rigidly enforced, the LA_{eq} event noise could exceed the LA_{eq} background noise by up to about 12 dB without major complaint. Given that background noise is not now normally measured in LA_{eq}, a 5 dB adjustment is needed to give an approximate equivalent LA_{90}, and on this basis 17 dB becomes the modified criterion.

Arising from the GLC work, two draft proposals for guidance were in circulation at the time of writing and, although some amendment may be incorporated into the final documents, the general tenor is unlikely to change significantly.

The Health and Safety Commission's *Guide to Health, Safety and Welfare at Pop Concerts and Other Similar Events* recommends that audience exposure level should not exceed 104 dB LA_{eq} over the duration of the event. For one event per year, and subject to a 2300 finishing time, the *Guide* recommends that event noise should not exceed 25 dB LA_{eq} above the LA_{90} background level but subject to a maximum level of 75 dB(A). For up to 12 events per year the excess figure is reduced to 15 dB, and for more than 12 events to 5 dB. After 2300 residual noise should be inaudible.

The Noise Council's *Draft Code of Practice for Environmental Control at Open Air Pop Concerts* suggests that for one event per year the LA_{eq} event noise should not exceed the LA_{eq} background noise by more than 20 dB but limited to 1200–2300, and that for up to 12 events per year this is reduced to 10 dB subject to a 2300 finishing time. Allowing for the 5 dB adjustment between LA_{eq} and LA_{90}, this, in effect, is the same as the HSC proposals. So it seems likely that whichever guidance

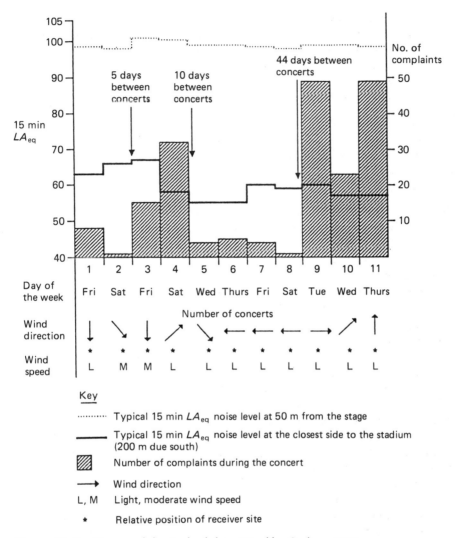

Figure 13.7 *Compounded noise level data, Wembley Stadium, 1986*

eventually becomes the norm, or whichever units of measurement are finally used, the outcome will be the same.

However, 25 dB LA_{eq} above the background LA_{90} is quite a high level of sound. Certainly the individual musical items being performed would be identifiable and the words of the song decipherable. Even at 15 dB above, the residual sound would be quite intrusive, so we are not talking of an overly restrictive criterion. Neither document is law, but both are intended to provide guidance as to what has been found in the past to be reasonable and to provide a workable solution. Also the existence of this guidance does not prevent a particular local authority, for reasons of its own, introducing an altogether different set of conditions on its own patch.

Means of compliance

The best solution is to select a site that is as far as possible from residential or other noise-sensitive premises. For any given venue, on a still day, there will be a particular ratio between the volume level inside the venue and that at the nearest noise-sensitive premises. This is the transmission loss (*TL*) figure. This ratio can be approximated by reading the level from Figure 13.3 and adding 3 dB to take account of façade and ground reflections. The level of sound emitted from the venue can be minimized by directing the loudspeaker system away from noise-sensitive areas and by angling the loudspeakers downwards so that as much sound as possible is absorbed by the audience. Wind blowing away from the noise-sensitive area will be beneficial, whilst wind blowing towards the noise-sensitive area will reduce the *TL* ratio. Also the humidity in the air can affect the propagation of sound, and under extreme conditions pop concert sound has

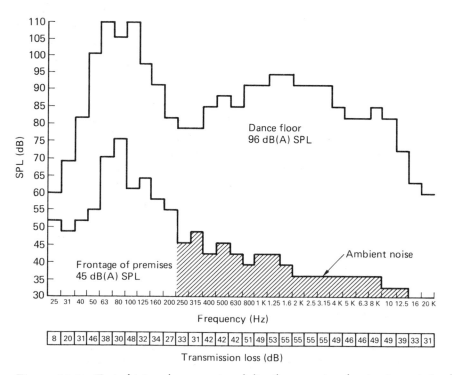

Figure 13.8   *Typical internal versus external discotheque spectra showing transmission loss through building façade, Romford Hollywood, 1988*

been known to travel several miles. So whilst a noise control strategy can be planned in advance, nothing is certain until the actual day of the event!

Because of the variability of the situation it is always advisable to adopt a noise control policy whereby noise levels outside the venue are monitored and communicated to the sound operators by a radio link. This task is often performed by a specialist independent consultant employed by the event promoters and liaising with the local environmental health official to avoid conflict.

The effects of enclosure

Many events take place inside buildings or inside marquees or other lightweight constructions such as warehouses. Whilst such structures do indeed provide some measure of noise containment, there are few buildings capable of providing total insulation against the type of noise spectrum shown in Figure 13.6(c), for example.

To illustrate the problem, the upper curve of Figure 13.8 shows the discotheque spectrum given in Figure 13.6(b) whilst the lower curve shows the resultant spectrum recorded outside the premises. It can be seen that whilst the building is providing effective screening over the middle and upper frequency bands, the low-frequency bass beat remains clearly in evidence. This is because of a phenomenon known as the mass law, which dictates that any building façade will provide the least amount of noise insulation at the lowest frequencies, which of course is exactly the opposite of what is required in a music situation. Figure 13.9 illustrates the mass law curve for a 400 mm concrete block wall and shows that at 100 Hz the sound reduction index of the wall is 27 dB lower than at 4 kHz.

In a lightweight building the problem is worse. Figure 13.10 shows an inside versus outside plot for a steel clad, steel framed warehouse-style building used as a roller skating rink. Note that only minimal attenuation is provided at the lowest frequencies, whilst 30–40 dB is provided at middle and high frequencies.

A marquee represents another oft-encountered situation. Figure 13.11 shows a set of four transmission loss plots taken at the four points of the compass at a pop music concert staged inside a large marquee. The results show the combined effect of the attenuation provided by the marquee and the directionality of the loudspeaker system.

An effective and convenient means of control is often provided by screening. Figure 13.12 shows the effect of parking a 12 m air ride trailer (used to carry the sound and lighting equipment to site) alongside a marquee at a rave event to screen a particularly noise-sensitive location.

Event noise management

Unless the venue is in the middle of nowhere there will be a finite limit to the *TL* rating that can be achieved, and at some point a limit on volume levels will be necessary. The HSC guidance document recommends a maximum audience exposure of 104 dB LA_{eq} over the duration of the event. This is an entirely realistic

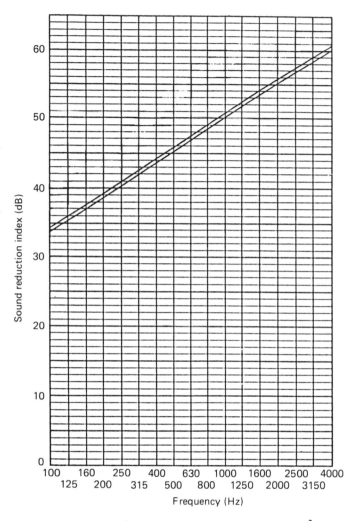

Figure 13.9   *Mass law curve for 400 mm, 300–320 kg/m² concrete block wall*

level and, given intelligent programming, should allow programme peaks of up to 110 dB(A) to be permitted whilst staying within the recommended event exposure level. This should not therefore present any difficulty. It is also a level which is likely to be achievable from an environmental or noise nuisance aspect, and so a few comments on volume levels *per se* are probably in order.

Whilst acknowledging that there exists a certain minimum volume level below which modern music-making is not viable, it will be found that the responsibility for the apparently insatiable demand for more and more volume lies primarily with MCs, DJs, artists or their sound engineers, rather than with the general public.

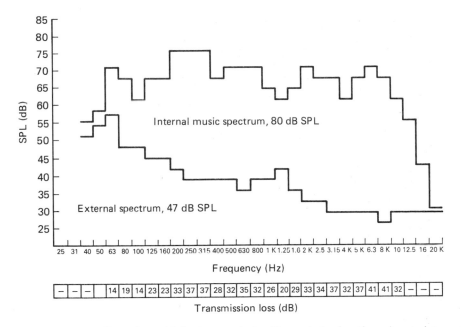

Figure 13.10 *Typical one-third octave analysis of transmission loss through a steel framed, steel clad industrial building*

Amongst other considerations this is due to a hearing phenomenon known as temporary threshold shift (TTS). It is caused by prolonged exposure to loud sound, and its effect is to reduce the hearing sensitivity of the listener by anything up to 20 dB. Thus an artist, a band, a DJ or an MC, working in a sound field of some 100 dB(A) or so for several hours at a stretch, would eventually perceive the volume as, say, 80 dB(A): this is below the satisfaction level mentioned earlier, and consequently up goes the volume control. Therefore, these are not the persons who should determine the volume setting of the equipment. The only certain way of control is to provide a sound level meter at the main mixing desk location and to ensure that the sound engineers keep to the agreed levels.

Another important aspect in the regulation of music volume levels is intelligent programme structuring. When patrons first enter the venue off the street, their hearing will be accustomed to normal street noises – perhaps 65–70 dB(A). Thus, during the warm-up period, a music level of say 90 dB(A) will be quite sufficient whilst the venue fills up. After an hour or so the volume level might need to be increased – perhaps towards 96 dB(A), with further increases as the event progresses. Exposure to the maximum volume levels should however be held in reserve for the high point of the evening's programme. This will probably only last an hour or so, after which volume levels can be progressively reduced as excitement levels are wound down towards the end, people thin out and the mood

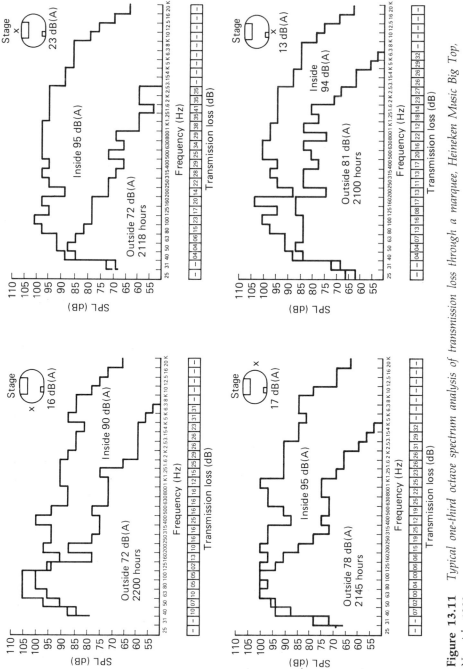

Figure 13.11 *Typical one-third octave spectrum analysis of transmission loss through a marquee, Heineken Music Big Top, Norwich, 1989*

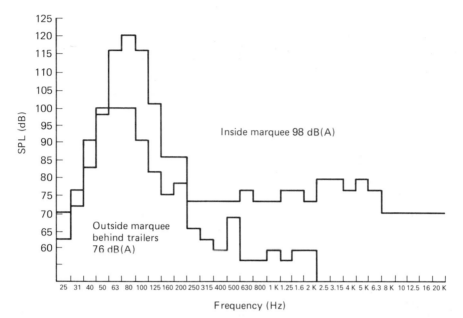

Figure 13.12   *Typical one-third octave spectrum analysis of screening by large vehicle at rave marquee*

relaxes, to end up back at around 96 dB(A) at finishing time. The psychology of the human perception of loudness is such that provided no one is allowed to experience the maximum volume setting in advance of the main session (and this is crucial to the implementation of the method), this form of structured programming will not in any way detract from the enjoyment of the music, will go a long way towards minimizing any nuisance complaints, and will lead to a general reduction in the likelihood of hearing impairment amongst patrons.

An important aspect of noise management is the way in which the sound is delivered to the audience. It can be seen from Figure 13.2 that the *TL* over say 50 m, is 34 dB. Therefore, to maintain 104 dB(A) at 50 m from a loudspeaker stack, the source SPL must be 138 dB(A). But Figure 13.1 shows that this is virtually at the threshold of pain and extremely dangerous. Therefore the loudspeakers should be elevated on scaffolding and protected by a crowd barrier to ensure that no one can get close to the source of sound. At many events the audience may extend well beyond 50 m, in which case repeater stacks should be used, fed via time-alignment delays to compensate for the relatively slow speed at which sound travels through air. Most large loudspeaker systems are fairly directional, with most of the output contained within a 90° cone. Thus, with careful aiming, the dispersion of sound can be largely restricted to the audience area where much of it will be absorbed by the audience themselves, thus minimizing the level of sound radiated outside the venue, or in the case of an indoor event, minimizing the generation of reverberant energy within the building.

Noise at work regulations

On 1 January 1990 the Noise at Work Regulations 1989 came into force. Although primarily directed at employees working in a noisy industrial environment, for the purposes of the legislation 'music' has been included in the general classification of noise, and the Regulations apply to everyone at work, whether an employee or self-employed. Therefore they will apply to everyone working on the site including promoters, artists, sound and lighting operatives, road crew, ushers, vendors, security staff etc., but do not apply to the audience.

As with noise nuisance, in so far as entertainment venues are concerned, the responsibility for enforcement lies with the local authority environmental health department.

The law

The principal instrument in law is the Health and Safety at Work Act 1974. Part 1, Section 2, places an obligation on every employer to 'ensure, so far as is reasonably practicable, the health, safety and welfare at work of all his employees'. Subsection 2(e) requires the employer to ensure 'the provision and maintenance of a working environment for his employees that is, so far as is reasonably practicable, safe, without risks to health, and adequate as regards facilities and arrangements for their welfare at work'.

As far as the law is concerned, the exposure of employees to loud sounds for prolonged periods is considered injurious to health and therefore to contravene the Act. Until 1990 the definition of what constitutes excessive noise exposure rested with a voluntary code of practice, but the Noise at Work Regulations 1989 are law and are enforceable as such.

Summary of the regulatory requirements

1 All employers are under a general duty to reduce the risk of hearing impairment to the lowest practicable level.
2 There are two specific 'Action levels'. These may be thought of as a measure of noise exposure or a noise dose and are similar to the LA_{eq} unit explained earlier:
   First Action Level   = 85 dB(A) for 8 hours
   Second Action Level = 90 dB(A) for 8 hours.
   Table 13.1 gives the equivalent dB(A) level for periods other than 8 hours.
3 In addition there is a peak action level which applies where a single 'noise event' is likely to exceed 140 dB. This is primarily concerned with impulsive sounds like cartridge-operated tools, blasting operations, shotguns etc. and will be of relevance where pyrotechnics are used.
4 When the personal noise exposure of an employee is likely to be at or above the First Action Level, a noise assessment must be carried out by a 'competent person' and a record of that assessment kept.

Table 13.1 *Noise action levels*

Period (hours)	First Action Level (dB(A))	Second Action Level (dB(A))
12	83.0	88.0
10	84.0	89.0
8	85.0	90.0
7	85.7	90.7
6	86.5	91.5
5	87.3	92.3
4	88.0	93.0
3	89.5	94.5
2	91.0	96.0
1	94.0	99.0
$\frac{1}{2}$	97.0	102.0

5 When the personal noise exposure of an employee is likely to be at or above the Second Action Level, the employer has an obligation to reduce the exposure as far as is reasonably practicable by controlling the sound level at source.

6 Some form of hearing protection – for example proprietary ear plugs – must be available if any employee exposed between the two action levels should feel discomfort or specifically ask for protection.

7 When the personal noise exposure of an employee is likely to remain at or above the Second Action Level, the employer is required to provide appropriate and effective hearing protection – i.e. ear muffs, ear plugs or in extreme cases a combination of both – and the employee is required to use the protection provided.

8 All work areas where exposure is likely to be at or above the Second Action Level are to be clearly marked as ear protection zones, and employers are required to ensure that anyone entering such a zone is wearing hearing protection.

9 The employer must ensure that all hearing protection apparatus provided is maintained in good working order and in clean and serviceable condition, and that it is not tampered with. This might include hearing protectors, any device used to restrict volume levels within the venue, acoustic screens, notices etc.

10 The employer must provide employees with information, instruction and training on the risk of hearing impairment associated with exposure to loud sounds, how the risk can be minimized, how to obtain hearing protection when exposure conditions so require, and on their statutory duties to cooperate with management in compliance with the Regulation. In the initial stages this might

simply involve making sure that employees are aware of the Regulations and of their basic requirements, that they are familiar with and know how to use the particular type of hearing protection to be issued, and that they know that prolonged exposure to loud music can lead to hearing impairment.

Compliance

Clearly the Regulations are primarily intended to cover an industrial workplace and a normally structured, permanently sited, working environment. Whilst this is not the case with a one-off entertainment event, the Regulations are nonetheless enforceable. Although it is usual to find the authorities relaxing enforcement on some of the finer points, they will usually be looking to the event organizers to show compliance with the main thrust of the requirements.

Although a noise assessment is called for, in practice there is little doubt that the majority of persons working on the site will be exposed above the First Action Level and that anyone working in the main arena or in the vicinity of the stage will be exposed above the Second Action Level. Given that compliance with the First Action Level requirements is not particularly onerous, it is suggested that these be implemented as a matter of course for everyone working on the site.

Given that the wearing of hearing protection is not always practicable in an entertainment environment, it is recommended that steps be taken to avoid breaching of the Second Action Level. If the loudspeaker orientation policy discussed in connection with the environmental and audience exposure guidance has been followed, then noise levels will already be fairly well controlled. Given these conditions, the most effective way of avoiding the Noise at Work Regulations Second Action Level requirements is to introduce a system of job rostering so that no one is required to work in the main audience area or in close proximity to any loudspeaker system for more than an hour or so at a time. The exposure table provided can be used to calculate the maximum time a particular employee can spend in a particular noise environment.

To consider a few examples, security staff working in the vicinity of the stage can change places with those at the gates at the far end or outside the venue, whilst food and beverage booths can be placed away from the main audience arena or can be screened from coverage from any nearby loudspeaker system. Clearly specific guidance applicable to all situations cannot possibly be given here, but there are all manner of common sense means by which the regulatory requirements can be met.

Summary

From the foregoing it will be clear that the days of unrestricted and uncontrolled use of high-power sound systems at music events have long gone. Partly for reasons of environmental protection and partly to reduce the risk of hearing damage to audience and to event management and staff, volume levels must be controlled.

To summarize the principal points arising frm this chapter:

1 Choose a venue which is as far away from any noise-sensitive location as possible.
2 Use a layout which will enable loudspeaker systems to be faced away from any noise-sensitive location, preferably directed into the prevailing wind.
3 Mount loudspeakers high up on scaffolding and angled down on to the audience, so as to minimize unwanted radiation outside the venue.
4 Use delayed loudspeakers to provide more uniform coverage of large areas and to avoid the need for excessively high SPL at each loudspeaker location.
5 Monitor the residual noise levels at the nearest noise-sensitive location and use a radio link to communicate any necessary adjustments to the mixing desk operators.
6 Provide a telephone complaints hot-line and take immediate action to deal with any complaint received.
7 Use barriers to keep the public away from the dangerously high SPL in the near field of the loudspeaker systems.
8 Provide a sound level meter at the mixing desk to enable the audience exposure limit to be monitored.
9 Implement a structured volume policy.
10 Implement all Noise at Work Regulations First Action Level requirements.
11 Use staff rostering to avoid breaching the hours-adjusted Second Action Level criterion.

Finally, the Regulations are there for very good reasons, and it is in the best interests of all concerned to recognize the importance of noise control and volume regulation as an integral aspect of event management. Whatever the personal feelings about volume levels, the facts are that if Wembley can work at event LA_{eq} levels of around 102 dB, then other venues should be able to operate within the HSE guidance level of 104 dB LA_{eq}. If help is needed, engage the services of a consultant with experience in this field of activity and used to working with the authorities.

Now that legislation has come and is here to stay, we must learn to live with it and cooperate in achieving an aural environment which is fair to all concerned and which will bring the benefit of a reduced risk of hearing impairment to performers, event staff and audience alike.

References

1 *Environmental Protection Act*, HMSO, 1990.
2 *Noise at Work Regulations 1989*, S.I. No. 1790, HMSO, 1989.
3 Health and Safety Commission and Home Office. *Draft Guide to Health, Safety and Welfare at Pop Concerts and other Similar Events*, HMSO, 1991.
4 Lord Wilson. *Report to Parliament*, Cmnd 2056, HMSO, 1963.
5 Noise Council. *Draft Code of Practice for Environmental Control at Open Air Pop Concerts*, HMSO.

14

COSHH Regulations in the theatre

Kevin Sivyer

Introduction

Prior to the Health and Safety at Work Act 1974, legislation tended only to reflect safety at work by avoidance of accidents. When the Act appeared, the consensus had changed so that occupational health was as important, if not more important, than safety. Regulations have now linked biological monitoring and medical surveillance to instruction and training of workers in health hazards. Disease prevention has become the 'in' phrase, rather than accident prevention.

The Control of Substances Hazardous to Health Regulations 1988 (COSHH), it seems no exaggeration to say, are the most important rules about the use of chemicals in the workplace this century and the most significant piece of legislation since the Health and Safety at Work Act was passed seventeen years ago, which itself was the first statute to concentrate on health awareness at work. COSHH builds on that awareness and turns the spotlight on to specific substances known to cause harm to workers if left uncontrolled.

The Regulations came into force on 1 October 1989 and enhance the Health and Safety at Work Act, applying to all work activities where hazardous substances are used or produced. They protect the workforce against risk to their health, whether immediate or delayed. The significant approach of the Regulations is that *all* employers, which category naturally includes theatre management, must make an assessment of the health risks that may arise from hazardous substances in their own particular work activities. They must then establish what measures are necessary to prevent, or adequately control, exposure to these hazards.

Duties under COSHH apply to self-employed people as well as employers. All duties owed by employers extend to persons foreseeably affected by the use and application of substances hazardous to health – not just employees, but everyone else working in the theatre. Only substances under the employer's control can be 'hazardous to health', i.e. hazards which an employer actually knows about, or ought as a reasonably prudent employer to know about, through official HSE guidance notes, codes of practice or trade journals.

Local management has responsibility for the implementation of the COSHH Regulations and also the control of contractors who may be using hazardous substances in their areas. Employees have a duty to comply with any requirements as to the use of control procedures and protective equipment and the reporting of any defects to management. They must also undergo any health surveillance or medical examinations required.

Principal elements of the COSHH Regulations

Duties of employers

The COSHH Regulations lay the following duties on employers:

- assessment of health risks to employees
- prevention and control of exposure to hazardous substances
- monitoring exposure to hazardous substances
- health surveillance
- informing and instructing employees in workplace health hazards
- keeping records.

Bearing in mind the wide definition of 'substances hazardous to health', these Regulations impose a considerable duty on employers.

Assessment of health risks

Employers must not carry out work liable to expose employees to substances hazardous to health unless they have first made an assessment of the risk created by the work to their employees, together with the steps necessary to comply with the COSHH Regulations. If necessary, such assessments must be updated periodically.

The Regulations do not specify who is to carry out the assessment. This will depend to a large extent on the size of the organization. In larger companies this work will probably be carried out by an in-house specialist, such as a qualified engineer, safety manager or occupational hygienist. Smaller companies should refer to occupational health consultancies or registered safety practitioners: information about both is available from the Institute of Occupational Safety and Health (see end of this chapter for details). Only work that is liable to expose people to hazardous substances needs to be assessed. If no substances hazardous to health within the meaning of COSHH are involved in any work, then the Regulations do not apply and no further action needs to be taken.

Prevention of exposure and control of hazardous substances

The assessment will specify controls which employers will have to introduce. Thus, employers are required to prevent exposure of employee to substances that are hazardous to health, but if this is not reasonably practicable, exposure should be adequately controlled. If the measures taken do not prevent or control exposure of employees to such substances as the limits require then employers must, in addition, provide suitable personal protection. It is insufficient merely to issue protective equipment once exposure to a hazardous substance has been identified.

'Adequate control' means one of the following:

- elimination or substitution of the offending substance(s)
- total or partial enclosure
- ventilation or extraction direct to atmosphere
- issue of personal protection.

In Britain, exposure limits for inhalation of all hazardous substances are laid down in the Health and Safety Executive's guidance note EH 40, published annually (note that the title will be changed in future years, but the number will remain). It is important that new issues are consulted as they appear, because later research may have found toxic properties in materials already in use.

Guidance note EH 40 includes two lists of dangerous substances: those having a maximum exposure limit (MEL) (Table 14.1), and those having an occupational exposure standard (OES). These can be defined as follows:

- An MEL is the maximum concentration of an airborne substance, measured over a defined period, to which an employee may be exposed by inhalation under any circumstances.
- An OES is the concentration of an airborne substance at which there is currently no evidence that it is likely to be injurious to employees if they are exposed by inhalation, day after day, to that concentration.

Four kinds of substances are deemed 'hazardous to health'. These are:

1 substances listed as 'dangerous for supply' and specified as
  (a) very toxic
  (b) toxic
  (c) harmful
  (d) corrosive
  (e) irritant
2 substances for which a maximum exposure limit (MEL) is specified, or, alternatively, for which there is an occupational exposure standard (OES)
3 micro-organisms
4 dust of any kind when present in substantial concentrations.

The above substances may be hazardous if:

- inhaled
- swallowed
- absorbed through the skin
- in contact with the skin surface.

Table 14.1 *Guidance note EH 40 Schedule 1: list of substances assigned maximum exposure limits (COSHH Regulations 2(1), 7(4) and 12(2))*

| | | Reference periods | | | |
| | | Long-term maximum exposure limit (8-hour TWA reference period) | | Short-term maximum exposure limit (10-minute reference period) | |
Substance	Formula	ppm	mg/m^3	ppm	mg/m^3
Acrylonitrile	$CH_2=CHCN$	2	4	—	—
Arsenic and compounds, except arsine and lead arsenate (as As)	As	—	0.2	—	—
Buta-1,3-diene	$CH_2=CHCH=CH_2$	10	—	—	—
2-Butoxyethanol	$C_4H_9OCH_2CH_2OH$	25	120	—	—
Cadmium and cadmium compounds, except cadmium oxide fume and cadmium sulphide pigments (as Cd)	Cd	—	0.05	—	—
Cadmium oxide fume (as Cd)	CdO	—	0.05	—	0.05
Cadmium sulphide pigments (respirable dust as Cd)	CdS	—	0.04	—	—
Carbon disulphide	CS_2	10	30	—	—
Dichloromethane	CH_2Cl_2	100	350	—	—
2,2'-Dichloro-4,4'-methylene dianiline (MbOCA)	$CH_2(C_6H_3ClNH_2)_2$	—	0.005	—	—
2-Ethoxyethanol	$C_2H_5OCH_2CH_2OH$	10	37	—	—
2-Ethoxyethyl acetate	$C_2H_5OCH_2OOCCH_3$	10	54	—	—
Ethylene dibromide	$BrCH_2CH_2Br$	1	8	—	—
Ethylene oxide	CH_2CH_2O	5	10	—	—
Formaldehyde	HCHO	2	2.5	2	2.5
Hydrogen cyanide	HCN	—	—	10	10
Isocyanates, all (as NCO)		—	0.02	—	0.07

Table 14.1   *continued*

| | | Reference periods | | | |
| | | Long-term maximum exposure limit (8-hour TWA reference period) | | Short-term maximum exposure limit (10-minute reference period) | |
Substance	Formula	ppm	mg/m^3	ppm	mg/m^3
Man-made mineral fibre		—	5	—	—
1-Methoxypropan-2-ol	$CH_3OCH_2CHOHCH_3$	100	360	—	—
2-Methoxyethanol	$CH_3OCH_2CH_2OH$	5	16	—	—
2-Methoxyethyl acetate	$CH_3COOCH_2CH_2OCH_3$	5	24	—	—
Rubber process dust		—	8	—	—
Rubber fume*		—	0.75	—	—
Styrene	$C_6H_5CH=CH_2$	100	420	250	1050
1,1,1-Trichloroethane	CH_3CCl_3	350	1900	450	2450
Trichloroethylene	$CCl_2=CHCl$	100	535	150	802
Vinyl chloride†	$CH_2=CHCl$	7	—	—	—
Vinylidene chloride	$CH_2=CCl_2$	10	40	—	—
Wood dust (hard wood)		—	5	—	—

*Limit relates to cyclohexane soluble material.
†Vinyl chloride is also subject to an overriding annual maximum exposure limit of 3 ppm.
Source: Health and Safety Executive guidance note EH 40.

Where substances have been assigned a maximum exposure limit (MEL), inhalation should not exceed that limit. Again, where an occupational exposure standard (OES) has been assigned, inhalation should be reduced to that standard and preferably below.

Use/maintenance/examination of control measures
Employers must ensure that:

1 Control measures and personal protective equipment are used and applied as specified in the Regulations.
2 Control measures are maintained in good working order.
3 Tests and examinations of local exhaust ventilation plant are carried out at least

once every year. Records of examinations, tests or repairs on such equipment must be kept for at least five years.

Monitoring workplace exposure

A constant feature of recent occupational health legislation is biological monitoring linked to regular health surveillance. This continues with COSHH. Employers must monitor exposure of employees to substances hazardous to health, and in specific cases there must be continuous monitoring. Methods of measuring exposure to airborne contaminants is contained in HSE guidance note EH 42. Records of monitoring must be kept for at least thirty years in the case of employees, and five years in other cases. Enforcing authorities will be particularly interested in these records in determining whether employers have complied with the Regulations. In the event of prosecution the records may constitute the only defence.

Health surveillance requirements

Employers must ensure that employees exposed to nominated substances are under ongoing health surveillance. Blood/urine tests should be carried out regularly as well as annual/biennial medical examinations, which employees cannot refuse to undergo. Health surveillance is also necessary where employees are exposed to hazardous substances which are accompanied by the risk of identifiable diseases.

Medical examinations must be carried out by employment medical advisers (EMAs) in cases where employees are exposed to certain substances at least every twelve months, or at shorter intervals, as necessary. Employers must also allow employees access to all records and not allow them to continue working in such conditions where a medical adviser certifies that they should not be further exposed to a hazardous substance.

Duty to inform/train

Where employees (as well as non-employees) are exposed to hazardous substances, employers must give them instruction and training in the hazards involved and precautions necessary to be taken. This includes, specifically, information about results of monitoring the exposure and collective results of health surveillance.

Duties of employees

Whilst these Regulations impose duties principally on employers, there are duties specifically laid on employees, namely:

1 Make full and proper use of control measures and protective equipment.
2 Report any defects to employers.
3 Undergo health surveillance or medical examinations during working hours.

Penalties/defences

Penalties for breach of these Regulations are the same as those for breach of the Health and Safety at Work Act. While it is a defence that a person took all reasonable precautions and exercised all due care to avoid committing an offence, this is an extremely difficult test to satisfy and the defence has rarely succeeded. It is better therefore to be vigilant and avoid a prosecution in the first place.

Application of the Regulations to theatrical activities

Theatrical activities most likely to be affected by the Regulations are workshops (design, scenic, props, paint and maintenance), production departments (wardrobes, wigs, hats, boots and dyeing) and graphic design studios. These areas tend to use various types of material in solid or liquid form (e.g. wood, metal, paint, solvents), which in turn may produce fumes or dusts in the working atmosphere. These may affect the workers themselves and any visitors to the area (e.g. cleaners, contractors).

Suppliers of substances brought into the workplace are legally obliged to provide information on any hazardous properties of their products, in the form of comprehensive labels or data sheets. Reference should be made to suppliers if the information is suspect or not understood.

Local management should then refer to HSE guidance note EH 40 to check if the substances are listed and, if so, what occupational exposure limits are imposed. If a substance is not listed there or in the COSHH code of practice then no further action is necessary, other than a common sense approach in the handling and use of the substance.

Particular references should be made to maximum exposure limits (MELs) imposed on dichloromethane, isocyanates, man-made mineral fibres, trichloroethylene and wood dusts. All these substances are used extensively in the various workshops, either in original form as solvents for cleaning purposes, or as mixtures in adhesives, or as propellants in aerosol sprays.

Wherever these are used, management must assess and/or measure the levels of exposure, so that appropriate protective measures may be taken. Measurements may be made by either static or personal sampling (i.e. suction filtration systems placed in strategic locations in the workplace or attached to a particular employee) over a defined period. Sampling systems may be purchased and operated by local managers, provided they have the appropriate knowledge and competency, or the services of a recognized professional consultancy may be employed. Analysis of the sampling will invariably have to be carried out by a recognized agency. Analysis of the results will decide if no further action is necessary (i.e. levels are below those listed in EH 40) or what additional measures have to be taken in order to protect staff.

Wherever possible, less toxic materials should be sought and used, thereby reducing or eliminating the hazard. This is often effective with regard to solvents and spray paints. If this proves to be impossible or impracticable, the work process should be partially or totally enclosed. Where necessary, spray booths or fume cupboards should be used, venting directly to fresh air.

An important consideration is the intrinsic safety features of such installations, e.g. flame/spark-proof motors and electrical fittings (sockets, lights). As a last

COSHH – What YOU need to know

In order to comply with the Control of Substances Hazardous to Health Regulations 1988, you must be aware of the following information. Make sure you are – it could save your life one day!

Department

Product Name

Uses

Composition

Physical and chemical properties

Risks to health

Factors which increase risks

Maximum/occupational exposure limits

Symptoms of overexposure

Storage precautions

Transport precautions

Handling/use precautions – including advice on personal protective equipment

Disposal precautions

Emergency action – fire, spillage, first aid

☐ Fire Officer ☐ Health & Safety Officer

Additional information – ecological hazards, relevant regulations, advice to occupational medical officers, references

Name, address and telephone number of supplier

Reference number, date of issue

Symbols to note

A substance which if it is inhaled or ingested or it penetrates the skin, may involve serious acute or chronic health risks and even death.	A substance which if it is inhaled or ingested or if it penetrates the skin, may involve limited health risks.	A non-corrosive substance which, through immediate, prolonged or repeated contact with the skin or mucous membrane, can cause inflammation.	A substance which may on contact with living tissues destroy them.
Toxic/ Very Toxic	**Harmful**	**Irritant**	**Corrosive**

FWD028

Figure 14.1 *COSHH Regulations staff information sheet*

resort and, in some cases, in addition to the above precautions, personal protection should be obtained and worn, i.e. masks and gloves, bearing in mind that masks are especially unpopular with employees. Advice on the choice and suitability of the equipment should be sought from suppliers, as there are many types and applications of both masks and gloves. Guidance note HS(G) 53 on respiratory protective equipment is available from HMSO. In paint shops, for instance, air-fed face masks (i.e. fresh air supplied via a compressor) may be appropriate, as a wide variety of materials are often sprayed, in high concentration, over long periods. Such equipment should also prove to be cost-effective, as many individual masks can be expensive and last for a very short time. Wood dusts should be extracted at source from the various machines in scenic and maintenance workshops which produce them.

Whatever form of control measure is employed, regular testing and maintenance of the equipment must be carried out and appropriate records kept.

An important part of the COSHH Regulations is the need to inform staff of the hazardous nature of the substances in use and associated risks in the handling, storage and disposal processes. Emergency action in case of fire or first aid is also a critical consideration. In addition to relevant training programmes, local management should compile all the necessary information and summarize this in an easy-to-read, single-sided notice, which can be posted on a wall alongside a particular work process, or filed in a register which is easily accessed by staff. An example of a typical information sheet may be found in Figure 14.1.

The disposal of hazardous material often poses certain problems and needs to be strictly controlled. Very little may be put into the drains or normal solid waste systems. Individual managers should ensure that disposal procedures which are included in hazchem data sheets are followed correctly. If there is any doubt, suppliers should be consulted or reference made to the local authority waste disposal department, who may offer disposal facilities for certain materials or recommend appropriate action. In some cases, authorized contractors must be used. Until a safe method for disposal is assured, materials must be kept safely in appropriate containers, usually plastic or metal, wherever possible those in which the material was originally supplied.

Useful addresses

The Institute of Occupational Safety and Health (IOSH), 222 Uppingham Road, Leicester LE5 0QC.

The Institute of Occupational Hygienists (IOH), 132 Oxgangs Road, Edinburgh EH10 7AZ.

Health and Safety Executive publications

Available from HMSO Publications Centre, PO Box 276, London SW8 5DT.

Control of Substances Hazardous to Health (general approved code of practice).
Control of Carcinogenic Substances.
COSHH Assessments.
Respiratory Protective Equipment: A Practical Guide for Users, HS(G) 53.
Health Surveillance under COSHH.
Occupational Exposure Limits, EH 40/92.
Monitoring Strategies for Toxic Substances, EH 42.
Surveillance of People Exposed to Health Risks at Work, HS(G) 61.
The Maintenance, Examination and Testing of Local Ventilation, HS(G) 54.
COSHH and Section 6 of the Health and Safety at Work Act, IND(G) 97(L).
Ventilation in the Workplace, EH 22.
Substances for Use at Work, HS(G) 27.

15

Training

Graham Walne

Safety is a subject about which there can be little room for subjectivity. A piece of equipment or a method of operation is either safe or it is not. These alternatives indicate that a precise position can be taken in each situation which informs the judgement and which will help clarify the position for the participant. However, subjectivity will undoubtedly creep into the assessment if there is no external force to monitor the process, resulting in activities which one person condemns and another condones. The process of making these decisions can also be either clarified or clouded by the wide variety of experiences usually enjoyed by the theatre's peripatetic personnel. Additionally, safety issues in the theatre are particularly vulnerable to the pressure both of the curtain rising on time, and of the need to save money. Under these circumstances, hasty and subjective judgements are more likely to take the place of wider safety agreements which were earlier reached without stress being present.

Hence there is a need for standards of safety which can be applied nationally and used when problems arise. There is some scepticism that in order to be capable of being applied nationally such standards would be too broad to be relevant, but we daily work within such a system when we drive our cars. Clearly, it is desirable that we can safely walk our pavements and travel our roads in the knowledge that those around us have been proven to be safe enough to control a lethal piece of equipment, and so most of us endure the inconvenience of a driving test and respect the need for its existence.

The driving test also carries a signal to employers that the prospective employee has attained a certain level of competence in this particular skill and is safe to use a car or other vehicle. Theatres also use considerable amounts of machinery and yet there is no 'driving test' for that. Prospective employers are obliged to judge job applicants on the strength of their claimed work experience. In some industries this situation would appear very curious because, unlike the entertainment industry, many others possess a recognized system of professional training which results in qualifications easily recognized by all.

By comparison, the UK entertainment industry's structure of training and qualifications is very patchy. Backstage there is a long tradition of training actors and stage managers at drama schools, and a more recent tradition of training for set and costume designers through further and higher education. The training of sound and lighting designers lags further behind, although much has been done in recent years in lighting. Education is often seen by some as an alternative to training instead of complementary to it, although others feel design cannot be taught at all (some interesting research has been carried out on this, as we shall see later). Technicians overall have fared less well, and currently their training relies upon theatres benevolent enough to spend extra time explaining processes, and/or sending their staff away on day release. Over the country as a whole only a handful of courses cater for technicians *per se* and, since there is little coherence between the diplomas available, few employers make such qualifications obligatory.

As a consequence of this erratic and deregulated structure, skill levels vary considerably from theatre to theatre. For example, an analysis made some years ago of the staff, equipment and general performance in delivering a particular production at over 100 venues indicated that 60% of the theatres were suffering a vast shortfall in the basic skills one would expect of staff. Major theatres were employing people unable to plot anything other than basic lighting cues on the control board, whilst others had staff who could not recognize the mainstream pieces of equipment (and thus did not know how to operate or focus them). Similar problems were reported in other departments.

At that time there seemed to be signs that the position was slowly deteriorating. Major touring productions began taking their own staff with them, thus denying the locals any experience. Management began employing work-experience students who were unpaid and often even came with a grant, in place of the regular army of experienced casuals which had been the core of theatre fit-ups for years. Outside contractors began installing scenery and rigging, again denying the residents any experience. Critically, the Association of British Theatre Technicians (ABTT) lost its grant to provide training for technicians.

It was against this background that in 1987 at a conference on training hosted by the northern branch of the ABTT at its trade show that the delegates clearly expressed their desire for action, and so an organization was formed to lead the debate on training issues. The organization was christened the Arts and Entertainment Technical Training Initiative (AETTI), with Graham Walne as chairman and Alan Stevenson as secretary. A first task was to contact every major employer, union and professional organization in the UK theatre industry. The AETTI flourished in the training vacuum and quickly became the focus of attention, in particular from the (then) Manpower Services Commission (MSC), which was establishing a network of organizations to develop national vocational qualifications (NVQs). The organizations were called industry lead bodies, or ILBs for short. In order to be recognized as an ILB, an organization had to command the respect of the majority of its industry. Thus with more employer, union and professional body representation than had apparently ever been gathered before, the AETTI was recognized as an ILB in 1988, the first such body in the arts and entertainment industry. The process of developing NVQs and Scottish vocational qualifications (SVQs) then became the AETTI's immediate concern. Other industries had already been through the process, and qualifications were available at this time for some hairdressing, catering, computing and engineering functions: and soon there were to be over 200 ILBs covering the whole of UK industry.

The procedure of developing a qualification begins with a research project into the size and nature of the industry itself. Little had been done on this in the theatre excepting the 1984 NOP survey, which had been jointly commissioned by the Theatres Advisory Council and the MSC; the latter saw the AETTI's work as a continuation of the 1984 research. The 1984 NOP survey provided valuable data about many aspects of theatre staffing: the high turnover (47% expect to leave within 5 years), the problems of understaffing (felt by 53% of managers and 45% of technicians), and significantly the lack of trained staff (felt by only 17% of technicians but by 40% of managers). The survey ended with a call for a 'national training initiative', a call clearly answered by the AETTI, whose own survey conducted in 1989 by Alan Stevenson found that nearly 40,000 people worked in the technical, stage management and design categories of live entertainment. This figure might seem high, but then it does include those working (in 1989 at least) in the 8000 discos or nightclubs, 1500 theatres and 500 arts centres, together with the 240 trade shows taking place annually in the UK.

The next stage in the process is to determine the functions involved in producing a defined result, known in the S/NVQ jargon as the 'key purpose'. Other industries and management systems perhaps call this their 'mission statement'. In order to undertake this task, teams of practitioners from all aspects of theatre kindly gave up their time to join working parties. The key purpose of the industry for which the AETTI was responsible was defined as 'to create, facilitate, and manage the matériel and environment of live performances'. The working parties then extrapolated a set of complementary functions, each essential if the key purpose was to be delivered. Table 15.1 gives some indication of what was produced, although the final model extended each of the sectional functions by two more stages, until considerable detail was available.

The working parties then analysed each function so that a definition of the minimum level of competence required to undertake it was achieved. This process involves identifying the criteria for specific aspects of performance. The competences which result are collated into units (and smaller divisions called elements) and the units are later assembled into qualifications. Before that can take place, however, the competences are tested nationally through working parties and by theatres using them in actual work situations. The resultant form is called a Standard of Occupational Competence, and the AETTI published its initial set in July 1991. Standards are useful in their own right, perhaps as the basis for a syllabus in a training environment, or as a job description until formal qualifications themselves are available.

Although the first, the AETTI is not the only ILB in the arts: it has now been

Table 15.1 *Arts and entertainment industry: key purpose and complementary functions*

Key purpose

To create, facilitate, and manage the matériel and environment of live performances.

A	*Establish the design*	A1	Establish the design brief.
		A2	Explore design possibilities.
		A3	Evaluate design ideas.
		A4	Present design solution.
B	*Manage the realization*	B1	Identify resources and needs.
		B2	Establish global costs.
		B3	Decide on nature of construction.
		B4	Establish human resource needs.
		B5	Establish and organize transport.
		B6	Negotiate tenders and contracts.
		B7	Meet regulatory requirements.
		B8	Monitor and adjust process.
		B9	Service rehearsal needs.
		B10	Recruit and supervise staff.
		B11	Operate PC and make purchases.
		B12	Initiate orders from suppliers.
		B13	Realize costume and wig design.
		B14	Realize scenery design.
		B15	Realize lighting design.
		B16	Realize sound design.
C	*Manage the installation and operation*	C1	Install sound components.
		C2	Install scenery components.
		C3	Install lighting components.
		C4	Install costume and wig components.
		C5	Install properties components.
		C6	Operate components in rehearsal.
		C7	Operate components in performance.
		C8	Operate running maintenance.
D	*Maintain environment and installations*	D1	Supervise preventive maintenance.
		D2	Identify fault and action required.
		D3	Liaise with external contractors.
		D4	Monitor operation of systems.
E	*Dismantle and pack the components*	E1	Identify storage areas.
		E2	Prepare for dismantling.
		E3	Operate dismantling procedure.
		E4	Fold/pack correctly.
		E5	Load as required.

Source: AETTI.

joined by Skillset, which covers occupations in film, television and radio, and by the Arts and Entertainment Training Council (AETC), which covers performers, administrators, musicians, writers, artists and crafts people. The AETC is also producing qualifications for stage management which will incorporate much of the technical units from the AETTI; indeed, there is much transference between ILBs to aid the mobility of labour. The AETTI is producing over 100 units for the backstage occupations and will also be working closely with the DESIGN ILB for the theatre design occupations. Part of a typical unit from the AETTI is reproduced in Table 15.2.

In order for someone to be judged competent, it is necessary to write the standards so that any assessor can easily reach a conclusion, and in that respect the performance has to result in a clear outcome. This makes it possible to enter a verdict that the candidate is competent 'now' or 'not yet' (which implies that further training is needed). Hence the actual wording of the standards and the nature of the evidence must be unequivocal in order to avoid confusions and subjective opinions.

Much therefore depends upon assessment, and in the S/NVQ system the assessors are trained individuals working out of recognized centres. The AETTI requires that the assessors are actually practitioners in whatever skill they are

Table 15.2   *Example AETTI qualification unit*

Unit: handle scenic elements

Element: pack flats and solid elements for travelling

Performance criteria
*Elements are carried clear of floor.
*Elements are stacked on side.
*Blocks are placed to prevent damage to fragile protrusions.
*Painted surfaces are protected.
*Sections of load are secured to prevent movement in transit.
*Boxes and containers are loaded to prevent compression damage.
*Loaded elements are protected from rubbing.

Range statement
Handling, packing, and unpacking scenery for travelling in pantechnicons or standard containers.

Performance evidence
Scenery and effects are packed and secured to maintain condition in transit.

Knowledge evidence
Relative weights of different materials.
Lorry hitch knot.
Strength of various methods of crating and boxing.

Source: AETTI.

assessing, making distinction between teaching which provides information, and assessment which checks that the knowledge has been ingested, understood and applied. Assessment centres also provide training or retraining and careers guidance. Candidates hold a record for life which contains all the information about their work, training, and units gained in the S/NVQ system, together with any other qualifications gained elsewhere. The record is in fact a complete document providing the employer with a single point of certificated reference. A key partner in this process is the body that will be awarding the qualifications, and in England the AETTI has formed a partnership with the City and Guilds Institute.

Assessment centres could easily be colleges or theatres, in fact anywhere which has the resources and trained staff to test the particular competence. In flying, for example, the ability to work at heights is paramount, and thus this competence can only be assessed in an actual flying situation. Herein lies the key of vocational qualifications, where, unlike almost all other kinds of qualification, the majority of a vocational qualification must be assessed either in the workplace or in a realistic simulation Theory alone is not allowed, and thus an employer looking at an individual with vocational qualifications knows he or she has had real practical experience.

The AETTI has to ensure that the qualifications also reflect all the legal requirements of the workplace (notably the safety legislation). In any debate about safety, someone usually voices the opinion that 'it's common sense', inferring that safety depends upon little else and that legislation is not required. Certainly one would hope that a sensible view of a particular matter would also be a safe one, presuming that a sensible person would not embark, unsupervised, on an action he or she knows would push them beyond the boundaries of their own experience or knowledge.

There are two major facets of that last sentence which require further consideration and which have major implications for safety legislation and any kind of training and qualification structure involved. Firstly, it is vital to create an environment in which it is possible for people to easily know their limitations. Without this understanding of the boundaries of knowledge and skills, the demands of the production might tempt people to take risks, but in law ignorance is no defence! In theory at least, the law requires each individual to have knowledge of the Health and Safety at Work Act, the Electricity at Work Regulations, the Control of Substances Hazardous to Health Regulations, and numerous other directives and codes of practice, in so far as they affect them. Recent conferences which have debated safety matters have highlighted that there is little cohesion across Europe, and certainly less adherence to or respect for the regulations in some European countries than there is in the UK, but this is no reason for slackness and incompetence.

Secondly, there is a clear danger that the weight of legislation could numb the industry's awareness of and response to safety issues, a situation which could be exacerbated by the proliferation of uninformed inspectors. Not surprisingly, therefore, at a safety conference in 1991 Joe Aveline of the AETTI was widely supported for calling for the industry to go on the initiative, become largely self-regulating and put the safety inspectorate on the defensive. This view had to some extent been influenced by a number of rulings which went against the industry's usual custom and practice. For example, a ruling that it was illegal for a technician to be in the platform or on the ladder of a moving tallescope at any time (thus obliging him or her to go up and down many more times during a focus session) was finally overturned in favour of a more sensible ruling that the technician should only descend when moving from one bar to another, an action which is frequently necessary anyway if the bars are not at the same height.

There can in reality be few people knowledgeable in the minutiae of the legislation, and fewer still of these people who can also run a flat, throw a cleat line, or work a memory board. Thus, in setting standards, surely people should only be required to know what it is 'reasonable' for them to know. The S/NVQ system, for example, has several levels which relate not to degrees of excellence but to increasingly complex functions and to responsibility. Thus one might 'reasonably' expect a lighting technician at the lower qualification level to be able to recognize and correctly cut and fit any of the main colour filter selections, but it might be 'unreasonable' to expect the same person, unsupervised, to make alternative suggestions and deal with multiplex changers and scrollers, a competence which would belong higher in the system. Again, the competence required in a temporary structure or fit-up is quite different from the competence required to handle the same piece of equipment in a permanent or purpose-built venue.

Once again we are back to subjectivity, and who is to define what it is 'reasonable' for this person to know? Is the assessment to be based on the individual in a specific environment, or on an average drawn from similar experiences across the nation? Clearly a key word in the previous paragraph is 'unsupervised'. This hints at a hierarchy in which someone else has the knowledge and is setting and adjusting the boundaries within which the trainees are working and developing. But again, who sets the boundaries for the supervisor?

The AETTI's work in setting national standards of occupational competence (on which the vocational qualifications are based) has encountered all of these problems, but standards are only required to encompass the minimum level of skill and knowledge involved in a particular function. Thus the many working parties of theatre practitioners have debated not local issues but core functions and skills. The acquisition and constant use of core skills is essential to the concept of safety. Studies of accidents show that they result not from sophisticated errors, but from basic fundamental mistakes. An interesting feature of safety investigations is the common fact that an increase in the ability of a piece of machinery to monitor its operation, and take preventive action when threatened, is usually accompanied by a decrease, sometimes only temporary, in the operator's vigilance. The Metropolitan Police, for example, reported a dramatic increase in minor accidents during the early use of seat-belts, and other authorities have reported a decrease in standards of electrical maintenance once residual current devices have been fitted to an installation. Thus the national standards seek to identify the basic core skills which serve each function and to link these to safety procedures. The aim is that individuals should be aware of a clear and assessed area within which to work, and should understand that, beyond that area, their ignorance may cause them to work in an unsafe manner.

It is this concept of ignorance which is the hardest to grasp when defining boundaries of knowledge. Theatre work is collaborative and each member of the team knows very well what the others do. Moreover most of this work is carried out under each other's gaze; there are few secrets for those on the inside. If a problem is encountered, the responsible person will be showered with opinions as to the correct solution. Additionally, the short-term nature of most productions results in the theatre having probably the highest turnover of personnel of any industry, as the 1984 NOP survey indicated. The survivors therefore tend to rely on a basket of complementary skills from which they can draw whatever the market requires at the time; economic survival is frequently linked to the freedom to move around and even to take several jobs simultaneously. The 1984 NOP survey indicated that most theatre departments relied heavily on freelance or casual staff (in some departments more than 50% of the labour force came into this category). With this amount of mobility in the labour force it is hard to collect feedback on the national effect of new materials, techniques or directives.

Figure 15.1 illustrates the complexity of the theatre industry. The diagram attempts to display the main functions of the technical workforce, namely to *make* the sets, props, costumes, to *install* them into a venue along with the lighting and sound equipment, and finally to *operate* these items in rehearsal and performance. The complexity of the theatre labour market is created because many people undertake two or three functions, requiring them to acquire different skills, and many of these people are freelance or casual, which makes them difficult to fit into a training or assessment network.

With such a flexibly skilled workforce, the concept of a boundary to their skill and knowledge is also hard to apply. People daily see various tasks being performed in front of them, and they subsequently claim these skills as their own in order to gain work. They may be able to deliver an acceptable result, but if they

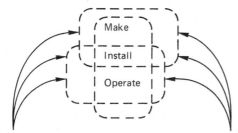

Resident staff   Casuals and freelance

Figure 15.1   *Complexity of the theatre industry*

have not witnessed proper safety procedures being carried out, then without adequate training they might not be able to respond properly to an emergency — just as it is wiser to attend a certificated driving school than to risk picking up the bad habits of a willing but unregistered friend.

Clearly, people need to know not only how to do their job, but also what action to take when things go wrong. This might involve calling on an artistic sense if something has to be substituted during a performance, when advice from designers and director is unavailable, but it might also involve a technical sense if the problem involves say electrical and structural elements. This requirement was identified by many practitioners when the AETTI asked the industry to respond to the drafts of the standards. The industry clearly saw that the competent person is one who is expected to know how to deal with everyday emergencies, but again definitions are needed: what is meant by 'everyday'?

Certainly one might 'reasonably' expect (that word again!) someone working with electrical equipment to know how to deal with electric shock. But how many theatre electricians actually do have this knowledge? The AETTI has attempted in its standards to establish minima so that an employer will at least know the person is safe to be allowed on the stage. There are parallels in other industries such as the Merchant Navy, in which no one is allowed on board ship until they have achieved the minimum qualification available. In the S/NVQ system there is a minimum level of competence which forms the bedrock for the qualifications, a minimum which has been agreed nationally by the working parties, employers, unions and professional bodies, and then tested.

Of course qualifications depend upon training, and people who deliver training tend to fall into two broad categories. On the one side are those whose career is specifically based on the delivery of training, many of these people having been taught to train people in a particular skill. On the other side are the practitioners in the field whose careers depend upon delivering a skill, but about which they can also lecture in training establishments. In both cases these people present advantages and disadvantages. Firstly, staff who remain in training establishments without refreshing their experience outside make it harder to expose themselves to new materials, techniques and regulations. In time this has the effect of making their experience itself appear stale and dated. Students tend to perceive this as irrelevant and, in overreacting, sadly cut themselves off from the ingrained practical help which the trainer may still have to offer. Secondly, with visiting lecturers who are still working in the field there is a high risk that they will be ignorant both of what the students already know, and also of the establishment's policy on various issues. Thus students are frequently obliged to listen to guidance which conflicts with previous information, but which is made the more attractive by being accompanied by anecdotes more contemporaneous than anything heard from resident staff.

The choice of designers and directors in training situations also has a profound influence on the quality of technical and stage management training. There are residents and visitors here too, with all the problems listed above. Young directors and designers tend to use training establishments as showcases first and teaching experience second (indeed they may not have acquired sufficient experiences to teach at all in the literal sense); but perhaps the most serious drawback is the employment of the untheatrical but fashionable, and whilst their indulgences might also provide valuable experience, this should not be gained at the expense of essential skills.

These conflicts can be eased or exacerbated by the physical properties of the training establishment itself. The lack of technical facilities tends to harden confusions and ignore omissions, because the students are denied the context of practical experience. By contrast, establishments which offer 'hands-on' work provide a reality in which all issues must be resolved if the curtain is to rise. However, the mere existence of practical work is insufficient to guarantee that anyone who undertakes it is safe to be employed. There may be serious gaps. For example, whilst formal drama training establishments do aim to expose the performing students to specific types of work, the productions are really chosen to absorb the quality and composition of the acting class. If the selection of productions omits a particular technical feature, then the syllabus of the actors takes precedence over the syllabus (if there is one!) of the backstage people. Most establishments do not have either the time or the resources to stage special classes to make good such omissions, and thus technical and stage management students servicing those productions tend to acquire an uneven range of skills.

What is quite often missing from training is the appreciation of the parameters within which the profession is obliged to work. For example, in order to be artistically and/or financially successful in the performing arts, it is necessary to understand economy. For stage managers and technicians, working in the most expensive labour-intensive areas, the efficient use of time is paramount, but many drama and technical training establishments mount productions in time frames which reflect neither the reality of the profession itself, nor the learning curve of the students. It is generally agreed that people learn more from their mistakes than from their successes, and so we might reasonably expect a good training environment to be one which encourages the student to experiment and caters for mistakes. But this takes time, and if this time is built into the production schedule, then will not the students absorb a distorted sense of the time they must take in order to complete a task professionally? Perhaps therefore the schedule of productions to which a particular student is exposed needs to tighten the time frame progressively as he or she passes through the course. The performing syllabus would need to change to accommodate this, but currently no performing course is run to take account of the needs of the technical course on this scale. There are also indications that EC legislation will recognize 'fatigue' and require a limit to the length of the working day and of breaks, which has major implications for both trainers and professionals alike.

Currently this state of affairs is compounded by the lack of a nationally recognized curriculum in drama and technical training. Thus without specific prior knowledge, an employer, faced with graduates from two establishments, cannot make selection on the diplomas alone unless he or she has personal experience of the colleges' output or course.

There are many establishments which do not operate any kind of performer course, and in which the whole time available is given over to projects and exercises. Many of these establishments are design schools, and these could suffer competition from the possible existence of a theatre design S/NVQ which could be delivered by a drama school through its many in-house productions. This reinvokes the question of whether design can be taught at all, or simply nourished and encouraged alongside an increased awareness of the technical processes involved. Interestingly, both the design ILB's and the AETC's (separate) researches into creativity to date have echoed the AETTI's own earlier and simpler research which also identified the process by which a design is produced. However, so far, there are doubts that a structure of creative assessment could be found that would meet the strict guidelines of the S/NVQ system. Should a theatre design S/NVQ become feasible (and cost-effective to assess – another difficulty), then the market will be able to choose between designers emerging from courses which have educated them to degree standard, and designers possessing a vocational qualification gained in a monitored workplace. Of course design schools could offer both simultaneously. Presumably any educational process for a designer would incorporate the foundation skills and technical knowledge which are also the cornerstore of S/NVQs.

What will be interesting to watch is the way in which the provision of designers, whether 'trained' or 'educated' or both, is influenced by their growing awareness that the Health and Safety at Work Act identifies specific responsibilities for designers. Already there have been rumours that prosecutions under the Act have been considered for designers whose work has allegedly been unsafe. The implications of this are that designers will need to have an even greater degree of technical awareness to match their creativity.

Both UK and EC legislatures are making vocational training a priority and, since this rationalization coincides with fluctuations in the number of young people, the market will increasingly influence training provision by funding the training of only those people it needs, by comparison with the current system of supporting a training industry which delivers too many people straight to the unemployment line. Wise establishments will recognize that retraining rather than pretraining will be the bigger market by the turn of the century, leading to shorter courses and a faster turnover of candidates.

This suggests that a modular approach would be the most versatile, and already some establishments have dissected their courses to find strengths and weaknesses. The latter are then related to a lack of a particular resource, often overcome by a partnership with the local theatre, which of course provides additional practical exposure. For example, there are clear safety implications involved in the rigging, operating and cueing of flying pieces, but many people who have successfully completed a stage management or technical course where flying systems were not featured would nevertheless consider themselves competent to work with flying systems because of the general nature of the diploma.

However, these people surely cannot be 'competent' as required by the safety legislation, and herein lies another factor which may have to be faced in the future. In many other industries (notably the professions) the definition of competence and the qualification which results from it provide the holder with a licence to practise, and this is frequently a requirement of the holder's indemnity insurance: no qualification, no insurance. It has been suggested that, in the future, a theatre's public liability insurance could be conditional upon the theatre meeting various standards of safety, one of which would directly relate to the competence of the staff. From this it has also been suggested that should a theatre's liability insurance be in question, presumably because the safety standards have not been met, then the theatre's performing licence might also be withheld until the relevant defects are rectified. Many other industries already take advantage of quality assurance standards, notably BS 5750 (which is paralleled by EN 29000 in Europe and ISO 9000 throughout the rest of the world), and enjoy benefits as a result, particularly in lower insurance premiums. The theatre is traditionally supposed to be short of funding (quality assurance certification is not cheap) and some pundits have assumed that the arts are above assessment and similar 'management gimmicks'. This may not be the case: insurance companies are becoming aware that accidents in the theatre industry are on the increase as rehearsal times are squeezed and as scenery is constructed of heavier materials and is more complex to fit up and operate. We have already seen that the 1984 survey proved there is a staff shortage as well.

There is thus a link between training, qualifications, safety and the ability to operate efficiently and legally. The following summary of the key points should prove helpful for those aiming to provide training:

1 Ensure that the training serves the needs of the industry and is not being provided merely because the college enjoys a particular resource. This implies that constant feedback from, and partnership with, the industry is vital at national and local levels. Monitor the take-up of the students by the industry and feed back the information into the course structure and content.

2 Ensure that the course only results in a nationally recognized qualification. However, in certifying the training, the requirements of the awarding body should not take precedence over the requirements of the industry.

3 Ensure that each part of the training results in a defined outcome easily recognizable by both employer and candidate. This implies that specific objectives must be set for each part of the course and that these objectives must be realistic (in terms of both what the industry requires and what the candidate needs) in order to provide satisfaction and encouragement to strive further.

4 Design the course so that the candidate has the flexibility to acquire new, additional, skills as he or she becomes more aware of the industry as a whole. Provide with this the opportunity for the candidate to switch disciplines as he or she becomes more conscious of personal abilities and shortcomings. Ensure that credit is given for work done on courses uncompleted, which implies a modular structure with modular assessment.

5 Publish assessment criteria so that the candidate is readily aware of the goals, in order to encourage self-assessment. Ensure that assessment can take place when the candidate feels able and not when the course dictates (but still set targets). This avoids time-serving, that is, 'they must be able to do that, they've been here two years.'

6 Ensure that resident staff are encouraged to take up work outside the establishment and actively support this by providing deputies and alternative contact time. Residents who do not do this must take sabbaticals. Visiting lecturers must be made aware of the progress of the people they are about to teach and thus where their particular contribution is placed. The curriculum must be designed so that staff and students can visit a wide range of trade shows, productions and venues regularly.

7 Work must be carried out in workplace situations (or simulated areas) and eventually reflect professional circumstances with regard to budget and time scale. This implies working within the terms of the agreements usual between union and employer organizations.

8 Equipment, infrastructure and procedures must comply at all times with legal requirements and related safety directives and practices. Candidates must be made aware of basic safety procedures, together with the preventive and remedial measures customary for their chosen discipline.

9 The curriculum should also provide for complementary studies in order to broaden the candidate's appreciation of the world and the industry in which the work is carried out. Additionally, seek to increase awareness of where information can be found and consulted.

10 The students should have access at all times to a grievance procedure which reflects the profession's respect for safety and quality and simultaneously addresses the requirements of any public bodies funding the training.

Finally, it has increasingly been suggested that the imposition of any kind of formal structure, be it for safety reasons, creation of qualifications, local authority audit or regional funding monitoring, is taking much of the essential fun out of the industry. It has been said that theatre is not a 'career' and not an 'industry'. Maybe this is why it has a growing accident record, a constant funding problem, a wasteful turnover of people, and a workforce closer to the poverty line than is desirable. It must be fun because there are few other compensations. Certainly something has attracted to the British theatre world-class actors, directors, writers, designers and technicians, and has been doing so for centuries.

The challenge is how to retain that unique contribution and at the same time to make improvements throughout the structure. The lack of adequate reward is causing good people to move to film, television and trade shows faster than ever before, and the lack of efficient production is wasting scarce resources. The partnership between the training industry and the employers, unions and professional bodies, embodied in organizations such as the AETTI, now has the responsibility of meeting that challenge.

Index